Kilimanjaro & Northern Tanzania

Lizzie Williams and Michael Hodd

Credits

Footprint credits
Editor: Alan Murphy
Production and Layout: Patrick Dawson, Elysia Alim, Danielle Bricker
Maps: Kevin Feeney

Managing Director: Andy Riddle
Commercial Director: Patrick Dawson
Publisher: Alan Murphy
Publishing Managers: Felicity Laughton, Nicola Gibbs
Digital Editors: Jo Williams, Tom Mellors
Marketing and PR: Liz Harper
Sales: Diane McEntee
Advertising: Renu Sibal
Finance and Administration: Elizabeth Taylor

Photography credits
Front cover: Mount Kilimanjaro, Graeme Shannon/Shutterstock
Back cover: Serengeti, Oleg Znamenskiy/Shutterstock

Printed in Great Britain by CPI Antony Rowe, Chippenham, Wiltshire

Every effort has been made to ensure that the facts in this guidebook are accurate. However, travellers should still obtain advice from consulates, airlines, etc about travel and visa requirements before travelling. The authors and publishers cannot accept responsibility for any loss, injury or inconvenience however caused.

Publishing information
Footprint *Focus Kilimanjaro & Northern Tanzania*
1st edition
© Footprint Handbooks Ltd
July 2011

ISBN: 978 1 908206 01 5
CIP DATA: A catalogue record for this book is available from the British Library

® Footprint Handbooks and the Footprint mark are a registered trademark of Footprint Handbooks Ltd

Published by Footprint
6 Riverside Court
Lower Bristol Road
Bath BA2 3DZ, UK
T +44 (0)1225 469141
F +44 (0)1225 469461
www.footprintbooks.com

Distributed in the USA by Globe Pequot Press, Guilford, Connecticut

All rights reserved. No part of this publication may be reproduced, stored in a retrieval system, or transmitted, in any form or by any means, electronic, mechanical, photocopying, recording, or otherwise without the prior permission of Footprint Handbooks Ltd.

The content of Footprint *Focus Kilimanjaro & Northern Tanzania* has been taken directly from Footprint's *Tanzania Handbook*, which was researched and written by Lizzie Williams and Mike Hodd.

Contents

- **5 Introduction**
  - 4 *Map: Northern Tanzania*

- **6 Planning your trip**
  - 6 Best time to visist
  - 6 Where to go
  - 7 Sleeping
  - 8 Eating
  - 9 Parks and safaris
  - 13 Essentials A-Z

- **19 Dar es Salaam**
  - 20 *Map: Dar es Salaam orientation*
  - 24 Sights
  - 26 *Map: Dar es Salaam centre*
  - 31 Around Dar
  - 32 *Map: Msasani Peninsula*
  - 35 Listings

- **53 North to Kilimanjaro and Moshi**
  - 54 *Map: North to Kilimanjaro and Moshi*
  - 56 The road from Dar to Moshi
  - 58 *Map: Lushoto*
  - 60 Listings
  - 64 Moshi and Marangu
  - 65 *Map: Moshi*
  - 67 Listings
  - 74 Kilimanjaro National Park
  - 75 *Map: Kilimanjaro National Park*
  - 74 Ins and outs
  - 78 Routes up the mountain

- **85 Arusha**
  - 86 *Map: Arusha region*
  - 89 Sights
  - 90 *Map: Arusha*
  - 93 Around Arusha
  - 96 Arusha National Park
  - 96 *Map: Arusha National Park*
  - 100 Listings

- **117 Northern Circuit game parks**
  - 118 *Map: Northern Circuit game parks*
  - 120 Ins and outs
  - 121 Tarangire National Park
  - 122 *Map: Tarangire National Park*
  - 123 *Map: Tarangire migrations*
  - 124 Listings
  - 127 Mto wa Mbu to Lake Natron
  - 128 Lake Manyara National Park
  - 128 *Map: Lake Manyara National Park*
  - 132 Listings
  - 135 Ngorongoro Conservation Area
  - 138 *Map: Ngorongoro Conservation Area*
  - 136 Ngorongoro Crater
  - 139 Olduvai Gorge
  - 142 Listings
  - 146 Serengeti National Park
  - 147 *Map: Serengeti National Park*
  - 148 *Map: Serengeti migrations*
  - 152 Listings

- **156 Index**

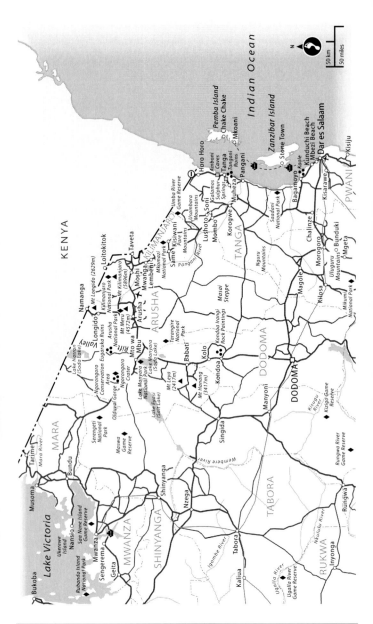

Four times the size of the United Kingdom, Tanzania is a country of enormous diversity, and roughly 1 million sq km of its land mass is dedicated to national parks and game reserves. Most people visit in pursuit of the 'Big Five' (safari means journey in Kiswahili), and, whilst the journey may be rough on the parks' bumpy and slippery roads, there is no denying that there is a wide range of locations in which to see an array of game. With the exception of the Ngorongoro Crater, which gets rather over-run with pop-up minibuses, the great game areas of Tanzania are less crowded than those in, say, Kenya or South Africa. The town of Arusha is the safari capital of East Africa, from where safaris depart all year round to visit the popular northern circuit parks: the vast plains of the Serengeti where the annual wildebeest migration is staged, the birthplace of man at the Olduvai Gorge, the natural beauty of Lake Manyara and the animal-stuffed Ngorongoro Crater. Tanzania's other popular attractions include snow-capped Mount Kilimanjaro, Africa's highest mountain and the world's tallest that can be walked up – for many people, to reach the summit at dawn counts as a memorable lifetime achievement.

Planning your trip

Best time to visit

Situated just south of the equator, Tanzanian temperatures average between 25 and 30°C. The hottest season is January-February and the coldest month is August. Humidity varies, being high along the coastal strip and on Zanzibar but much lower in the interior highlands. There are long rains, *masika*, from March to May and short rains, *mvuli*, fall from October to December. In addition there are frequently heavy rains in the south of Tanzania from December until April. On the coast, high temperatures are cooled by ocean breezes so it is rarely overpoweringly hot, although humidity levels peak just before the rains arrive and it can become unbearably uncomfortable. Away from the coast, it is much drier and the rains are a little kinder. On peaks above 1500 m the climate is cooler, with permanent snow on the highest peaks such as Kilimanjaro where nightime temperatures drop well below zero. In terms of avoiding the rains, the best time to visit is between May and October, but Tanzania has much to offer all year round. The wildebeest migration in the Serengeti occurs from November to June. If you are planning a trekking holiday the best months are May to September. Travelling by road, especially in the more remote areas or through the national parks, is easier during the dry months, as road conditions deteriorate significantly in the rainy seasons. March, April and May can be months of heavy rain making travel on unsealed roads difficult. Even in these months, however, there is an average of four to six hours of sunshine each day. Finally, bear in mind that malaria peaks during the rainy seasons, when the mosquitoes are prolific. Most of the lodges drop their rates significantly, sometimes by as much as 50%, during low season from the beginning of April to the end of June.

Where to go

The obvious choice of arrival is the balmy seaside capital of Dar es Salaam, although there are also direct flights to Zanzibar and Kilimanjaro. For those visitors heading to the northern circuit parks, the other option is to fly to Nairobi, which has a better choice of international flights, and then get a transfer to Arusha which is less than 300 km away due south. This opens up more opportunities to combine a safari in Tanzania with other places in East Africa – maybe a safari to Kenya's southern parks and reserves and the Rift Valley lakes, or a trip to Uganda to perhaps see the rare mountain gorillas in the impenetrable forests that straddle the borders with Rwanda and the Democratic Republic of Congo.

Tanzania's northern circuit alone easily attracts the majority of tourists and it is an extremely popular route as it includes the best known of the national parks. All the safari operators offer combinations of a few or all of the following parks, and how long you go for depends on how many parks you want to visit and how many nights you want to stay in each. Popular routes take in Lake Manyara National Park, Ngorongoro Crater Conservation Area (with Olduvai Gorge) and the Serengeti National Park. Less visited, the Tarangire National Park, as a dry season retreat for many animals, is also a splendid game-viewing opportunity. To see Ngorongoro Crater and Lake Manyara you will need three days and two nights. To see these two plus the Serengeti you will need four days and three nights, and if you add Tarangire to these three you will need six days and five nights. For those on a very tight budget, the shortest camping safari on offer typically spends one night in the Serengeti and one night at Ngorongoro or at a campsite in Karatu before returning to Arusha, though this for most will feel a little rushed. Also allow for one night's accommodation in Arusha before and at the end of your safari. If possible, time your safari with the annual wildebeest migration, which can usually be seen in the Serengeti from November to June.

Getting there

The majority of travellers arrive in Tanzania through Dar es Salaam's **Julius Nyerere International Airport** (JNIA). There are also direct international flights to **Kilimanjaro Airport** (between Arusha and Moshi, see page 56). There is a departure tax of US$50 on all international flights leaving Tanzanian airports but this is usually included in the price of the ticket. When flying to Tanzania, getting a window seat is definitely a good option, as cloud permitting, you may be lucky enough to get a glimpse of the gleaming top of Mount Kilimanjaro. It is not generally cheaper to arrange a return to Nairobi and a connecting return flight to Dar es Salaam. But for travellers who are only visiting the northern circuit parks, it is easier to fly to Nairobi, given that Arusha is only 273 km to the south of Nairobi, and enter Tanzania through the Namanga land border from Kenya. There are regular shuttle buses between Nairobi and Arusha and Moshi. You can also fly from Nairobi to Kilimanjaro. Nairobi is served by more airlines than Dar es Salaam so air fares are more competitively priced.

Sleeping

There is a wide range of accommodation on offer from top-of-the-range lodges and tented camps that charge US$300-1000 per couple per day, to mid-range safari lodges and beach resorts with double rooms with air conditioning and bathroom for around US$150-250, standard and faded small town hotels used by local business people for around US$50-100 per room, and basic board and lodgings used by local travellers at under US$10 a day. At the top end of the market, Tanzania now boasts some accommodation options that would rival the luxurious camps in southern Africa – intimate safari camps with unrivalled degrees of comfort and service in stunning settings. The beach resorts too have improved considerably in recent years, and there are some highly luxurious and romantic beach lodges and hotels that again are in commanding positions

Generally, accommodation booked through a European agent will be more expensive than if you contact the hotel or lodge directly. Tanzania's hoteliers are embracing the age of the internet, and an ever-increasing number can take a reservation by email or through their websites. Low season in East Africa is generally around the long rainy season from the beginning of April to the end of June, when most room rates drop considerably. Some establishments even close during this period, though the resorts on Zanzibar remain open throughout the year.

For the more expensive hotels, the airlines, and game park entrance and camping fees, a system operates whereby tourists are charged approximately double the local rate and

Sleeping and eating price codes

Sleeping

$$$$	over US$300	**$$$**	US$100-299
$$	US$50-99	**$**	Under US$50

Unless otherwise stated, prices refer to the cost of a double room including tax, not including service charge or meals.

Eating

🍴🍴🍴 Expensive over US$30   🍴🍴 Mid-range US$15-30
🍴 Cheap under US$15

Prices refer to the cost of a main course with either a soft drink, a glass of wine or a beer.

---

this must be paid in foreign currency and not TSh. In the cheaper hotels you should get away with paying in TSh but always ask before checking in.

Eating

Cuisine on mainland Tanzania is not one of the country's main attractions. There is a legacy of uninspired British catering (soups, steaks, grilled chicken, chips, boiled vegetables, puddings, instant coffee). Tanzanians are largely big meat eaters and a standard meal is *nyama choma*, roasted beef or goat meat, usually served with a spicy relish, although some like it with a mixture of raw peppers, onions and tomato known as *kachumbari*. The main staple or starch in Tanzania is *ugali*, a mealie porridge eaten all over Africa. Small town hotels and restaurants tend to serve a limited amount of bland processed food, omelette or chicken and chips, and perhaps a meat stew but not much else. Asian eating places can be better, but are seldom of a high standard. There is a much greater variety in the cities and the tourist spots; both Dar es Salaam and Zanzibar in particular (with its exquisite coastal seafood) do a fine line in eateries. The Swahili style of cooking features aromatic curries using coconut milk, fragrant steamed rice, grilled fish and calamari, and delicious bisques made from lobster and crab. A speciality is *halau*, a sweet dessert made from almonds. Some of the larger beach resorts and safari lodges offer breakfast, lunch and dinner buffets for their all-inclusive guests, some of which can be excellent while others can be of a poor standard and there's no real way of knowing what you'll get. The most important thing is to avoid food sitting around for a long time on a buffet table, so ensure it's freshly prepared and served. Vegetarians are catered for, and fruit and vegetables are used frequently, though there is a limited choice of dishes specifically made for vegetarians on menus and you may have to make special requests. The service in Tanzanian restaurants can be somewhat slower than you are used to and it can take hours for something to materialize from a kitchen. Rather than complain just enjoy the laid-back pace and order another beer.

Various dishes can be bought at temporary roadside shelters from street vendors who prepare and cook over charcoal. It's pretty safe, despite hygiene being fairly basic, because most of the items are cooked or peeled. **Savouries** include: barbecued beef on skewers (*mishkaki*), roast maize (corn), samosas, kebabs, hard-boiled eggs and roast cassava (looks like white, peeled turnips) with red chilli-pepper garnish. **Fruits** include: oranges (peeled and halved), grapes, pineapples, bananas, mangoes (slices scored and turned inside-out), paw-paw (*papaya*) and watermelon.

Most food is bought in open air markets. In the larger towns and cities these are held daily, and as well as fresh fruit and vegetables sell eggs, bread and meat. In the smaller villages, markets are usually held on one day of the week. Markets are very colourful places to visit and as Tanzania is very fertile, just about any fruit or vegetable is available.

Parks and safaris

National parks and reserves Going on safari can be a most rewarding experience. However, it is something to be prepared for, as it will almost certainly involve a degree of discomfort and long journeys. Some of the roads in Tanzania can be very exhausting. The unsealed roads are bumpy and dusty, and it will be hot. It is also important to remember that despite the expert knowledge of the drivers, they cannot guarantee that you will see any animals. When they do spot one of the rarer animals, however, watching their pleasure is almost as enjoyable as seeing the animal itself. To get the best from your safari, approach it with humour, look after the driver as well as you are able (a disgruntled driver will quickly ruin your safari), and do your best to get on with, and be considerate to, your fellow travellers. Safaris to Serengeti National Park, Ngorongoro Conservation Area, Lake Manyara, Tarangire and Arusha National Parks are best arranged from Arusha (see page 109). For trips to Mikumi and Ruaha National Parks and Selous Game Reserve, arrangements are best made in Dar es Salaam (see page 46).

It is essential to tour the parks by vehicle and walking is prohibited in most of the parks. You will either have to join an organized tour by a safari company, or hire or have your own vehicle. Being with a guide is the best option as without one, you will miss a lot of game. There are a huge number of companies offering safaris which are listed in the relevant chapters. Safaris can be booked either at home or once in Tanzania. If you go for the latter it may be possible to obtain substantial discounts, but ensure that the company is properly licensed and is a member of the **Tanzania Association of Tour Operators (TATO)**, www.tatotz.org, which represents over 240 of Tanzania's tour operators and is a good place to start when looking for a safari. If you elect to book in Tanzania, avoid companies offering cheap deals on the street – they will almost always turn out to be a disaster and may appear cheap because they do not include national park entrance fees. At the tourist office in Arusha there is a blacklist of unlicensed operators and people with convictions for cheating tourists. Safaris do not run on every day of the week, and in the low season you may also find that they will be combined, meaning if you are on a six-day safari you could expect to be joined by another party say on a four-day safari.

Safaris vary in cost and duration, but on the whole you get what you pay for. The costs will also vary enormously depending on where you stay and how many of you there are in a group. For an all-inclusive safari staying in the large safari lodges that offer twice daily game drives and buffet meals, expect to pay around US$150-250 per person per day, more if you opt for air transfers. At the very top end of the scale, staying in the most **exclusive tented camps and lodges** and flying between destinations, expect to pay in excess of US$500 per person per day. At the lower end of the market, a **camping safari**

Game viewing rules

→ Keep on the well-marked roads and track; off-road driving is harmful because smoke, oil and destruction of the grass layer cause soil erosion.

→ Do not drive through closed roads or park areas. It is mandatory to enter and exit the parks through the authorized gates.

→ For your own safety, stay in your vehicle at all times. Your vehicle serves as a blind or hide, since animals will not usually identify it with humans. In all the parks that are visited by car it is forbidden to leave the vehicle except in designated places, such as picnic sites or walking trails.

→ Stick to the parks' opening hours; it is usually forbidden to drive from dusk to dawn unless you are granted special authorization. At night you are requested to stay at your lodge or campsite.

→ Never harass the animals. Make as little noise as possible; do not flash lights or make sudden movements to scare them away; never try and attract the animals' attention by calling out or whistling.

→ Never chase the animals and remember that they always have right of way.

→ Do not feed the animals; the food you provide might make them ill, and once animals such as elephants learn that food is available from humans they can become aggressive and dangerous when looking for more and will eventually have to be shot.

→ If camping at night in the parks, ensure that the animals cannot gain access to any food you are carrying.

→ Do not throw any litter, including used matches and cigarette butts; this not only increases fire risk in the dry season, but also some animals will eat whatever they find.

→ Do not disturb other visitors. They have the same right as you to enjoy nature. If you discover a stationary vehicle and you want to check what they are looking at, never hinder their sight nor stop within their photographic field. If there is no room for another car, wait patiently for your turn, the others will finally leave and the animals will still be there. If there is a group of vehicles, most drivers will take it in turns to occupy the prime viewing spot.

→ Always turn the engine off when you are watching game up close.

→ Do not speed; the speed limit is usually 50 kph. Speeding damages road surfaces, increases noise and raises the risk of running over animals. Wild animals are dangerous; despite their beauty their reactions are unpredictable. Don't expose yourself to unnecessary risks; excessive confidence can lead to serious accidents.

using the basic national park campsites is about US$140-180 per person per day, which given that the park fees alone in some of the parks is US$50 per day, this is not unreasonable. These rates include park entrance fees, cost of vehicle and driver, and food. You'll need to take your own sleeping bag, and possibly a roll mat. Few companies provide drinking water and it is important to buy enough bottles to last your trip before you set off. It is surprising how much you get through and restocking is not easy. See page 111 for 'How to organize a safari'.

Park fees

Park permit entry fees
(In any period of 24 hours, or part thereof. Children under 5, free entry)

Kilimanjaro
Adult	US$60
Child 5-16 years	US$10

Serengeti and Ngorongoro Conservation area
Adult	US$50
Child 5-16 years	US$10

Arusha, Tarangire and Lake Manyara
Adult	US$35
Child 5-16	US$10

Katavi, Mikumi, Ruaha, Rubondo and Udzungwa National Parks
Adult	US$20
Child 5-16 years	US$5

Gombe Stream
Adult	US$100
Child 5-16 years	US$20
Child under 5	Free

Mahale
Adult	US$80
Child 5-16	US$30

Vehicle entry to parks
Up to 2,000 kg	US$40 (foreign)
	TSh 10,000 (Tanzanian)
2,000-3000 kg	US$150 (foreign)
	TSh 25,000 (Tanzanian)

Note Only Tanzanian registered vehicles are allowed down into the crater itself, for which the additional Crater Service Fee is US$200 per vehicle.

Camping permit
(In any period of 24 hours, or part thereof. Fees as of May 2011)

Established campsites
Adult	US$30
Child 5-16	US$5

Special campsites
Adult	US$50
Child 5-16	US$10

Guide fees
Service of official guide	US$10
(outside his working hours)	US$15
Walking safaris guides	US$20

Special sport fishing fees
Applicable only to Gombe, Mahale and Rubondo Island National Parks (sport fishing allowed between 0700 and 1700 only)

Adult	US$50
Child 5-16	US$25
Child under 5 years	Free

Hut, hostel and rest house fees
(rates per head per night)

Kilimanjaro National Park: Mandara, Horombo and Kibo	US$50
Meru – Miriakamba and Saddle	US$20
Other huts – Manyara, Ruaha, Mikumi etc	US$20
Hostels – Marangu, Manyara, Serengeti, Mikumi, Ruaha and Gombe Stream (strictly for organized groups with permission of park wardens in charge)	US$10
Rest houses – Serengeti, Ruaha, Mikumi, Arusha, Katavi	US$30
Rest house – Gombe Stream	US$20

Rescue fees
Mounts Kilimanjaro and Meru: the park will be responsible for rescue between the point of incident to the gate on any route. The climber will take care of other expenses from gate to KCMC or other destination as he/she chooses.
The rates are payable per person
for trip   US$20

Tipping How much to tip the driver and guide on safari is tricky. It is best to enquire from the company at the time of booking what the going rate is. As a rough guide you should allow about 10% of your safari cost. Always try to come to an agreement with other members of the group and put the tip into a common kitty. Remember that wages are low and there can be long lay-offs during the low season. Despite this there is also the problem of excessive tipping, which can cause problems for future clients being asked to give more than they should.

Transport It is worth emphasizing that most parks are some way from departure points, and obviously the longer you spend actually in the parks, rather than just driving to and from them, the better. If you go on a three- day safari by road, you will often find that at least one day is taken up with travelling to and from the park, often on bad bumpy and dusty roads – leaving you with a limited amount of time in the park itself. The easiest option, which is of course the most expensive, is to fly, and most parks and reserves have a good network of airstrips and there are daily flights. This gives you the optimum time game viewing in the parks themselves. On most safaris, vehicles will almost certainly be a Landrover, Land- cruiser or minibus accommodating six to eight people. They will have a viewing point through the roof (the really upmarket ones will also have a sun shade). In practice this means that only three to four people can view out through the roof at any one time – passengers usually take turns to stick their heads and cameras out of the top.

What to take There is very little room in the vehicles and you will be asked to limit the amount you bring with you. You'll have to leave excess luggage at a hotel or with the tour operator. There is very little point in taking too much clothing – expect to get dirty, particularly during the dry season when dust can be a problem. Try to have a clean set of clothes to change into at night when it can also get quite cold. Loose clothing and sensible footwear is best. The other important items are binoculars, a camera with a telephoto lens (you will not get close enough to the animals without one). You may also wish to take a more detailed field guide. The Collins series is particularly recommended. The drivers are usually a mine of information. Take a notebook and pen – write down the number of species of animals and birds you spot (anything over 100 is pretty good).

Essentials A-Z

Accident and Emergency
Police, fire and ambulance T112.

Electricity
230 volts (50 cycles). The system is notorious for power surges. Computers are particularly vulnerable so take a surge protector plug (obtainable from computer stores) if you are using a laptop. New socket installations are square 3-pin but do not be surprised to encounter round 3-pin (large), round 3-pin (small) and 2-pin (small) sockets in old hotels – a multi-socket adaptor is essential. Some hotels and businesses have back-up generators in case of power cuts, which are more common at the end of the dry seasons.

Embassies and consulates
Australia, 23 Barrack St, Perth WA 6000, T08-9221 0033, www.tanzaniaconsul.com.
Canada, 50 Range Rd, Ottawa, Ontario KIN 8J4, T613-232 1509, www.tzrepottawa.ca.
France, 13 Av Raymond, Pointcare, 75116 Paris, T01-5370 6366, www.amb-tanzanie.fr.
Germany, Eschenallee 11, Berlin 14050 T030-303 0800, www.tanzania-gov.de.
Kenya, Continental House, Harambee Av/Uhuru Highway, Nairobi, T020-331056, tanzania@users.africaonline.co.ke.
Malawi, Capital City, Lilongwe, T01-775038, wwwtzhighcomm@tz.lilongwe.mw.
Mozambique, Ujamaa House, Av Marites Da Machava 852, Maputo, T01-491165, safina@zebra.eum.mz.
South Africa, 822 George Av, Arcadia, 0007, Pretoria, T012-342 4371/93, www.tanzania.org.za.
Uganda, 6 Kagera Rd, Kampala, T041-256272, tzrepkla@imul.com.
UK, Tanzania House, 3 Stratford Pl, London W1C 1AS, T020-7569 1470, www.tanzania-online.gov.uk.
US, 2139 R Street NW Washington D.C. 20008, T202-939 6125, www.tanzaniaembassy-us.org.
Zambia, Ujamaa House, No 5200, United Nations Av, 10101 Lusaka, T01-227698, tzreplsk@zamnet.zm.
Zimbabwe, Ujamaa House, 23 Baines Av, Harare, 04-721870, tanrep@icon.co.zw.

Health
The health care in the region is varied and few medical facilities are available outside the big towns. There are many excellent private and government clinics/hospitals. As with all medical care, first impressions count. If a facility is grubby then be wary of the general standard of medicine and hygiene. It's worth contacting your embassy or consulate on arrival and asking where the recommended clinics are. If you do get ill, and you have the opportunity, you should also ask your medical insurer whether they are satisfied that the medical centre or hospital that you have been referred to is of a suitable standard.

The Flying Doctors, at Wilson Airport in Nairobi covers Tanzania. A 2-week tourist membership costs US$30, 2 months US$50. It offers free evacuation by air to a medical centre or hospital. You can contact them in advance for membership and information on T+254 (0)20 315454/5, www.amref.org.

Ideally, you should see your GP or travel clinic at least 6 weeks before your departure for general advice on travel risks, antibiotics for travellers' bacterial diarrhoea, malaria and vaccinations. Make sure you have travel insurance, The Flying Doctors based at Wilson Airport in Nairobi cover Tanzania, see above and page 16); get a dental check (especially if you are going to be away for more than a month); know your own blood group; and if you suffer a long-term condition such as diabetes or epilepsy make sure someone knows or that you have a Medic Alert bracelet/necklace with this information on it. Basic vaccinations recommended include polio, tetanus, diphtheria, typhoid and hepatitis A. If you are entering the country overland, you may well be asked for a yellow fever vaccination certificate.

Further information

www.bloodcare.org.uk The Blood Care Foundation (UK) will dispatch certified non-infected blood of the right type to your hospital/clinic.

www.btha.org British Travel Health Association (UK). This is the official website of an organization of travel health professionals.

www.fitfortravel.scot.nhs.uk Fit for Travel (UK). A-Z of vaccine and travel health advice requirements for each country.

www.fco.gov.uk Foreign and Commonwealth Office (FCO). This is a key travel advice site, with useful information on the country, people and climate and lists of the UK embassies/consulates.

www.masta.org Medical Advisory Service for Travellers Abroad (MASTA). A-Z of vaccine and travel health advice and requirements.

www.medicalert.co.uk Medic Alert. Produces bracelets and necklaces for those with existing medical problems, where key medical details are engraved, so that if you collapse, a medical person can identify you.

www.travelscreening.co.uk Travel Screening Services. A private clinic that gives vaccine and travel health advice.

www.who.int World Health Organization. The WHO site has links to the WHO Blue Book on travel advice.

Lankester T, *Travellers' Good Health Guide* (2nd edition, Sheldon Press, 2006).

Money → *US$1=TSh 2141, £1=TSh 1518, €1=TSh 2456 (May 2011)*

Currency The Tanzanian currency is the Tanzanian Shilling (TSh), not to be confused with the Kenyan and Uganda Shilling which are different currencies. Notes currently in circulation are TSh 200, 500, 1,000, 5,000 and 10,000. Coins are TSh 50, 10 and 20 but these are hardly worth anything and are rarely used. As it is not a hard currency, it cannot be brought into or taken out of the country, however there are no restrictions on the amount of foreign currency that can be brought into Tanzania. There are banks with ATMs and bureaux de change at both Julius Nyerere International and Zanzibar International airports. The easiest currencies to exchange are US dollars, UK pounds and euros. If you are bringing US dollars in cash, try and bring newer notes – because of the prevalence of forgery, many banks and bureaux de change do not accept US dollar bills printed before 2000. Sometimes lower denomination bills attract a lower exchange rate than higher denominations. Travellers' cheques (TCs) are widely accepted, and many hotels, travel agencies, safari companies and restaurants accept credit cards. Most banks in Tanzania are equipped to advance cash on credit cards, and increasingly most now have ATM machines that accept Visa and MasterCard. Departure taxes can be paid in local or foreign currency, but they are usually included in the price of an air ticket.

Exchange Visitors to Tanzania should change foreign currency at banks, bureaux de change or authorized hotels, and under no circumstances change money on the black market which is highly illegal. All banks have a foreign exchange service, and bank hours are Mon-Fri 0830-1500, Sat 0830-1330. The government has authorized bureaux de change known as forex bureaux to set rates for buying foreign currency from the public. Forex bureaux are open longer hours and offer faster service than banks and, although the exchange rates are only nominally different, the bureaux usually offer a better rate on TCs. In the large private hotels, rates are calculated directly in US$, although they can be paid in foreign or local currency. Airline fares, game park entrance fees and other odd payments to the government (such as the airport international departure tax) are also quoted in dollars, though again these can be paid for in both foreign or local currency. Just ensure that you are getting a reasonable exchange rate when the hotel or airline, etc converts US$ to TSh.

Credit cards and travellers' cheques
These are now accepted by large hotels, upmarket shops, airlines, major tour operators and travel agencies, but of course will not be taken by small hotels, restaurants and so on. There may also be a 5% fee to use them. In any town of a reasonable size you will be able to use an ATM that allow you to withdraw cash from Visa, MasterCard, Plus and Cirrus cards. Diners Club and American Express are, however, limited. Your bank will probably charge a small fee for withdrawing cash from an ATM overseas. Most banks can also organize a cash advance off your credit card. Many banks refuse to exchange travellers' cheques without being shown the purchase agreement that is, the slip issued at the point of sale that in theory you are supposed to keep separately from your travellers' cheques. Travellers' cheques are now accepted as payment for park entry fees by Tanzania National Parks, as well as cash.

Cost of travelling In first-rate luxury lodges and tented camps expect to pay in excess of US$150 per person per night for a double rising to US$500 per night per person in the most exclusive establishments. There are half a dozen places aimed at the very top of the range tourist or honeymooner that charge nearer US$1000 per person per night. For this you will get impeccable service, cuisine and decor in fantastic locations either in the parks or on the coast. In 4- to 5-star hotels and lodges expect to spend US$200-300 a day. Careful tourists can live reasonably comfortably on US$100 a day staying in the mid-range places, though to stay in anything other than campsites on safaris, they will have to spend a little more for the cheapest accommodation in the national parks. Budget travellers can get by on US$20-30 per day using cheap guest-houses and public transport. However, with additional park entry fees and related costs, organized camping safari costs can exceed US$400 for a 3-day trip and climbing Mt Kilimanjaro is an expensive experience whatever your budget. Commodities such as chocolate and toiletries are on the expensive side, as they are imported but they are readily available. Restaurants vary widely from side-of-the-road local eateries where a simple meal of chicken and chips will cost no more than US$2-3, to the upmarket restaurants in the cities and tourists spots that can charge in excess of US$60 for 2 people with drinks.

Opening hours
Most offices will start at 0800, lunch between 1200-1300, finish business at 1700, Mon-Fri; 0900-1200 on Sat. Small shops and kiosks and markets in the bigger towns are open daily. Banks are open Mon-Fri, 0830-1530, and Sat 0830-1330. Post offices are open Mon-Fri 0800-1630, Sat 0900-1200.

Police
Calling a policeman 'sir' is customary in Tanzania. If you get in trouble with the law or have to report to the police – for any reason – *always* be exceptionally polite, even if you are reporting a crime against yourself. Tanzania police generally enjoy their authoritative status and to rant and rave and demand attention will get you absolutely nowhere. For petty offences (driving without lights switched on, for example) police will often try to solicit a bribe, masked as an 'on-the-spot' fine. Establish the amount being requested, and then offer to go to the police station to pay, at which point you will be released with a warning. For any serious charges, immediately contact your embassy or consulate.

Post

The postal system is fairly reliable. Airmail takes about 2 weeks to destinations in Europe and North America. Buy stamps at the hotel or at a postcard shop, as post offices are crowded and chaotic. If sending parcels, they must be no longer than 105 cm long and have to be wrapped in brown paper and string. There is no point doing this before getting to the post office as you will be asked to undo it to be checked for export duty. Items have been known to go missing, so post anything of personal value through the fast post service known as EMS; a registered postal service available at all post offices, or with a courier company. DHL has offices in the major cities, TNT and Fedex have offices in Dar es Salaam. Letters to Europe take 3 working days, to North America, 5 days. If sending post to Tanzania, note there is no home delivery and addresses use post office box numbers; known as 'private bag', and the location of the relevant post office.

Safety

The majority of the people you will meet are honest and ready to help you so there is no need to get paranoid about your safety. However, theft from tourists in Tanzania does occur and it will be assumed that foreigners in the country have relative wealth. Visitors on tours or who are staying in upmarket hotels are generally very safe. Otherwise, it is sensible to take reasonable precautions by not walking around at night, and by avoiding places of known risk during the day. Petty theft and snatch robberies can be a problem, particularly in the urban areas. Don't wear jewellery or carry cameras in busy public places. Bum-bags are also very vulnerable as the belt can be cut easily. Day packs have also been known to be slashed, their entire contents drifting out on to the street without the wearer knowing. Carry money and any valuables in a slim belt under clothing. Always lock room doors at night as noisy fans and a/c can provide cover for sneak thieves. Be wary of a driver being distracted in a parked vehicle, whilst an accomplice gets in on the other side – always keep car doors locked and windows wound up. You also need to be vigilant of thieves on public transport and guard your possessions fiercely and be wary of pickpockets in busy places like the bus and train stations. Never accept food and drink from a stranger on public transport as it might be doped so they can rob you.

It's not only crime that may affect your personal safety; you must also take safety precautions when visiting the game reserves and national parks. If camping, it is not advisable to leave your tent or banda during the night. Wild animals wander around the camps freely in the hours of darkness, and a protruding leg may seem like a tasty takeaway to a hungry hyena. This is especially true at organized campsites, where the local animals have got so used to humans that they have lost much of their inherent fear of man. Exercise care during daylight hours too – remember wild animals can be dangerous.

Telephone → *IDD 000. Country code 255.*
In most towns there is an efficient international service from the Tanzania Telecoms (TTCL) offices (www.ttcl.co.tz) are usually within the post office or nearby. Connections are quick and about a third of the price of a call through hotels, which are expensive for phone calls and faxes. You pay in advance and the minimum time is 3 mins, but you get your money back if the call fails to connect. Fairly new card phone boxes are appearing in the cities and in theory you buy cards from the TTCL office, but they don't always have stock. You can also try shops and stalls near to the phones. In larger towns, private telecommunication centres also offer international services. Telephone calls from Tanzania to Kenya and Uganda are charged at long-distance tariffs rather than international. If you have a mobile phone

with a roaming connection, then you can make use of Tanzania's cellular networks, which cover most larger towns, the urban sections of the coast, Zanzibar and the tourist areas but not some of the parks and reserves or the southwest of Tanzania away from the towns and the main road. SIM and top-up cards for the pay-as-you-go mobile providers are available just about everywhere; in the towns and cities these often have their own shops, but you can buy cards from roadside vendors anywhere, even in the smallest of settlements. Indeed, mobile phones are now such a part of everyday life in Tanzania, many establishments have abandoned the less reliable local landline services and use the mobile network instead. You will see from listings such as hotels and restaurants in this book, mobile numbers are sometimes offered instead of landline numbers, they start T07. Indeed, if you find a taxi driver or tour guide you like, get their cell phone numbers as this is the best way to reach them. Quite remarkably, fishermen now use mobile phones to check the market prices of fish in the fish markets on Zanzibar and in Dar es Salaam before deciding to which they are going to sail to sell their catch. One of the cell phone providers Zain, have been operating a system called One Network since 2006, which is the world's first borderless network. It now covers 22 African countries from Zambia to Gabon and enables callers to use their phones without roaming and all calls across this vast region are at local (not international) rates. The network now has a rather staggeringly 25 million subscribers. If you are travelling on, say to Kenya or Uganda, it's a good idea to opt for a Zain SIM card. The network was called Celtel before being rebranded under the Zain telecommunications umbrella so look out for both cards.

Time
GMT + 3. Malawi and Zambia are GMT+2 so when crossing from Tanzania, clocks go back 1 hr.

Tipping
It is customary to tip around 10% for good service and this is greatly appreciated by hotel and restaurant staff, most of whom receive very low pay. Some of the more upmarket establishments may add a service charge to the bill. It is also expected that you tip safari guides, and if climbing Kilimanjaro, porters too (see page 76). For information on tipping when on safari or visiting parks, see page 12.Tourist information
The **Tanzania Tourist Board**, has its offices in the IPS Building, 3rd Floor, Samora Av/ Azikiwe St, Dar es Salaam, T022-2111 2244, www.tanzaniatouristboard.com. Contact them in advance and they will send you a brochure. The **Tourist Information Office** for drop in visitors is at the Matasalamat Mansion, Samora Av, Dar, T022-213 1555. Mon-Fri 0800-1630, and Sat 0830-1230. Staff can make reservations at any of the larger hotels in Tanzania and national park lodges (payment in foreign currency only) but they can't help you with budget accommodation. It's better to book national park lodges through a travel agency or tour operator, as they may offer special deals. Brochures and maps can also be picked up from the tourist offices in Zanzibar and Arusha (see page 89). **Tanzania National Parks (TANAPA)** has an office in Arusha, T027-250 3471, www.tanzania parks.com (see page 89).

Useful websites
www.absolutetanzania.com Tourist information with interesting articles about the economy, government and conservation.
www.africaonline.com Comprehensive website covering news, sport and travel all over Africa.
www.go2africa.com Full accommodation and safari booking service for East Africa, with useful practical information.

www.overlandafrica.com Sells a variety of overland tours throughout East Africa.

www.tfcg.org The website for the Tanzania Forest Conservation Group, with more information on the mountains and forests in the region.

Visas and immigration

Visas are required by all visitors except citizens of the Commonwealth (excluding citizens of the UK, Australia, New Zealand, South Africa, Canada, India and Nigeria who *do* require visas), Republic of Ireland and Iceland. Citizens of neighbouring countries do not normally require visas. For more information visit Tanzania's Ministry of Home Affairs website; www.moha.go.tz.

It is straightforward to get a visa at the point of entry (ie border crossing or airport) and many visitors find this more convenient than going to an embassy. Visas are issued at the following entry points: The road borders of Namanga, Taveta, Isebbania and Lunga Lunga (all with Kenya), Tunduma (with Zambia), Mutakula (Uganda), Rusomu (Rwanda) Songwe (Malawi, and Kilambo (Mozambique), as well as Julius Nyerere International Airport, Kilimanjaro International Airport, Zanzibar International Airport, and the ports in Zanzibar and Kigoma. Visas are paid for in US dollars, Euros or UK pounds and have been set at US$50 or €50.

Visas obtained from Tanzanian Embassies require 2 passport photographs and are issued in 24 hrs. Visitors who do not need a visa are issued with a visitor's pass on arrival, valid for 1-3 months. Your passport must be valid for a minimum of 6 months after your planned departure date from Tanzania; required whether you need a visa or not.

It is worth remembering that there is an agreement between Tanzania, Kenya and Uganda that allows holders of single entry visas to move freely between all 3 countries without the need for re-entry permits. Also remember that although part of Tanzania, Zanzibar has its own immigration procedures and you are required to show your passport on entry and exit to the islands. You'll be stamped in and out but ensure your 3-month Tanzania doesn't expire when on Zanzibar.

Visas can be extended at the **Immigration Headquarters**, Ohio/Ghana Av, Dar es Salaam, T022-211 8637/40/43, www.moha.go.tz. Mon-Fri, 0730-1530. There are also immigration offices in Arusha and Mwanza (see pages 115). You will be asked to show proof of funds (an amount of US$1000 or a credit card should be sufficient) and your return or onward airline ticket. Occasionally, independent travellers not on a tour may be asked for these at point of entry.

Contents

22 Dar es Salaam
- 20 *Map: Dar es Salaam orientation*
- 22 Ins and outs
- 24 Sights
- 26 *Map: Dar es Salaam centre*
- 31 Around Dar
- 32 *Map: Msasani Peninsula*
- 34 Listings

Footprint features

- 20 Don't miss …
- 23 24 hours in the city
- 29 Casuarina cones
- 48 The dala-dalas of Dar es Salaam

At a glance

Getting around Taxis are available on every street corner and plenty of *dala-dalas* and local buses. But traffic can be chaotic and the city is compact enough to walk around the main sites.

Time required 1-2 days, an extra day if you want to explore the coastal suburbs.

Weather Uncomfortably sticky and humid in Mar before the rains, with high temperatures. Pleasantly warm for the rest of the year and wet towards end Mar-May.

When not to go A good year-round destination.

Daar es Salaam

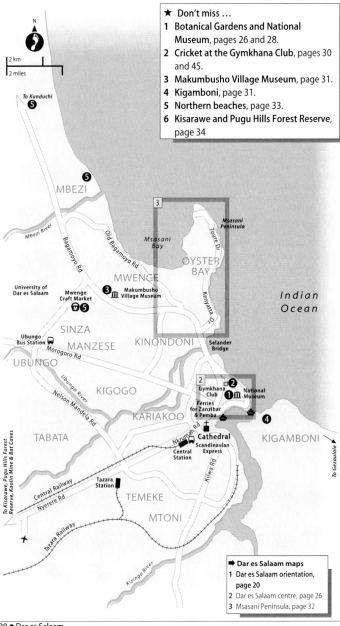

Dar es Salaam, meaning 'haven of peace' in Arabic, is far from peaceful these days but, by African standards at least, is a relatively relaxed, unassuming yet atmospheric city. It's hardly a hive of activity for tourists – there are a handful of local museums, art galleries and craft markets to visit, and some interesting architecture of the 'faded colonial grandeur' category alongside mosques, an attractive Lutheran church and a Roman Catholic cathedral that dominate the harbour front. But, with a rapidly increasing population estimated at 4 million, it is a thriving port, business centre and administrative base for the country (even though its status of capital city was removed in 1973), and you could do far worse than spend a couple of days here simply watching urban Tanzanian life go by. People are relaxed and friendly, the main sights of the city centre are easily walkable and it's home to some excellent international-standard hotels and restaurants.

The city dates from 1857 and was successively under the control of Zanzibar, Germany and Britain before self-determination in 1961, with all these influences leaving their mark on its character. During German occupation in the early 20th century, it was the centre of colonial administration and the main contact point between the agricultural mainland and the world of trade and commerce in the Indian Ocean and the Swahili Coast. Today, the ocean provides a sparkling backdrop to the city, with everything from small fishing boats to cruise liners and tankers visiting the port. And should the urban bustle prove too much, nearby beaches to the north and south of town provide an easy escape. Further afield, Dar is the main springboard for ferries or flights to the islands of Zanzibar, Pemba and Mafia and to game parks across the country.

Ins and outs → *Phone code: 022. Population estimated at 4,000,000. Altitude: sea level.*

Getting there

Air International and domestic flights depart from **Julius Nyerere International Airport** ⓘ *flight information T022-284 4212, www.jnia.aero*, along Nyerere (formerly Pugu) Road, 13 km from the city centre. The airlines have desks at the airport and there are a range of facilities. For those international visitors requiring a visa for Tanzania, the visa desk is just before immigration at international arrivals. To get from the airport to the city, *dala-dala* and minibuses run regularly, are cheaper than regular taxis, but are crowded and there can be a problem with luggage, which will normally have to be accommodated on your knees. Taxis are the better option with fixed fares costing between US$25-35, depending on your destination. ▸▸ *For airline office details, see page 47.*

Bus The main bus station for up-country travel is on Morogoro Road in the Ubungo area, 6 km to the west of the centre. It is well organized and modern with cafés and shops and ticket offices on the main road outside. It is also reasonably secure as only ticket holders and registered taxi drivers are allowed inside; nevertheless watch out for pick pocketing. For a few shillings you can hire a porter with a trolley for luggage. A taxi into the city should cost around US$8-10. Outside on Morogoro Road, you can also catch a local bus or *dala-dala* to the centre, though again these are crowded and there is a problem if you are carrying a large amount of luggage. The best bus company recommended for foreigners, Scandinavia Express, has an office at the Ubungo Bus Station where all their buses stop, though it also has a downtown terminal on Nyerere Road where all their services start and finish. ▸▸ *For details, see page 49.*

Ferry Ferries leave from the jetty on Sokoine Drive opposite St Joseph's Cathedral. Dhows and motorized boats leave from the wharf just to the south of the boat jetty, but it is now illegal for foreigners to take dhows along the coast and you would be ill-advised to arrange such a journey. The ferry companies request payment in US$ cash only and each company has a ticket office on or around the wharf. ▸▸ *For details, see page 49.*

Train Trains to the central regions of Tanzania (the Dar–Tabora–Kigoma/Mwanza line), run from the **Central Railway Station** ⓘ *Sokoine Dr, T022-211 0600*. It is convenient for most hotels and is only a short walk to the ferry terminal. Trains for the southwest (the Dar–Mbeya–Zambia line) leave from **TAZARA Station** ⓘ *T022-286 5187, www.tazara.co.tz for online reservations*, some 5 km from the centre. There are plenty of *dala-dala* and a taxi costs about US$7. ▸▸ *For details, see page 50.*

Getting around

Dala-dalas These are cheap at around US$0.40 for any journey (see page 48). The front of the vehicle usually has two destinations painted on the bonnet or a sign stating its destination, and sometimes another stating the fare. The main terminals in town are at the Central Railway Station (Stesheni) and the New Post Office (Posta) on Azikiwe Street. From both, if there are not enough passengers, the *dala-dala* will also make a detour to the Old Post Office on Sokoine Drive to pick up more people.

24 hours in the city

Dar es Salaam isn't brimming with life in the small hours but it is possible to spend a varied and active 24 hours here.

Start with a morning walk around the old town before it gets too hot and wander around the faded colonial architecture through to the **Botanical Gardens** and the **National Museum**. A guided walk will take you a good couple of hours. For a light lunch, call in at **L'Epi d'Or** patisserie on Samora Avenue and treat yourself to a freshly made sandwich and the best coffee in town. Then jump on a *dala-dala* to the **Makumbusho Village Museum** for a glimpse of tribal Tanzania's way of life, and take in one of their colourful dance displays in the afternoon. Make sure you spare some time for nearby **Mwenge Craft Market**, and watch expert carvers create wooden carvings and handicrafts – the best place for souvenir shopping in the city. Then head back to **Msasani Peninsula** in time for a sundowner on the terrace overlooking the bay at the **Peninsula Seaview Hotel**.

Dinner time could take you to the newest restaurant on the block – the **Oriental** at the trendy Kilimanjaro Hotel Kempinski or if you want to make the most of the seafood here, try the **Oyster Bay Grill**. **Q Bar** is the place for live music most evenings, then round off the night at **Club Bilicanos**, a world class nightclub that will keep you dancing till dawn. Just as the sun's rising, take a cab to the colourful **fish market** off Ocean Road and watch it come alive with fishermen bringing in their catch and stall-holders setting up for another busy day. Finally, wander over to the **Kigamboni** ferry port and join the locals heading south on the ferry for a brief 10-minute journey, before taking a cab a couple of kilometres to **Mikadi Beach** for a refreshing dip in the ocean or a plunge in their pool, and recover with an all-day breakfast.

Taxis Taxis are readily available in the city centre and are parked on just about every street corner. They cost around US$2-3 per km. Any car can serve as a taxi, they are not painted in a specific colour, and they may be new or battered but serviceable. If you are visiting a non-central location and there is no taxi stand at the destination, you can always ask the driver to wait or come back and pick you up at an allotted time. These days most of Dar's taxi drivers have mobile phones, so it is easy enough to get the number and call the driver when you want to be picked up. Taxis do not have meters so always negotiate taxi fares before setting off on your journey.

Tuk-tuks (bajajis) These have increased in numbers over the past few years and are at least half the price of regular taxis. They don't go very fast, though, and are quite uncomfortable so for longer journeys stick to taxis.

Tourist offices

If you contact the **Tanzania Tourist Board** ⓘ *IPS Building, 3rd Fl, Samora Av/Azikiwe St, T022-211 1244, www.tanzaniatouristboard.com*, in advance they will post out brochures. The **Tourist Information Office** ⓘ *Matasalamat Mansion, Samora Av, T022-213 1555, Mon-Fri 0800-1600, Sat 0830-1230*, for drop-in visitors has a limited range of glossy leaflets about the national parks and other places of interest, a noticeboard with transport timetables and fares, a (not too good) map of the city and, sometimes, a 1:2,000,000 scale map of Tanzania. Staff are very helpful, however and can also make reservations at any of the larger hotels in Tanzania and national park lodges (payment in foreign currency only) but they can't help you with budget accommodation. However, it's generally better to book the larger resort hotels and national park lodges through a travel agency or tour operator as they may offer special deals.

There are two free monthly publications available from some hotels and travel agencies; the *Dar es Salaam Guide*, which has transport timetables and good articles about destinations and sights in the city; and *What's Happening in Dar es Salaam*. The latter is better for information about upcoming events.

When to visit
The hottest months are December to the end of March, when the Indian Ocean is warm enough to swim in at night. The long rains are from March-May and the short rains November-December. The best season to visit is June-October, although there is sun all the year round, even during the rains, which are short and heavy and bring on intense humidity.

Sights

The best way to discover the heart of Dar es Salaam is on foot and we have suggested two half-day walks that take in most of the historic buildings. An alternative is to join a guided **walking tour** ① *2½ hr morning walks through the old town cost around US$35 adult, US$15 child depending on the tour operator, with discounts for groups, and including tastings of Swahili, Arab and Indian foods.* Ask the tourist office to recommend a tour operator.

Walking tour of the old town
A walking tour (about half a day) of the historic parts of old Dar es Salaam might start at the **Askari Monument** at the junction of Samora Avenue and Azikwe Street. Originally on this site was a statue to Major Hermann von Wissmann, the German explorer and soldier, who suppressed the coastal Arab Revolt of 1888-1889 and went on to become governor of German East Africa in 1895-1896. This first statue erected in 1911 depicted a pith-helmeted Wissmann, one hand on hip, the other on his sword, gazing out over the harbour with an African soldier at the base of the plinth draping a German flag over a reclining lion. It was demolished in 1916 when the British occupied Dar es Salaam, as were statues to Bismarck and Carl Peters. The present bronze statue, in memory of all those who died in the First World War, but principally dedicated to the African troops and porters, was unveiled in 1927. The statue was cast by Morris Bronze Founders of Westminster, London, and the sculptor was James Alexander Stevenson (1881-1937), who signed himself 'Myrander'. There are two bronze bas-reliefs on the sides of the plinth by the same sculptor, and the inscription, in English and Swahili, is from Rudyard Kipling.

Proceeding towards the harbour, on the left is the **New Africa Hotel** on the site where the old **Kaiserhof Hotel** stood. This was once the finest building in Dar es Salaam, the venue for the expat community to meet for sundowners. The terrace outside overlooked the Lutheran church and the harbour, while a band played in the inner courtyard. Across Sokoine Drive, on the left is the **Lutheran cathedral** with its distinctive red-tiled spire and tiled canopies over the windows to provide shade. Construction began in 1898. Opposite is the **Cenotaph**, again commemorating the 1914-1918 war, which was unveiled in 1927 and restored in 1992.

Turning left along Kivukoni Front, there is a fine view through the palm trees across the harbour. Just past Ohio Street, on the shore side, is the **Old Yacht Club**. Prior to the removal of the club to its present site on the west side of Msasani Peninsula in 1967, small boats bobbing at anchor in the bay were a feature of the harbour. The Old Yacht Club buildings now house the harbour police headquarters.

Opposite the Old Yacht Club is the site of the German Club for civilians, which was expanded to form the Dar es Salaam (DSM) Club in the British period. It used to have a spacious terrace and a handsome bar. On the first floor are rooms that were used for accommodation, with verandas facing inward and outside stone staircases. Evelyn Waugh once stayed here. Today, after substantial renovation, this building is the smart new **Kilimanjaro Hotel Kempinski**, one of Dar's most luxurious hotels.

Further along Kivukoni Front is the first of an impressive series of German government buildings. The first two, one now the High Court, and the other the present Magistrates' Court on the corner of Luthuli Road, were for senior officials. In between is the old **Secretariat**, which housed the governor's offices. On the other corner of Luthuli Road is the German Officers' Mess, where some gambling evidently took place as it became known as the **Casino**. These buildings are exceptional, and it is a tribute to the high quality construction of the German period that they have survived, with virtually no maintenance for the past 30 years. Construction was completed in 1893. On the high ground further along Kivukoni Front is the site of the first European building in Dar, the **Berlin Mission**. It was built in 1887, extensively damaged in the 1888-1889 uprising and demolished in 1959 to make way for a hotel, which, in the event, was not constructed.

The eastern part of the city resembles an eagle's head (it is said the Msasani Peninsula is one of the eagle's wings). At the tip of the eagle's beak was a pier, just where the fish market (see page 30) stands today, constructed in the British period for the use of the governor. This was just a little further round the promontory from the present ramp for the ferry that goes over to Kigamboni. Past Magogoni Street is the **Swimming Club** (see page 46), constructed in the British period and now mostly used by the Asian community.

Following Ocean Road, on the left is the present **State House**, with a drive coming down to gates. This was the original German governor's residence. It had tall, Islamic-style arches on the ground floor rather similar to those in the building today, but the upper storey was a veranda with a parapet and the roof was supported on cast-iron columns. The building was bombarded by British warships in 1914 and extensively damaged. In 1922 it was rebuilt and the present scalloped upper-storey arches added, as well as the tower with the crenellated parapet.

The **German Hospital** is further along Ocean Road with its distinctive domed towers topped by a clusters of iron spikes. It is an uneasy mixture of the grand (the towers) and the utilitarian (the corrugated-iron roofing). It was completed in 1897 and was added to during the British period with single-storey, bungalow-style wards to the rear.

Turning left past the baobab tree down Chimera Road and taking the left fork, Luthuli Road leads to the junction with Samora Avenue. Here stood the statue of Bismarck, a replica of the celebrated Regas bust. The area either side of this boulevard, one of the glories of Dar es Salaam in the German era, was laid out as an extensive park. The flamboyant trees and *oreodoxa* (Royal Palms) still border it.

The first Director of Agriculture, Professor Stuhlmann, began laying out the **Botanical Gardens** in 1893. The building that houses the Agriculture Department as well as the Meteorological Station and the Government Geographer lies just to the southwest and was completed in 1903, by which time the gardens were well established, Stuhlmann using his position as Chief Secretary from 1900-1903 to channel resources to their development. The gardens became the home of the Dar es Salaam Horticultural Society, which still has a building on the site, and has undergone some rehabilitation with most of the exhibits labelled. Now, though, it's in need of some further care and attention, although it's a welcome escape from the city and the peacocks give it an air of exoticism. It is one of the few places in the world to see the coco-de-mer palm tree apart from the Seychelles.

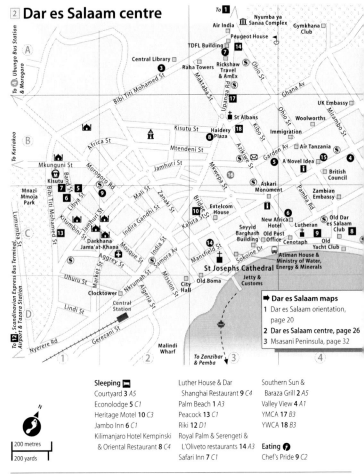

Dar es Salaam centre

➡ **Dar es Salaam maps**
1 Dar es Salaam orientation, page 20
2 Dar es Salaam centre, page 26
3 Msasani Peninsula, page 32

Sleeping
Courtyard **3** *A5*
Econolodge **5** *C1*
Heritage Motel **10** *C3*
Jambo Inn **6** *C1*
Kilimanjaro Hotel Kempinski & Oriental Restaurant **8** *C4*
Luther House & Dar Shanghai Restaurant **9** *C4*
Palm Beach **1** *A3*
Peacock **13** *C1*
Riki **12** *D1*
Royal Palm & Serengeti & L'Oliveto restaurants **14** *A3*
Safari Inn **7** *C1*
Southern Sun & Baraza Grill **2** *A5*
Valley View **4** *A1*
YMCA **17** *B3*
YWCA **18** *B3*

Eating
Chef's Pride **9** *C2*

To the left of the gardens is **Karimjee Hall**, built by the British and which served as the home of the Legislative Council prior to independence. It then became the home of the National Assembly, the Bunge. In the same area is the original **National Museum** (see page 28), a single-storey stone building with a red-tiled roof and arched windows constructed as the King George V Memorial Museum in 1940, changing its name in 1963. A larger, modern building was constructed later to house exhibits, and the old building was used as offices.

Turning left down Shaaban Robert Street, on the other side of Sokoine Drive, in a crescent behind the Speaker's Office is the first school built in Dar es Salaam (1899) by the German government. It was predominantly for Africans, but also had a few Indian pupils, all children of state-employed officials (*akidas*). Walking west down Sokoine Drive you return to the New Africa Hotel.

Walking tour of the City

A second half-day walking tour might begin at the New Africa Hotel and proceed west along Sokoine Street past the National Bank of Commerce building on the right. On the corner with Mkwepa Street is the German **Post Office** completed in 1893. Although the façade has been remodelled to give it a more modern appearance, the structure is basically unchanged. Just inside the entrance is a plaque to the memory of members of the Signals Corps who lost their lives in the First World War in East Africa. There are some 200 names listed with particularly heavy representation from South Africa and India whose loyalty to the British Empire drew them into the conflict.

On the opposite corner to the post office is the site of the old customs headquarters, the **Seyyid Barghash Building**, constructed around 1869. The building on the corner with Bridge Street is the modern multi-storey **Wizaraya Maji, Nishati na Madim** (Ministry of Water, Energy and Minerals), which is on the site of the old Customs House. Next door, sandwiched between the ministry building and Forodhani Secondary School, is the **White Fathers' House** – called **Atiman House**. It is named after a

Chinese **4** *B4*
City Garden **5** *B4*
Cynics' Café & Wine Bar **7** *A3*
Debonair's & Steer's **15** *B4*
Garden Food Court at
 Haidery Plaza **8** *B3*
Sawasdee **6** *C4*
Sichaun **3** *A2*
Sno-cream **14** *C3*

Bars & clubs
Club Bilicanas **16** *B3*

heroic and dedicated doctor, Adrian Atiman, who was redeemed from slavery in Niger by White Father missionaries, educated in North Africa and Europe, and who worked for decades as a doctor in Tanzania until his death, circa 1924. Atiman House was constructed in the 1860s in the Zanzibar period and is the oldest surviving house in the city, excluding administrative buildings. It was built as a residence for the Sultan of Zanzibar's Dar es Salaam wives, and sold by the Sultan to the White Fathers in 1922. In the visitors' parlour are two extremely interesting old photographs of the waterfront at Dar es Salaam as it was in German colonial times.

Continuing along Sokoine Drive to the west, the next building is **St Joseph's Roman Catholic Cathedral**. Construction began in 1897 and took five years to complete. St Joseph's remains one of the most striking buildings in Dar es Salaam, dominating the harbour front. It has an impressive vaulted interior, shingle spire and a fine arrangement of arches and gables. Next to the cathedral was Akida's Court.

On the corner of Morogoro Road is Dar's oldest surviving building, the **Old Boma** dating from 1867. It was built to accommodate the visitors of Sultan Majid and features a fine Zanzibar door and coral-rag walls. On the opposite corner is the **City Hall**, a very handsome building with an impressive façade and elaborate decoration.

On the corner of Uhuru Street is the **Railway Station**, a double-storey building with arches and a pitched-tile roof, the construction of which began in 1897. Between the station and the shore was the site of the palace of Sultan Majid and of the hospital for Africans constructed in 1895 by Sewa Haji, but which was demolished in 1959.

Turning right in front of the railway station leads to the **clock tower**, a post-war concrete construction erected to celebrate the elevation of Dar es Salaam to city status in 1961. A right turn at the clock tower leads along Samora Avenue and back to the Askari Monument.

There are other notable buildings in the City. On Mosque Street is the ornate **Darkhana Jama'at-Khana** of the Ismaili community, three storeys high with a six-storey tower on the corner topped by a clock, a pitched roof and a weathervane.

There are several other mosques, two (**Ibaddhi Mosque** and **Memon Mosque**) on Mosque Street itself (clearly signposted and stringed with coloured lights used for religious occasions), one on Kitumbini Street, one block to the southwest of Mosque Street, (a **Sunni mosque** with an impressive dome), and there are two mosques on Bibi Titi Mohamed Street, the **Ahmadiyya mosque** near the junction with Pugu Road and the other close by. On Kitsu Street, there are two Hindu temples, and on Upanga Road is a grand Ismaili building decorated with coloured lights during festivals.

St Alban's Church on the corner of Upanga Road and Maktaba Street was constructed in the interwar period. St Alban's is a grand building modelled on the Anglican church in Zanzibar. This is the Anglican Church of the Province of Tanzania, and was the Governor's church in colonial times. The **Greek Orthodox church**, further along Upanga Street, was constructed in the 1940s. **St Peter's Catholic Church**, off the Bagamoyo Road, was constructed in 1962, and is in modern style with delicate concrete columns and arches.

The Museum and House of Culture Dar es Salaam (formerly National Museum)

ⓘ *Shaaban Robert St next to the Botanical Gardens, between Sokoine Dr and Samora Av, T022-211 7508, www.houseofculture.or.tz. Daily 0930-1800. Entry US$5. Student US$2.*

The Museum opened in 1940 in the former King George V Memorial Museum building next to the Botanical Gardens. King George V's car can still be seen in the newer wing,

Casuarina cones

A particularly fine set of casuarina trees can be found along Ocean Road in Dar es Salaam. Strangely, they are also found in Australia. Quite unlike most other trees in East Africa, the theory is that the seed-bearing cones were carried by the cold tidal currents from the west coast of Australia into the equatorial waters flowing west across the Indian Ocean to the shore of Tanzania and then north along the East African coast in the Somalia current, eventually germinating after a journey of about 10,000 km.

---

which was built in front of the old museum in 1963. The museum is in a garden where a few peacocks stroll and where there is a sculpture in memory of victims of the 1989 American Embassy bombing. Created in 2004 by US artist Elyn Zimmerman, it comprises a group of six related geometric forms that surround a granite-rimmed pool. Their flatness and thinness, as well as their striking silhouettes and outlines, were inspired by shapes used in traditional African art, shields and other objects including Tanzanian stools, which Zimmerman said greatly influenced her work. Very interestingly, the very same artist designed the World Trade Centre Memorial in 1993, after a bomb set by terrorists exploded on the site of the World Trade Centre in New York. That sculpture was a cenotaph to an attack that predated both the 7 August 1998 bombings in Dar es Salaam and Nairobi, and the 11 September 2001 attacks in New York. Zimmerman's 1993 sculpture was destroyed in the 2001 attack at the World Trade centre.

The museum has excellent ethnographic, historical and archaeological collections. The old photographs are particularly interesting. Traditional craft items, headdresses, ornaments, musical instruments and witchcraft accoutrements are on display. Artefacts representing Tanzanian history date from the slave trade to the post-colonial period. Fossils from Olduvai Gorge kept there include those of Zinjanthropus – sometimes referred to as Zinj or 'nutcracker man' – the first of a new group of hominid remains collectively known as *Australopithecus boisei*, discovered by Mary Leakey. The coastal history is represented by glazed Chinese porcelain pottery and a range of copper coins from Kilwa. One of the more unusual exhibits is a bicycle in working order made entirely of wood. The museum also regularly stages exhibitions – see press for details.

West towards Kariakoo

The area to the northwest of India Street, on either side of Morogoro Road, was an Asian section of the city in the colonial period, and to a large extent still is. Buildings are typically several storeys high, the ground floor being given over to business with the upper storeys being used for residential accommodation. The façades are often ornate, with the name of the proprietor and the date of construction prominently displayed. Two superb examples on Morogoro Road, near Africa Street, are the premises of M Jessa. One was a cigarette and tobacco factory and the other a rice mill.

Further to the west is the open Mnazi Mmoja (coconut grove) with the **Uhuru Monument** dedicated to the freedom that came with independence, and celebrations take place here every year on 9 December to commemorate Independence Day. The original Uhuru monument is a white obelisk with a flame – the Freedom Torch. A second concrete monument, designed by R Ashdown, was erected to commemorate 10 years of independence. This was enlivened with panels by a local artist. On the far side of the space is **Kariakoo**, laid out in a grid pattern and predominantly an African area. It became known as Kariakoo during the latter part of the First World War when African porters (the carrier corps, from which the current name is derived) were billeted here after the British took over the city in 1916. The houses are Swahili style. The colourful **market** in the centre and the shark market on the junction of Msimbazi and Tandamuti streets are well worth a visit but watch out for pickpockets.

Fish market and Banda Beach

At the point of the eagle's beak, where the ferry leaves for Kigamboni, is the **Integrated Fish Market Complex**. A fish market has been on this site since time immemorial, formerly part of an old fishing village called Mzizima, which was located between what is now State House and Ocean Road Hospital. The village met its demise when Seyyid Majid founded Dar es Salaam in 1862, although the fish market survived. In 2002, the Japanese government funded a substantial expansion programme and a new fish market was built. There are now zones for fish cleaning, fish frying, one for shellfish and vegetables, another for firewood and charcoal, an auction hall for wholesale vendors and buyers, and a maintenance area for the repair of boats, fishing nets and other tools of the trade. The complex is one of a kind and provides employment for 100 fishermen catering to thousands of daily shoppers. As you can imagine, this is an extremely smelly place. Fresh fish can be bought here and there is an astonishingly wide variety of seafood from blue fish, lobster, red snapper, to calamari and prawns. Be warned though, the vendors are quite aggressive and you'll need to haggle hard. You can also buy ice here to pack the fish.

Just north of the market is a stretch of sand known as **Banda Beach**, a well-known place for sittin' on the dock of the bay. Fishing boats, mostly lateen-sailed *ngalawas*, are beached on the shore.

Gymkhana Club

Further along Ocean Road, past State House and the hospital, are the grounds of the Gymkhana Club, which extend down to the shore. Amongst other sports practised here (see page 45) is golf, and there is an 18-hole course featuring what are called 'browns' as opposed to 'greens'. There were various cemeteries on the shore side of the golf course, a European cemetery between the hospital and Ghana Avenue, and a Hindu crematorium beyond.

Nyumba ya Sanaa Complex

ⓘ *Junction of Ohio St, Ali Mwinyi Rd and Bibi Titi Mohammed St, northwest of the Royal Palm Hotel, T022-213 1727. Open Mon-Fri 0800-2000, Sat-Sun 0800-1600.*

This art gallery has displays of paintings in various styles including oil, watercolour and chalk, as well as carvings and batiks. You can see the artists at work, and there is also a café on site. The centre was started by a nun and the present building was constructed with help from a Norwegian donation in the early 1980s. Traditional dances are held here on Friday evenings at 1930.

Oyster Bay

At the intersection of Ocean Road and Ufukoni Road on the shore side is a rocky promontory which was the site of European residential dwellings constructed in the interwar period by the British. These are either side of Labon Drive (previously Seaview Road). Continuing along Ocean Road is Selander Bridge, a causeway over the Msimbazi Creek, a small river edged by marsh that circles back to the south behind the main part of the city. Beyond Selander Bridge, on the ocean side, is Oyster Bay, which became the main European residential area in the colonial era (Rita Hayworth had a house here), and today is the location of many diplomatic missions. There are many spacious dwellings, particularly along Kenyatta Drive, which looks across the bay. The area in front of the recently refurbished **Oysterbay Hotel** is a favourite place for parking and socializing in the evenings and at weekends, particularly by the Asian community. Ice cream sellers and barbecue kiosks have sprung up on the shore in the last few years.

Around Dar

Makumbusho Village Museum

ⓘ *Bagamoyo Rd, about 9 km from the city centre, on the right-hand side of the road just before the Peacock Hotel Millennium Towers, T022-270 0437, www.villagemuseum.home stead.com. Open daily 0930-1900, US$3, Tanzanians and children US$1, photos US$3, video cameras US$20. Taxis cost about US$10 from the city centre, or dala-dala from the New Post Office (Posta) heading towards Mwenge, which pass the entrance. Ask for Makumbusho bus stop or get off when you see the tall Millennium Towers Hotel and walk back a few metres.*

The museum gives a compact view of the main traditional dwelling styles of Tanzania, with examples of artists and craftsmen at work. There are constructions of tribal homesteads from 18 ethnic groups with examples of furnished dwelling huts, cattle pens, meeting huts and, in one case, an iron-smelting kiln. Traditional dances are performed daily from 1400 to 1800 with performers recruited from all over Tanzania. It's worthwhile having a guide to explain the origin of the dances, which end with a display of tumbling and acrobatics. There is a café, and an unusual compound, the Makumbusho Social Club, where the public is welcome. The small, corrugated-iron, partly open-sided huts are each named after one of Tanzania's game parks.

Kigamboni

The beaches on Kigamboni are the best close to the city and, like on the beaches to the north, the resorts here (see Sleeping page 38) are popular with day visitors especially at the weekends. The Kigamboni ferry (which takes cars) leaves from the harbour mouth close to the fish market, just before Kivukoni Front becomes Ocean Road, at regular intervals during the day. The ferry runs from 0600 to midnight and costs US$1 per vehicle and US$0.25 per person. Foot passengers can walk directly on to the ferry from the city side and at Kigamboni catch taxis and *dala-dala* that follow the beach road for several kilometres to where most of the more accessible resorts are. Hotels such as **Ras Kutani** and the **Amani Beach Hotel** are further down this road, around 30 km from the ferry, and you will need to contact these lodges to arrange transport if you are not driving yourself.

The small town of Kigamboni spreads up from where the ferry docks and is the site of Kivukoni College, which provided training for CCM party members, but has now been

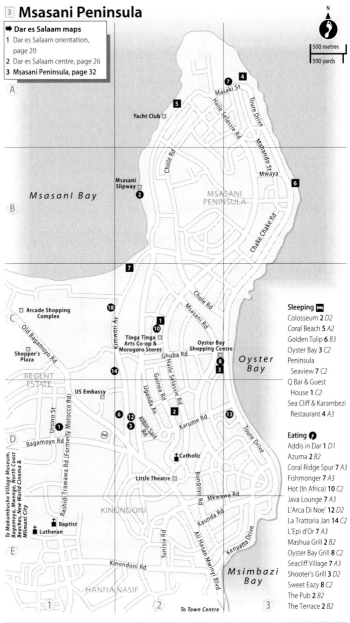

turned into a school and a social science academy. Just before the college, which faces across the harbour to Kivukoni Front, is the Anglican church and a free-standing bell. The Anglican church was formerly a Lutheran church. The new Lutheran church, a fine modern building, lies 500 m into Kigamboni. On the Indian Ocean shore side there are several small enterprises making lime by burning cairns of coral.

Gezaulole

ⓘ *Part of the Cultural Tourism Programme operated from Arusha. Further details can be obtained from the Tanzanian tourist information centre in Arusha, T027-2503 8403, www.infojep.com/culturaltours. Brochures for each project can be downloaded from the website.*

The coastal village of Gezaulole lies 13 km or half an hour's drive southeast of the ferry at Kigamboni, reachable by *dala-dala*. This was chosen as one of the first Ujamaa villages, part of an ultimately unsuccessful settlement policy of the early 1970s, in which people from many areas of the country were relocated to form agricultural communes. In earlier days it was a Zaramo settlement and they gave the village the name Gezaulole, which means 'Try and See' in the Kizaramo language. Today, the community has an active role in a cultural tourism programme that offers walks through the village and on the beach, short trips on a local dhow and visits to an old slave depot and a 400-year-old mosque. It is possible to stay with a local family, though it is easy enough to reach on a day trip. Inexpensive and tasty local meals are available and can be eaten with one of the families even if you are not staying for the night. Locally made handicrafts are also for sale. Profits from the programme go towards buying equipment for the local school.

Northern beaches

ⓘ *To get to either beach, a taxi from the city will cost in the region of US$15. To get to Kunduchi by public transport take a* dala-dala *from the New Post Office (Posta) in the city to Mwenge about 10 km along the Bagomoyo Rd, then change to one heading to Kunduchi (clearly signposted on the bonnet of the vehicle). Both rides will cost US$0.30. To get to Mbezi, take the same Kunduchi* dala-dala *from Mwenge, and at the sign for the White Sands Hotel on Bagamoyo Rd a couple of kilometres before the Kunduchi turn off, ask to get off (look out for the Kobil service station). At this junction you can catch a bicycle taxi for US$0.70 or a tuk-tuk for US$2, the couple of kilometres to the hotels. Do not walk along this road, as there have been muggings.*

The shore close to Dar es Salaam is not particularly good for swimming. The best beaches are at **Kunduchi**, some 25 km north of the city, and **Mbezi Beach,** 20 km north of the city. These beaches are separated by a lagoon but both are accessed along side roads off the Bagamoyo Road and are easily reached by good tarmac roads. Most of the hotels and resorts along this coast (see page 39) welcome day visitors who want to enjoy the facilities and beaches, including Silver Sands Hotel, Kunduchi Beach Hotel, Bahari Beach Hotel, Jangwani Sea Breeze Resort and the White Sands Hotel. Some charge a fee of US$5-10 for the day, and it's worth paying to use the hotels' private (and guarded) beaches – the stretches of beach between the hotels should not be visited unaccompanied, people have been mugged here. Some also charge an extra fee if you bring your own food and drink. This is because many Indian families bring full-on picnics for a day at the beach and the hotel benefits little from selling food and drink. Most have restaurants and bars with bands playing at weekends and public holidays, and some offer a variety of excursions to nearby islands and also windsurfing. Snorkelling is a bit hit and miss because the water is not always very clear, especially during the rainy seasons.

There is a good beach on the uninhabited **Bongoyo Island**, 2 km north of Msasani Peninsula. The island is a marine reserve popular for diving and snorkelling, and there are a few short walking trails, good beaches and simple seafood meals are available. A popular destination for a day trip from Dar es Salaam, boats take 30 minutes, cost US$14 return and leave from **The Slipway** on Msasani Peninsula at 0930,1130, 1330 and 1530, returning approximately one hour later. A similarly good beach can be found on **Mbudya Island**, 4 km north of Bongoyo Island, but there are no facilities here. Boat rides are available from **White Sands Hotel**, **Jangwani Sea Breeze Resort** and **Bahari Beach Hotel**.

Diving

On the mainland, local divers recommend the offshore islands around Dar es Salaam, though mainland reefs accessible from Tanga and Dar have been damaged through the illegal practice of dynamite fishing, which, through slack policing, is still a problem today. However, if you are not visiting Pemba or Zanzibar and need to get wet, there are a number of memorable dive sites around Dar worth a dip or two. Of particular note is Ferns Wall, which is on the seaward side of Fungu Yasin Reef, where you'll find large barrel sponges, gorgonian fans and 2-m long whip corals. Reef sharks are often spotted here. Because of its depth this site is for advanced divers only. Another favourite is Mwamba, a unique reef comprising large fields of pristine brain, rose and plate corals. Although slightly further out, Big T reef is a must dive for the experienced diver but only on a calm day. Latham Island, southwest of Dar, is an area surrounded by deep water where big game fish and elusive schools of hammerheads can be found. It can only be dived with a very experienced skipper who knows the area. ▶▶ *For further details, see Activities and tours, page 45.*

Kisarawe and Pugu Hills Forest Reserve

ⓘ *Follow the airport road to the south of the city. Buses to Kisarawe leave from Narungumbe St (next to the Tanzania Postal Bank on Msimbazi St in Kariakoo) about once an hour and cost US$2. To get to Pugu, turn left at the Agip petrol station in Kisarawe and the track into the reserve is a little further along on the right. It's 3 km from Kisarawe and if you're driving you'll need a 4WD.*

In the peaceful rural hill town of Kisarawe it is hard to believe that you are just 32 km southwest from the hustle and bustle of Dar es Salaam. During the colonial period Kisarawe was used by European residents of the capital as a kind of hill station to escape from the coastal heat. It receives a higher rainfall than Dar because of its slightly increased elevation. There is little to see in the town itself but the surrounding countryside is very attractive, in particular the nearby rainforest at Pugu Hills Forest Reserve about 3-4 km from the centre of Kisarawe town. It constitutes one of the few remaining parts of a coastal forest, which 10 million years ago extended from Mozambique to northern Kenya. It was gazetted as a reserve in 1954, at which time it stretched all the way to Dar's international airport and was home to many big game animals, including lions, hippos and elephants. Since then the natural growth of the metropolis, as well as the urban demand for charcoal (coupled with the lack of alternative sources of income), has seen a large reduction in the forested area. In the past few years a concerted effort has been made to counter this process and a nature trail has been established in order to encourage people to visit the area. Although Pugu contains flora and fauna which are unique to the forests of this district, you are unlikely to come across many animals in the forest; but it is a very beautiful spot and the perfect tonic for those in need of a break from Dar es Salaam. Most visitors spend the night in the new lodge here (**Pugu Hills**), though you can visit just for the day but still need to make a reservation for this with the lodge (see page 40).

Pugu Kaolin Mine and the Bat Caves

A further 3-4 km on from the Pugu Hills Reserve is Pugu Kaolin mine, which was established by the Germans in the early 1900s. Kaolin is a type of fine white clay that is used in the manufacture of porcelain, paper and textiles. The deposits here at Pugu are reputed to be the second largest in the world and should the market for it pick up, the mining of kaolin will clearly constitute a further threat to the survival of the remaining rainforest. If you continue through the mine compound you come to a disused railway tunnel, 100 m long and German built (the railway was re-routed after the discovery of kaolin). On the other side of this are a series of man-made caves housing a huge colony of bats. In the early evening at around 1800 or 1900 (depending on the time of year) the bats begin to fly out of the caves for feeding. It is a remarkable experience to stand in the mouth of the caves surrounded by the patter of wings as huge numbers of bats come streaming past you.

Dar es Salaam listings

For Sleeping and Eating price codes and other relevant information, see pages 7-9.

Sleeping

As far as top-grade accommodation is concerned, hotels in Dar es Salaam have improved in recent years and there is excellent international standard accommodation in the city centre, Msasani Peninsula and on the beaches to the north and south of the city. The lower end of the market is reasonable value, although it is always sensible to check the room and the bathroom facilities and enquire what is provided for breakfast. Also check on the security of any parked vehicle. Bear in mind that it is possible to negotiate lower rates, especially if you plan to stay a few days. Most upmarket hotels will ask visitors to pay in foreign currency – this really makes no difference but just check the rates in TSh and US$ against the current exchange rate, and make a fuss if you are charged more than the US$ equivalent of the TSh rate. Increasingly, more and more establishments are accepting credit cards, but this often incurs a commission of around 8-15%. In the middle and lower range it is usually possible to pay in TSh, and this is an advantage if money is changed at the favourable bureau rate. VAT at 20% was officially introduced in 1998 and is added to all service charges, though this is usually included in the bill.

Dar es Salaam *p22, maps p26 and p32*
The listings below are split between the city centre and the Msasani Peninsula. Msasani is the European side of town and is where most of the nice hotels can be found.

City centre
$$$$ Kilimanjaro Hotel Kempinski,
Kivukoni Front, T022-213 1111,
www.kempminski-dar essalaam.com.

Occupying a commanding position in the centre of the city overlooking the harbour, this new hotel offers 5-star luxury with contemporary decor and excellent restaurants. A large 5-storey building enclosed in blue glass, it has 180 rooms with all the facilities you'd expect of a top class business hotel. Prices start at US$310 for a de luxe room. There's also a spa, a beautiful swimming pool on the 1st floor and a gym. The **Level 8** nightclub has live music and stunning views over the city. Despite all this, it's slightly lacking in character and service is efficient but impersonal.

$$$ Heritage Motel, Kaluta/Bridge St, T022- 211 7471, www.heritagemotel.co.tz. Easy to locate in the city centre, this new hotel in a tall, yellow building is conveniently located for the Zanzibar ferry terminal, and is excellent value for money. It has comfortable, spotless rooms (although single rooms are cramped). At the time of visiting, there was a noisy building site next door.

$$$ Palm Beach, 305 Ali Hassan Mwinyi Rd, opposite the junction with Ocean Rd, T022-213 0985, www.pbhtz.com. Stylish art deco hotel, completely refurbished, a little away from the centre of town. Cool and modern decor, 32 rooms, Wi-Fi available, airy bar and restaurant. Popular beer garden with BBQ.

$$$ Peacock Hotel – Millenium Towers, 10 km north of the city on Ali Hassan Mwinyi Rd, (New Bagomoyo Rd), part of the Millennium Towers shopping centre, T022-277 3431, www.peacock-hotel.co.tz. In a glass tower block with ultra modern decor and facilities, all 60 rooms have a/c, satellite TV and internet access. The executive suites are twice the size of the standard rooms, and the junior suites have an extra spare bedroom, both for only US$20 more. Swimming pool, gym, 2 restaurants and bars. A smart business hotel near the **Makumbusho Village Museum** and **Mwenge Craft Market**.

$$$ Peacock Hotel, Bibi Titi Mohamed St, T022-212 0334, www.peacock-hotel.co.tz. Well run and centrally located modern hotel with 69 rooms, with a/c and TV, in a tower block. Great views of downtown Dar from the restaurant on the top floor, which serves good food with occasional theme nights. The unmistakable building was recently 'cocooned' in blue glass to make it cooler inside.

$$$ Protea Hotel Courtyard, Ocean Rd, T022- 213 0130, www.proteahotels.com/courtyard. A quality small hotel with good facilities, a bit more character than some of the larger hotels and with excellent food and service. Standard, superior and de luxe rooms, with a/c, TV and minibar. Wi-Fi, bar, restaurant and pool.

$$$ Royal Palm, Ohio St, T022-211 2416, www. moevenpick-daressalaam.com. Part of the Moevenpick chain, this hotel has conference and banqueting facilities, a shopping arcade and recreation centre, an outdoor swimming pool and lovely gardens. The 230 recently renovated rooms all have a/c and mod cons. The best rooms are at the rear. There's a British Airways office and several restaurants, a coffee shop and a bakery. Wi-Fi available.

$$$ Southern Sun Hotel, Garden Av, T022-213 7575, www.southernsun.com. The former Holiday Inn, this is one of the nicest hotels in Dar town centre, conveniently located next to the Botanical Gardens (their peacocks regularly fly into the hotel's gardens) and close to the National Museum. 152 well- equipped rooms with Wi-Fi access, a business centre, gym, swimming pool and a popular restaurant and bar (see Eating, page 40). Recommended for its relaxing ambience and friendly and helpful staff.

$$ Riki Hill Hotel, Kleist Sykes St, west of Mnazi Mmoja Park, T022-218 1820, www.rikihotel.com. 40 rooms in a smart white block several storeys high, comfortable a/c rooms with bathrooms. Restaurant with very good à la carte food, bar and shops, 24-hr bureau de change. Will arrange a free pick up from the airport.

$$ Valley View Hotel, on the corner of Congo St and Matumba A St, T022-218 4556, www. valleyview-hotel.co.tz. A bit out of the way, off Morogoro Rd, a turning opposite United Nations Rd, about 1 km from the intersection with Bibi Titi Mohamed St. A friendly hotel in a neat white and stone building with 41 slightly dated rooms with a/c, TVs, fridge and 24 hr room service. Buffet breakfast.

$$-$ Luther House Hotel, on the corner of Sokoine Dr and Pamba Rd, T022-212 0734, luther@simbanet.com, behind the Lutheran church on the waterfront. Central and in considerable demand, so it's necessary to book. Simple freshly painted rooms with basic shower and toilet, TVs and a/c. The **Dar Shanghai** restaurant is on the ground floor (see Eating, page 41).

$ Econolodge, corner of Libya St and Band St, T022-211 6048/50, econolodge@raha.com. A plain but functional place with sparsely furnished, clean self-contained rooms, the cheaper ones have fans, the more expensive have a/c. Small TV lounge. Price includes continental breakfast. Cheapest double US$21.

$ Jambo Inn, Libya St, T022-211 4293, www.jamboinnhotel.com. Centrally located reasonable budget option popular with backpackers. With reliable hot water and working fans, the 28 rooms are self-contained. Rates are as low as US$20 for a double and for a little more you can get a/c. The affordable restaurant serves Indian food (no booze), fresh juice and ice cream; if you are staying in the hotel you get 10% off meals. Internet café downstairs.

$ Safari Inn, Band St, T022-211 9104, safari-inn@lycos.com. Very central, similar to the nearby **Jambo Inn**, fairly simple but sound. 40 rooms, only 3 with a/c, in a square concrete block down an alleyway (there are security guards are at the entrance). Continental breakfast is included but there's no restaurant. Doubles are US$20 and a single is US$15.

$ YWCA, corner of Azikiwe St and Ghana Av, T022-213 5457, ywca.tanzania@africa online.co.tz, and the **YMCA**, T022-212 1196, are 1 block apart across Maktaba St. (The YWCA is above the Tanzania Post Bank on Azikiwe St). Both offer simple, clean and cheap accommodation with mosquito nets and fans. Men and women are accepted in both establishments.

Msasani Peninsula

$$$$ Oyster Bay Hotel, Toure Dr, T022-260 0530, www.theoysterbayhotel.com. This beautifully chic boutique hotel has recently opened, with 8 stylish bedrooms facing the Indian Ocean. Its British owners also own **Beho Beho** in Selous and place the same emphasis on luxury and relaxation. There's a quiet lawned garden with swimming pool and outdoor eating terrace and the interior is furnished with a mix of contemporary and antique African crafts. Rates are from US$300 per person full board.

$$$$-$$$ Hotel Sea Cliff, northern end of the peninsula, Toure Dr, T022-260 03807, www.hotelseacliff.com. Stylish hotel with whitewashed walls and thatched makuti roofing set in manicured grounds. 94 spacious and modern a/c rooms, most with ocean view, and 20 more units in garden cottages, all with satellite TV. **Coral Cliff** and **Ngalawa** bars, **Calabash Restaurant**, and the beautifully positioned **Karambezi** café bar over the bay. Also has a health club, gift shop, casino, bowling alley and shopping centre. One of the most luxurious hotels in Dar.

$$$ Colosseum Hotel, Haille Selassie Rd, T022-266 6655, www.colosseumtz.com. 42 rooms with a/c, plasma TVs and internet. Guests have free use of the sports facilities, which include a 20 m pool, a gym on 2 floors and 2 squash courts, and can then visit the exotic Cleopatra Spa to help soothe away the aches and pains afterwards. There's a pizzeria and a continental restaurant.

$$$ Coral Beach Hotel, Coral La, T022-260

1928, www.coralbeach-tz.com. A new wing to this hotel opened in Jan 2009, with smart, boutique style rooms, far nicer than those in the old wing. The lobby is bright and breezy; a restaurant and bar overlook the pool set in slightly unkempt gardens, and there's a business centre, gym, sauna and jacuzzi.

$$$ Golden Tulip, Toure Dr, T022-260 0288, www.goldentulipdaressalaam.com. The best thing about this hotel is the huge infinity pool that faces the ocean, set in lovely gardens, which non-residents can use for US$7. The **Maasai Grill** serves good brunches at weekends. The hotel itself looks quite smart from the lobby, but the rooms are tired and shabby. All 91 rooms have TV, a/c and minibar. The Presidential Suite has an exercise bike.

$$$-$$ Peninsula Seaview Hotel, Chuibay Rd, T0787-330888 (mob), www.peninsulaseaviewhotel.com. 12 modern en suite bedrooms with TV, Wi-Fi, fridge and fans (no mosquito nets). Food is available at **O'Willie's Irish Whiskey Tavern** on the ground floor with a restaurant terrace outside near the beach, although a sign warns not to walk on the shore without an *askari* (guard).

$$-$ Q Bar and Guest House, off Haile Selassie Rd, behind the Morogoro Stores, T0754-282474 (mob), www.qbardar.com. 20 comfortable, if a little noisy, rooms in a smart 4 storey block. All have a/c, fridge, bathroom, cool tiled floors and Tingatinga paintings on the walls. Also offer 6 dorm beds for US$12 each. A friendly and popular expat venue with live music and DJs. The bar and restaurant has 3 pool tables, a big screen for watching sport, and plenty of draught beer and cocktails (see Eating, page 42). Separate dining room for guests on the 2nd floor, breakfast included.

Around Dar *p31*
Southern beaches

$$$$ Amani Beach Hotel, 30 km south from the Kigamboni ferry, or air transfers can be arranged from Dar by the resort, T0754-410033 (mob), www.amanibeach.com for online information and reservations. Quality hotel, with a/c, en suite rooms in 10 individual whitewashed cottages decorated with African art, and with garden terraces and hammocks where breakfast is delivered. Swimming pool, tennis courts, horse riding, restaurant, bar, conference facilities and TVs. Set in 30 ha of tropical woodland around a wide bay. Rates are from US$250 per person full board.

$$$$ Ras Kutani, T022-213 4802, www.raskutani.com. 28 km further south of Kigamboni ferry, 2-hr road journey or a short charter flight from Dar es Salaam arranged by the resort. This resort is small and intimate with only 9 luxurious cottages, 4 suites and a family house beautifully decorated, in a superb location on a hill overlooking the ocean and the wide arch of white sandy isolated beach and freshwater lagoon. Windsurfing, swimming pool, watersports and snorkelling available but no diving. All rates are full board and are about US$400 per person, resident rates are considerably lower with specials on weekdays.

$$ South Beach Resort, 8 km south of the Kigamboni ferry, Mjimwema, T022-282 0666, www.southbeachresort-tz.com. A brash new resort with a large swimming pool and jacuzzi set in a huge paved area with an outdoor disco, pool tables, shisha lounge and **Whisky Shack** bar. 36 en suite rooms in a characterless block overlooking the pool. The camping ground is shadeless and a long walk from facilities. Day passes are available – Mon-Fri US$4, Sat-Sun US$6, with fines if you bring in your own food or fail to wear your wristband 'tag' which proves payment.

$$ Sunrise Beach Resort, Kipepeo Beach near Mjimwema, 7 km south of Kigamboni ferry, T022-550 7038, www.sunrisebeachresort.co.tz. Characterless 2-storey bandas with balconies and bathrooms, thatched restaurant and bar, Wi-Fi zones, sun loungers on the beach, watersports including jet skiing, quad bikes available for hire. Far better option for camping than the neighbouring **South Beach Resort**, tents are available for US$15 with decent ablutions blocks nearby.

$$-$ Kipepeo, Kipepeo Beach next to the **Sunrise Beach Resort** (above), near the village of Mjimwema, 7 km south of the Kigamboni ferry, T 0754-276178 (mob), www.kipepeovillage.com. 20 rustic beach huts built on stilts in a grove of coconut palms with en suite bathrooms. Plenty of space for vehicles and camping (separate hot showers). Overlanders can leave vehicles for a small daily fee while they go to Zanzibar. Very good food and drinks are served on the beach or at the beach bar. A relaxed and affordable option close to the city. Camping US$ 5 per person, basic beach bandas US$25, huts from US$65 including full English breakfast. Recommended.

$ Mikadi Beach, 2 km from the Kigamboni ferry, T0754-370269 (mob), www.mikadibeach.com. Recently upgraded by new management, this popular campsite in a grove of coconut palms is right on the beach. Secure parking, clean ablutions, 12 simple double bandas, a swimming pool and a very good bar that gets busy at the weekends. Day rates US$4. For a small fee you can park vehicles here whilst you visit Zanzibar.

Northern beaches

Note It is unsafe to walk along the beach between the northern hotels. The hotels' private beaches are watched by security guards and at the end of the beaches are signs warning guests of the danger of mugging – take heed.

$$$ Beachcomber Hotel, Mbezi Beach, T022-264 7772/4, www.beachcomber.co.tz. Rather concrety development, a/c rooms with TV, minibar and phone. Swahili decor, health club with sauna, steambath and massage, watersports facilities and swimming pool. Offer a free shuttle between the hotel and the airport.

$$$ Kunduchi Resort, Kunduchi, T0748-612231 (mob), www.kunduchiresort.com. Very elegantly decorated modern rooms with a/c, TV and minibar, a mixture of African and Islamic-style architecture and decor for main service areas. Bar, pool bar, excellent restaurants serving continental, seafood and Japanese food, swimming pool, tennis and squash courts, gym, beach with palms and flowers, live music at weekends, watersports facilities and trips to off-shore islands. The **Wet n Wild Water Park** is just next door.

$$$ White Sands, Mbezi Beach, T022- 264 7620/6, www.hotelwhitesands.com. Offers 88 sea-facing rooms in thatched villas with TVs, a/c and minibar, and 28 apartments for short and long term lets. Swimming pool, gym, beauty centre and watersports including a PADI dive centre. Several restaurants, one off which (Indian) is superb, and bars. **Water World Waterpark** is adjacent to the hotel. Free shuttle service into the city.

$$ Jangwani Sea Breeze Resort, Mbezi Beach, T022-264 7215, www.jangwani.org. 34 a/c rooms with flatscreen TVs and en suite bathrooms. Swimming pool set in pretty gardens with lots of flowering shrubs, right on the beach. 2 other pools (1 just for toddlers), watersports, gym, go-karting, 3 restaurants, pool bar, barbecues and live music at the weekends. Can organize excursions, free shuttle to town centre.

$$-$ Bahari Beach, Kunduchi, T022-265 0352, www.twiga.ch/tz/bahari.htm. With renovations planned at the time of writing, this hotel has self-contained accommodation in thatched rondavaals with a/c and TV. There's a large bar and restaurant area under the high thatched roofing (limited menu but good food). Swimming pool with bar, band at the weekends and public holidays, traditional dancing Wed night, sandy beach, garden surroundings, gift shop, tour agency and watersports centre. Reports welcome.

$ Silver Sands, Kunduchi, T022-265 0567, www.silversands.netfirms.com. Pleasant old hotel with restaurant, bar and basic accommodation, some rooms have fans and are cheaper than those with a/c. The weekends attract a number of day visitors when a band plays on the terrace. The food is good and not badly priced. There is also a campsite with a well-maintained ablutions block and it is possible to pitch your tent right on the beach. You can leave a vehicle here while you make a trip to Zanzibar.

Kisarawe and Pugu Hills Forest Reserve *p33*
$$-$ Pugu Hills, Pugu Hills Forest Reserve, 35 km south of Dar, T0754-56 5498 (mob), www.puguhills.com. 4 smart bamboo huts erected above the forest floor on poles, with hardwood floors and Swahili furnishings. Swimming pool, fabulously rustic restaurant offering snacks and 4 dishes a day including one vegetarian dish, and lovely nature trails through the forest (non-residents have to pay a US$30 fee for hiking in the reserve). The resort can also arrange visits to a local cattle market. Camping available, US$7 per person.

Eating

Most of the hotels, including those on the beach out of town, have restaurants and bars. While the city centre has a fair number of good places to eat, many of these are only open during the day, cater for office workers and do not serve alcohol. The best places for dinner and evening drinks are out of the centre on the Msasani Peninsula.

Dar es Salaam *p22, maps p26 and p32*
City centre
††† Baraza Bar & Grill, Southern Sun Hotel, see Sleeping, above. A deservedly popular restaurant serving a mix of Swahili and continental food, including pastas, curries, grills, seafood and vegetarian dishes. Outdoor terrace onto pool area and a relaxed bar.
††† Istana, Ali Hassan Mwinyi Rd, opposite Caltex petrol station, a few kilometres out of the city on the Bagamoyo Rd, T022-276 1348. Specializes in Malaysian cuisine. Theme nights throughout the week, Chinese on Tue, meat grill on Wed, satay buffet on Thu, etc. Specialities include *roti canai*, puffed bread filled with meat, chicken and apples and served with hot curries. Good value all you can eat buffets. Open kitchen, tables in the garden, play area with staff to look after children.
††† Oriental, Kilimanjaro Hotel Kempinski, see Sleeping, above. Open Tue-Sun. Smart, 1st floor restaurant serving a varied Southeast Asian menu with an excellent wine list and impeccable service. Bookings advised.
††† Sawasdee, top floor of **New Africa Hotel**, Azikwe St, T022-211 7050. Exceptionally good and very authentic Thai food, wonderful harbour views, buffet on Tue and Fri.
††† Serengeti and **L'Oliveto**, Royal Palm Hotel, see Sleeping, above. **Serengeti** open daily, **L'Oliveto** open Mon-Sat. Upmarket Italian restaurants, reservations recommended and you need to dress up. At the Serengeti there are themed nights every day of the week: Mediterranean on Mon, Italian on Tue, Oriental on Wed, seafood on Thu, popular fondue night on Fri, Tex-Mex on Sat and Indian on Sun. Serve good value buffet lunches with freshly made pasta or salads.
†† Chef's Pride Restaurant, virtually opposite **Jambo Inn Hotel**, on road between Libya St and Jamhuri St. Closed evenings. Good food at excellent prices, fast service. Italian, Chinese, Indian and local dishes available.
†† Mediterraneo, Kawe Beach off Old Bagomoyo Rd, midway between the city and the northern beaches, T022-261 8359. Italian pastas, salads and Chinese, occasional live music and Swahili-style buffets. On Sat afternoon there is a barbecue from 1200-2000. Overlooks the ocean, a good place for kids.

¶ Sichuan Restaurant, Bibi Titi Mohamed St, T022-215 0548. Excellent and authentic Chinese restaurant. Most main course dishes are around US$5, and there is a large range to choose from. Plenty of vegetarian options.
¶ Chinese Restaurant, basement of **NIC**, Samora Av. Good, inexpensive Chinese cuisine, also African and some continental dishes. Has been going some 30 years.
¶ City Garden Restaurant, corner of Garden Av and Pamba St, T022-213 4211. African, Indian and Western meals, buffets at lunchtime, excellent juices, tables are set in garden, good service and consistently popular, especially at lunchtime. A new branch has opened on Bridge St. Highly recommended.
¶ Cynics' Café and Wine Bar, in the TDFL building opposite the **Royal Palm Hotel**. Open Mon-Thu until 1800, Fri until 2100. Fresh pastries, salads, sandwiches, wine by the glass, beer and coffee.
¶ Dar Shanghai, behind the Swiss Air office in Luther House Hotel, Sokoine Dr, T022-213 4397. Chinese and Tanzanian menus, canteen-style atmosphere. The food's not brilliant but it's quick and filling. No booze but soft drinks.
¶ Debonair's and **Steer's**, corner of Ohio St and Samora Av, T022-212 2855. Quality South African chains. **Debonair's** serves pizza and salads, while **Steer's** offers burgers, ribs and chips. Also in the Steer's Complex is **Hurry Curry**, an Indian takeaway, **Chop Chop, Chinese**, and a coffee shop. Eat at plastic tables in a/c surroundings.
¶ Garden Food Court, on the 2nd floor of the Haidery Plaza, Kisutu St. Daily 1100-2300. Here you'll find the **Red Onion**, a fairly formal Indian and Pakistani restaurant serving good value lunchtime buffets for US$8; **Natasha Spiced Chicken** for barbecued fast food; and the **Coffee Bud** for snacks and drinks. Food can be taken out of each restaurant and eaten on the outside terrace.
¶ Jambo Inn, Libya St, T022-211 0711. Excellent cheap Indian menu, huge inflated chapattis like air-cushions, also Chinese and European dishes. Outside and inside dining.

Ice cream parlours ¶ Sno-cream, Mansfield St. An old-fashioned ice cream parlour serving excellent ice cream. Incredibly elaborate sundaes with all the trimmings.

Msasani Peninsula

¶¶¶ Addis in Dar, 35 Ursino St, off Migombani St/Old Bagamoyo Rd in the Oyster Bay area, near the site of the new US Embassy, T0713-266299 (mob). Open Mon-Sat 1200-1430, 1800-2300. Small and charming Ethiopian restaurant with an outside terrace. Plenty of choice for vegetarians. It is wise to drop in and book ahead.
¶¶¶ Azuma, 1st floor at **The Slipway**, T022-260 0893. Open Tue-Fri for dinner, Sat-Sun for lunch and dinner. Japanese and Indonesian restaurant, authentic cuisine with good views over the bay. Very good sushi. If you book ahead, the chef will come out from the kitchen and prepare food at your table.
¶¶¶ Fishmonger, upstairs, Sea Cliff Village Food Court, T0754-30 4733 (mob). Excellent fish and seafood from US$12-20, nice outdoor terrace. Non-fishy options are limited.
¶¶¶ Hot (in Africa), off Haile Selassie Rd, T0784-839607 (mob). Afro-European food, some of the most inventive cuisine in Dar, traditional roast lunches on a Sun, very trendy decor and a good atmosphere.
¶¶¶ Karambezi, Hotel Sea Cliff, see Sleeping, above, T0787-044555 (mob). Beautiful setting on wooden decking overlooking the ocean. Good selection of wines and a varied menu with pizzas, pastas, seafood and grills. Treat yourself to the seafood platter for 2, for US$46.
¶¶¶ Oyster Bay Grill, Oyster Bay Shopping Centre, T022-260 0133. Daily 1800-2300. Very elegant and some of the best food in Dar, specializing in steak, seafood and fondue. Average price with wine US$30 per head, much more if you go for the lobster

Coral Ridge Spur, Sea Cliff Village Food Court, T0752-201745 (mob). South African steak and ribs chain, geared up for families with a play area, Wild West themed decor, big portions and help-yourself salad bar. The meat is good but if you have eaten at a Spur elsewhere in Africa there are no surprises.

L'Arca di Noe', Kimweri Av, T0713-601 282 (mob). Open Wed-Mon. Italian pastas, seafood, pizzas from US$5, range of desserts, wide selection of wines, pleasant atmosphere. Wed night is an all you can eat buffet with 26 different pastas and sauces, and on Thu you get a free glass of wine with every pizza.

La Trattoria Jan, Kimweri Av, T0754-282969 (mob). Excellent Italian cuisine, ice creams, open air seating at the rear, pleasant atmosphere and good value. The pizzas are some of the best in town, takeaway available.

Mashua Bar and Grill, at The Slipway, T022-260 0893. Open evenings only. Grills, burgers, salads and pizza. Offers ocean views and live music and dancing on Thu.

Q Bar and Guest House, see Sleeping, above. Open daily 1700 until late, happy hour 1700-1900. The bar has 3 pool tables, a big screen for watching sport, pub grub and plenty of draft beer and cocktails. Live music on Fri and Sat is 1970s soul night.

Shooter's Grill, 86 Kimweri Av, Namanga, T0754-304733 (mob). Very good steaks, ladies get a free glass of wine on Wed and men get a free beer with every T-bone steak sold on a Thu. Live music on Sun, good atmosphere.

Sweet Eazy, Oyster Bay Shopping Centre, Toure Dr, T0755-754074 (mob). Open daily until midnight, happy hour 1700-1900 and all night on Fri. Cocktail bar and restaurant, African and Thai cuisine. Jazz band on Sat.

The Pub, at The Slipway, T022-260 0893. International food, mainly French and Italian in an English-style pub setting, also serves burgers, sandwiches and grills, draft beer and there are good Sun roast lunch specials.

The Terrace, at The Slipway, T022-260 0893. Open Mon-Sat. Italian cuisine and barbecued grills and seafood. Moorish painted arches and outside dining area.

Java Lounge, Sea Cliff Village Food Court, T0748-467149 (mob). Very good service, outdoor deck, range of cocktails and 20 different coffees. Good breakfasts, light meals.

L'Epi d'Or, Samora Av and Sea Cliff Village, T022-213 6006. Mon-Sat 0700-1900. Coffee shop and bakery serving very good sandwiches with imaginative fillings, cappuccino and fresh juice, croissants, pastries and salads.

Around Dar *p31*
Southern beaches

Mikadi Beach, see Sleeping, above. A great spot on the beach for weekend lunch or all-day breakfasts if you want to escape the city. Speciality alcoholic slushies and a varied menu including fish and chips, home-made burgers, steak sandwiches, vegetarian crêpes and a seafood platter. Day rate of US$4 covers use of the swimming pool next to the shore.

Bars and clubs

Dar es Salaam *p22, maps p26 and p32*
There are few nightclubs as such in Dar, though many of the hotels and restaurants mentioned above crank it up late in the evening with live music or a DJ, especially at weekends when tables are cleared away for dancing. Some discos are in attractive outdoor settings. Those hotels and restaurants that have regular discos and/or live music are notably **Jangwani Sea Breeze Resort**, and **White Sands Hotel** on the northern beaches; **South Beach Resort** on the southern beaches; **O'Willie's Irish Whisky Tavern** at the Peninsula Sea View Hotel; and the **Q bar** on the Msasani Peninsula. In the city centre, **Level 8** cocktail bar on the 8th floor of the Kilimanjaro Hotel Kempinski,

Kivukoni, T022- 213 1111, provides mesmerizing views of downtown Dar at night and occasional live jazz

Club Bilicanas, Mkwepu St, T 0788-904169 (mob). Open every night until around 0400. Entry at weekends is US$23 per person (half of this is redeemable against food and drink). Reopened in Jan 2009 after an extensive 2 year renovation programme, this is far and away the most popular club in Dar. It has been imaginatively designed, with a VIP lounge, 7 bars and glass decor, and has all the effects you'd expect from a world-class night club. Drink prices are reasonable and the place is fully a/c.

Entertainment

Dar es Salaam *p22, maps p26 and p32*

Casinos

Las Vegas Casino, corner of Upanga Rd and Ufukoni Rd, T022-211 6512. Roulette, poker, blackjack, vingt-et-un and slot machines.

There are also casinos at the **Kilimanjaro Hotel Kempinski,** T022-213 1111 (open until 0400) and **Hotel Sea Cliff**, T022-260 0380.

Cinema

Visitors seldom go to the cinema, which is a pity as the audience reaction makes for an exciting experience. Programmes are in the newspapers or monthly guides such as *Dar Life* and *Dar es Salaam Guide*. The cinemas show mostly Indian, martial arts or adventure films. Entrance is about US$4.

British Council, Ohio St, T022-211 6574. Shows films fairly regular film on a Wed.
Century Cinemax, in the Mlimani City Shopping Mall near the university, T022-277 3053. New complex, discounts on Thu.
New World Cinemas, New Bagamoyo Rd, T022-277 1409. Discounts on Tue.

Live music

Concerts of classical music by touring artists are presented by the **British Council**, the **Alliance Française** and occasionally other embassies. African bands and artists and Indian groups play regularly at the hotels and restaurants especially at weekends. Look for announcements in the *Dar es Salaam Guide*, and *What's Happening in Dar es Salaam*.

Theatre

British Council, Ohio St. Occasionally presents productions, check the papers.
Little Theatre, Haile Selassie Rd, off Ali Hassan Mwinyi Rd, next door to the Protea Apartments, T0784-277388 (mob), daressalaamplayers@raha.com. Presents productions on an occasional basis, perhaps half a dozen a year, usually drama and comedy and 1 musical a year. Very popular, particularly the Christmas pantomime.

Shopping

Dar es Salaam *p22, maps p26 and p32*
There are shops along Samora Av (electrical goods, clothing, footwear) and on Libya St (clothing and footwear). Supermarkets, with a wide variety of imported foods and wines, are on Samora Av between Pamba Av and Azikawe St; on the corner of Kaluta St and Bridge St; opposite Woolworth's on Garden Av; in Shopper's Plaza; and in the Oyster Bay Hotel Shopping Mall. The new Mlimani City Shopping Mall, Sam Nujoma Rd near Dar University is also home to a huge **Shoprite** supermarket. A popular location for buying fruit and vegetables is the market on Kinondoni Rd, just north of Msimbuzi Creek.

The Namanga shops are at the corner of Old and New Bagamoyo Rd, and are basically stalls selling household supplies and food; there's a good butcher's towards the back. **Manzese Mitumba Stalls**, Morogoro Rd, Manzese, has great bargains for second- hand clothing and Uhuru St has several *kanga* shops (the traditional wrap-arounds worn by women) usually for little more than US$3. **Ilala Market**, on Uhuru St, sells vegetables, fresh and dried fish and second-hand clothing. Fresh fish and seafood can be bought at the **Fish Market** on Ocean Rd, just past the Kigamboni ferry.

Shopping centres and department stores

Haidery Plaza, at the corner of Upanga Rd and Kisutu St in the city centre. A small shopping centre that as well as shops has an internet café and a popular food court.

Mayfair Plaza, opposite TMJ Hospital, Old Bagamoyo Rd, Oyster Bay, www.mayfairplaza.co.za. This centre has a number of quality shops, including upmarket clothes and shoe shops, jewellers, dry cleaners, banks, pharmacies and a branch of **Shoprite**, plus coffee shops and a food court.

Mlimani City Shopping Mall, San Nujoma Rd, near the university. Dar's latest shopping centre with a huge cinema complex, one of the biggest **Shoprite** supermarkets in Tanzania, and a plethora of smaller shops covering everything from clothes to electronics.

Oyster Bay Hotel Shopping Centre, see Sleeping, page 37. Supermarket, internet café, and gift and art shops. There are plans to renovate this centre.

Sea Cliff Village, Hotel Sea Cliff, see Sleeping, page 37. Has a branch of the excellent bookshop **A Novel Idea** (see below), a French bakery, and a good shop upstairs called **Mswumbi** that sells fresh coffee beans. There are 'day rooms' for rent here – bedrooms that are only let out during the day for people who have returned to Dar from safari and are not flying out until the evening (contact the hotel). There's also a vastly overpriced supermarket catering for expats.

Shoppers' Plaza, Old Bagamoyo Rd, on the Msasani Peninsula. Has a good variety of shops, including a large supermarket. The Arcade nearby, has a travel agency, boutiques, hairdresser, nail technician, glass and framing shop, and restaurants.

The Slipway complex, on the Msasani Peninsula, facing Msasani Bay. Expensive, high quality goods can be found here. Another branch of **Shoprite**, an internet café, a craft market, a hair and beauty salon, several restaurants and a branch of Barclay's Bank with an ATM. There are also a few 'day rooms'. To book these contact Coastal Air, T022-260 0893, www.slipway.net.

Woolworths, in the New PPF Towers building on Ohio St. The only department store in Dar, this is a South African clothing store very similar to the UK's Marks & Spencer.

Bookshops

Second-hand books can be found at the stalls on Samora Av, on Pamba St (off Samora), on Maktaba St and outside Tancot House, opposite Luther House. Most of these also sell international news magazines such as *Time*, *Newsweek*, *New African*, etc.

A Novel Idea, branches at **The Slipway**, Msasani Peninsula, at the **Hotel Sea Cliff**, and on the corner of Ohio St and Samora Av, T022-260 1088, www.anovelidea-africa.com. The best bookshop in Dar by far, this is perhaps the most comprehensive bookshop in East Africa with a full range of new novels, coffee table books, maps and guide books.

Other bookshops are the **Tanzanian Bookshop**, Indira Gandhi St, leading from the Askari Monument; and **Tanzania Publishing House**, Samora Av. Both have only limited selections.

Curios and crafts

Traditional crafts, particularly wooden carvings, are sold along Samora Av to the south of the Askari Monument. Good value crafts can be purchased from stalls along Ali Hassan Mwinyi Rd near the intersection with Haile Selassie Rd and, in particular, at **Mwenge**, along Sam Njoma Rd, close to the intersection with Ali Hassan Mwinyi Rd. This is the best place for handicrafts in Dar, and for ethnographia from all over Tanzania and further afield (notably the Congo). There are a large number of shops and stalls offering goods at very reasonable prices and you can watch the carvers at work. The market is 10 km or about 30 mins from the town centre towards the northern beaches, easily reached by *dala-dala*. It is just around the corner from the *dala-dala* stand.

More expensive, quality modern wood products can be obtained from **Domus**, in The Slipway complex, which also houses **The Gallery**, selling wood products as well as paintings by local artists. There is a craft market here selling tablecloths, cushions and beadwork, and a Tingatinga workshop.

Activities and tours

Dar es Salaam *p22, maps p26 and p32*
Athletics
Meetings at the National Stadium, Mandela Rd to the south of the city.

Cricket
Almost entirely a pursuit of the Asian community. There are regular games at week-ends at: **Annadil Burhani Cricket Ground**, off Aly Khan Rd; **Gymkhana Club**, off Ghana Av; **Jangwani Playing Fields**, off Morogoro Rd, in the valley of Msimbazi Creek; and **Leaders Club**, Dahomey Rd, off Ali Hassan Mwinyi Rd.

Diving
Sea Breeze Marine Ltd, White Sands Hotel, T022-264 7620, www.seabreezemarine.org.

Fishing
Marine fishing can be arranged through many of the hotels on the beaches.

Fitness and running
The **Hash House Harriers** meet at 1730 on Mon afternoons, details are available from the British Council, Ohio St, T022-211 6574.
Colosseum Hotel & Fitness Club, Haille Selassie Rd, T022-266 6655. Has a state-of-the-art gym spread over 2 floors, a range of fitness classes, 2 squash courts, a swimming pool and spa. A day pass is US$15 with discounts for multiple days.
The Fitness Centre, off Chole Rd on Msasani Peninsula, T022-260 0786. A gym with weights and also aerobics and yoga classes.
Millenium Health Club, Mahando St, at the north end of Msasani Peninsula, T022- 260 2609. Has a gym, aerobics, sauna and beauty parlour.

There are also gyms at the **Hotel Sea Cliff** and **White Sands Hotel**.

Golf
Gymkhana Club, Ghana Av, T022-212 0519. Only guests are permitted to play golf at the club. Costs are around US$28 for 18 holes, you can hire very good quality clubs and shoes . Here, because of a shortage of water, you will be playing on browns not greens.

Sailing
Yacht Club, Chole Rd, Msasani Peninsula, T022-260 0132. Visitors can obtain temporary membership here. The club organizes East Africa's premier sailing event, the Dar to Tanga (and back) Yacht Race every Dec.

Soccer
The main African pursuit, followed by everyone from the President and the Cabinet down. Matches are exciting occasions, with radios throughout the city tuned to the commentary. Terrace entrance is around US$2 (more for important matches). It is worth paying extra to sit in the stand. There are 2 divisions of the National league, and Dar es Salaam has 2 representatives – **Simba** and **Young Africans** (often called Yanga) – and there is intense rivalry between them. Simba, the best- known Tanzanian club, have their origins in Kariakoo and are sometimes referred to as the 'Msimbazi Street Boys' – they have a club bar in Msimbazi St. Initially

formed in the 1920s as 'Eagles of the Night', they changed their name to 'Sunderland FC' in the 1950s. After independence all teams had to choose African names and they became Simba. See www.simbasportsclub.com, for more information.

The 2 main venues for watching soccer: **Karume Stadium**, just beyond the Kariakoo area, off Uhuru St.

National Stadium, Mandela Rd to the south of the city. This has recently been renovated. The national team **Taifa Stars** play regularly here, mostly against other African teams.

Swimming

Many of the larger hotels have swimming pools that charge a small fee for non-guests.
Swimming Club, Ocean Rd near Magogoni St. This is the best place to swim in the sea. Otherwise, the best sea beaches are some distance to the north and south of the city.
Water World, next to **White Sands Hotel**, Mbezi Beach. Tue-Sun. US$5 adults, US$4 children. Has several different water slides and games for children.
Wet 'n' Wild, Kunduchi Beach, T022-265 0326. This is an enormous complex largely, though not exclusively, for children. There are 7 swimming pools with 22 water slides, 2 are very high and 1 twists and turns for 250 m. There is an area for younger children, tennis and squash courts, go-karting, an internet café, hair and beauty parlour, fast food outlets and a main restaurant, and also facilities for watersports on the open ocean, including windsurfing and fishing trips; there is even a qualified diving instructor.

Tour operators

A variety of companies offer tours to the game parks, the islands (Zanzibar, Pemba, Mafia) and to places of historical interest (Kilwa, Bagamoyo). It is well worth shopping around as prices (and degrees of luxury) vary. It is important to find an operator that you like, offers good service, and does not pressure you into booking something.
Bon Voyage Travel, Ohio St, T022-211 8198, www.bonvoyagetz.com.
Cordial Tours, Sokoine Rd T 027-250 6495, www.cordialtours.com.
Easy Travel & Tours, Raha Towers, Bibi Titi Mohamed St, T022-212 3526, T022-212 3842, www.easytravel.co.tz.
Ebony Tours & Safaris, T0773-011153 (mob), www.ebony-safaris.com.
Emslies Travel Ltd, NIC Investment House, 3rd Flr, Samora Av, opposite Royal Palm Hotel, T022-211 4065, www.emsliestravel.biz.
Fortune Travels & Tours Ltd, Jamhuri St, T022-213 8288, www.fortunetz.com.
Hakuna Matata, The Arcade, Old Bagamoyo Rd, T022-270 0231.
Hima Tours & Travel, Simu St, T022-211 1083, www.himatours.com.
Hippo Tours & Safaris, Mwalimu Nyerere Cultural Centre (Nyumba ya Sanaa), T022-212 8662, www.hippotours.com.
Hit Holidays, Bibi Titi Mohamed St (near Rickshaw Travel), T022-211 9024, www.hitholidays.com.
Holiday Africa Tours & Safaris, TDFL Bldg, Ohio St, T022-212 7746.
Interline Travel & Tours, NIC Life House, Sokoine Dr/Ohio St, T022-213 7433.
Kearsley Travel and Tours, Kearsley House, Indira Gandhi St, T022-211 5026/30, www.kearsley.net.
Leopard Tours, Movenpick Royal Palm Hotel, Ohio St, T022-211 9754/6, www.leopard-tours.com.
Lions of Tanzania Safari & Tours, Peugeot House, Bibi Titi Mohamed Rd, T022-212 8161, www.lions.co.tz.
Luft Travel & Cargo Ltd, GAK Patel Bldg, Maktaba St, T022-213 8843.
Planet Safaris, Ohio St, T022-213 7456, www.planetsafaris.com.
Reza Travel & Tours, Jamhuri St, opposite Caltex Station, T022-213 4458, reza@rezatravel.com.
Rickshaw Travel (American Express Agents),

Royal Palm Hotel, Ohio St, T022-211 4094, www.rickshawtravels.com.
Skylink Travel & Tours, TDFL Bldg, Ohio St, opposite Royal Palm Hotel, T022-211 5381; airport, T022-284 2738; Mayfair Plaza, T022-277 3983, www.skylinktanzania.com.
Sykes, Indira Ghandi St, T022-211 5542, www.sykestours.co.uk.
Takims Holidays Tours and Safaris, Mtendeni St, T022-211 0346/8, www.takimsholidays.com.
A Tent with a View Safaris, Zahara Towers, Zanaki St, T022-211 0507, www.saadani.com, www.selouslodge.com, www.safariscene.com.
Walji's Travel Bureau, Zanaki St/Indira Ghandi St corner, T022-211 0321, www.waljistravel.com.
Wild Thing Safaris, corner of Makunganya St and Simu St, www.wildthingsafaris.com.

Transport

Dar es Salaam *p22, maps p26 and p32*
Air
Domestic flight schedules change regularly and it's always best to check with the airlines before making plans. It's also necessary to reconfirm your bookings a day or so before flying since timings often change. **Precision Air** depart from the International Terminal at Dar airport, the other airlines all depart from the domestic terminal. Most domestic flights have a baggage limit of 15 kg per person.
Air Tanzania, T022-211 8411, www.air tanzania.com, has 2 daily flights from Dar to **Zanzibar** at 0900 and 1600 (25 mins); a daily flight to **Kilimanjaro** at either 0910 or 2000 (55 mins) depending on the day of the week; and 2 daily flights to **Mwanza** at 0700 and 1600 (1 hr 30 mins).

Coastal Air, T022-284 2700/1, www.coastal.cc, has a scheduled service from Dar to **Arusha** (2 hrs) via **Zanzibar** daily at 0900. This service continues on to the **Serengeti**. To **Kilwa** (1 hr) via **Mafia Island** (30 mins) at 1500. To **Pemba** at 1400 (1 hr). Flights to **Ruaha** (3 hrs) via **Selous** (30 mins) depart at 0830. There's another daily flight to the Selous at 1430 which stops at all the camps. **Tanga** (1 hr 30 mins) daily via Zanzibar and Pemba at 1400. Flights to **Zanzibar** daily every 1½ hrs from 0730-1530, and 1645 and 1745 (20 mins, US$75).

Precision Air, T022-213 0800, T022-212 1718, www.precisionairtz.com, flies to **Mwanza** Wed, Fri and Sun at 0810, Mon, Tue, Thu and Sat at 1055 (2 hrs). To **Tabora** (2 hrs) and **Kigoma** (3 hrs 15 mins) Fri-Wed at 1100. To **Zanzibar** daily 0650 and 1320 (20 mins). There are additional flights to Zanzibar on Thu and Fri at 0830, and on Mon, Tue, Wed, Sat and Sun 1100. To **Arusha** daily 0820 and 1320 (1 hr 15 mins). To **Shinyanga** on Mon, Wed, Fri and Sun at 1330 (2 hrs).

Zanair, T024-223 3768, www.zanair.com, have daily flights from Dar to **Zanzibar** at 0900, 1215, 1645 and 1815; direct to **Pemba** at 1345; and to the **Selous** at 0840.

Airline offices Air India, Bibi Titi Mohamed St, opposite Peugeot House, T022-215 2642, www.airindia.com. **Air Malawi**, JM Mall, Samora Av, T022-212 4280, www.airmalawi.com. **Air Tanzania**, ATC Bldg, Ohio St, T022-211 8411, www.airtanzania.com. **British Airways**, based at the Royal Palm Hotel, Ohio St, T022-2113 8202, www.britishairways.com. **Emirates**, Haidery Plaza, Kisutu St, T022-2116 1003, www.emirates.com. **Ethiopian Airlines**, TDFL Bldg, Ohio St, T022-2117 0635, www.flyethiopia.com. **Gulf Air**, Raha Towers, Bibi Titi Mohamed St/Maktaba St, T022-2137 8526, www.gulfairco.com. **Kenya Airways**, Peugeot House, Bibi Titi Mohammed/Ali Hassan Mwinyi Rd, T022-211 9376, www.kenya-airways.com. **KLM**, Peugeot House as above T022-211 3336, www.klm.com. **Oman Air**, airport, T022-213 5660, www.oman-air.com. **Qatar Airways**, Barclays House, Ohio St, T022-211 8870, www.qatarairways.com. **South Africa**

The dala-dalas of Dar es Salaam

Ownership of one or more minibuses, or *dala-dalas*, remains a favourite *mradi* (income-generating project) for Dar es Salaam's middle class and, judging by the numbers squeezed into their interiors and the speed at which they travel between destinations, those returns are handsome. Realizing that they can't monitor the number of passengers using their buses, the *dala-dala* owners stipulate how much they expect to receive at the end of the day from the 'crew' they hire to operate the vehicle; anything left over constitutes the crew's wages. It is a system that appears to work to everyone's advantage other than that of the passenger, who suffers the consequent overcrowding and the suicidal driving as *dala-dala* competes with *dala-dala* to arrive first and leave fullest.

In a forlorn attempt to reduce the number of accidents, the Tanzanian government passed a law in early 1997 requiring all public service vehicles to install governors restricting speeds to under 80 kph. However, *dala-dala* and coach operators soon worked out ways to override them, or simply disconnected them completely, and within weeks the drivers were proceeding with their old reckless abandon.

The basic crew of each *dala-dala* is made up of two people: the driver (clearly picked for the ability to drive fast rather than well) and the turnboy (in Dar slang *Mgiga debe* – literally 'he who forces things into a tin can'), whose job it is to collect money and issue tickets, harangue passengers who fail to make room for one more, as well as to entertain the remainder of the bus with hair-raising acrobatic stunts hanging from the door of the bus (there is at least one *Mpiga debe* currently working in Dar who has just one leg – it's not hard to imagine how he lost the other one). Supplementing this basic crew at either end of the journey is a tout, who bawls out the intended destination and route, attempting to attract or, if necessary, intimidate people (at times this stretches to actual manhandling of passengers) into entering his *dala-dala*. He is paid a fixed amount for each bus that he touts for. In addition, when business is slow, there are people who are paid a small amount to sit on the bus pretending to be passengers in order to give the impression that it is fuller than it actually is to the potential passenger, who will then enter the *dala-dala*, assuming it will be leaving sooner than the next one along.

The *dala-dala* network radiates from three main termini in the town centre, Posta at Minazi Mirefu ('Tall palm trees') on the Kivukoni Front opposite the Old Post Office; Stesheni, close to the Central Railway Station; and Kariakoo, around the Uhuru/Msimbazi Street roundabout for destinations south and at the central market for those in the north. From each of these you can catch *dala-dalas* to destinations throughout Dar es Salaam, although the four main routes are along Ali Hassan Mwinyi to Mwenge (for the Makumbusho Village Museum, Mwenge handicrafts market and the university); along the Kilwa Road to Temeke, Mtoni and Mbagala (these take you to the Salvation Army); to Vingunguti via Kariakoo and Ilala (for the TAZARA Railway Station); and along the Morogoro Road to Magomeni, Manzese and Ubongo. For a *dala-dala* going to the airport ask for Uwanja wa Ndege at Minazi Miretu.

Airways, Raha Tower, Bibi Titi Mohammed St, T022-2117 0447, www.flysaa.com. **Swiss Air**, Luther House, Sokoine Dr, T022-211 8 8703, www.swiss.com.

Bus

The main bus station is **Ubungo Bus Station** on Morogoro Rd, 6 km from the city centre, which can be reached by bus, *dala-dala* or taxi. Outside on the road is a long line of booking offices. Recommended for safety and reliability is **Scandinavia Express**, which has its own terminal on Nyerere Rd at the corner of Msimbazi St (taxi from the city centre approximately US$2), though all buses also stop at the Ubungo bus station, T022-285 0847, www.scandinaviagroup.com. There is a small airport-style arrival and departure lounge at the terminal with its own restaurant. Buses are speed limited, luggage is securely locked up either under the bus or in overhead compartments, and complimentary video, drinks, sweets and biscuits are offered. Buses depart daily for **Arusha** at 0745, 0830 and 0915 (9 hrs, US$30 luxury service, US$20 standard); **Mbeya** at 0645 and 0745 (12 hrs, US$20); **Tanga** at 0800 (6 hrs, US$8.50), and **Dodoma** at 0915 and 1100 (4 hrs, US$10). **International destinations Mombasa** and **Nairobi** in Kenya, **Kampala** in Uganda and **Lusaka** in Zambia.

Other bus companies include **Dar Express** T0754-373415 (mob) and **Royal Coaches** T022-212 4073.

Car hire

Car hire can be arranged through most of the tour operators. Alternatively try:
Avis, in the TDFL building, opposite the Royal Palm Hotel, Ohio St, run by Skylink Travel & Tours, T022-211 5381, www.avis.com;
Business Rent a Car, 16 Kisitu St, T022-212 2852, www.businessrentacar.com; **Green Car Rentals**, Nukrumah St, along Nyerere Rd, T022-218 3718, T0713-227788 (mob), www. greencarstz.com; **Hertz**, airport, T022-211 2967, www.hertz.com; or **Tanzania Rent-A-Car**, airport, T022-212 8062.

Ferry

All ticket offices of the ferry companies with services to **Zanzibar** and **Pemba** are on Sokoine Dr adjacent to the jetty. Ignore the touts who may follow you to the offices to claim credit and take commission. The companies themselves advise travellers to completely ignore them and it is easy enough to book a ticket on your own.

Most ferries are fast and comfortable hydrofoils or catamarans that take on average 90 mins to reach Zanzibar, and the tourist fare is fixed at US$45 one way (including port tax) for all companies. The slow over-night boat back from Zanzibar with **Flying Horse** is US$25. Payment for tickets is in US$ cash. Companies no longer accept TCs.

Services to **Zanzibar and Pemba**:
Azam Marine, T022-213 4013, www.azam-marine.com. Australian-built Seabus catamarans that take 1 hr 40 mins to Zanzibar. They depart daily at 0800, 1115, 1330, 1400 and 1600. From Zanzibar to Dar, ferries depart at 0700, 0930, 1330 and 1630. On Tue and Fri they also operate a service from Dar es Salaam to Pemba via Zanzibar at 0730 which arrives in Zanzibar at 0855, departs again at 1000 and arrives in Pemba at 1205. The return boat on Tue and Fri departs Pemba at 1230, arrives in Zanzibar at 1435, departs again at 1630 and arrives in Dar at 1755.
Flying Horse (Africa Shipping Corporation), T022-212 4507. Outward journey to Zanzibar departs at 1200 and takes 2 hrs, the overnight return from Zanzibar departs 2200. For some this return journey is inconvenient as passengers are not let off at Dar until 0600, when Customs open. However, tourists are accommodated in comfortable, a/c compartments, and provided with mattresses to sleep on until 0600. A good option for budget

travellers as the fare is only US$20 each way and you save on accommodation for 1 night. **Sea Express**, T022-213 7049, www.sea-express.net. Daily ferry from Dar at 0715 which arrives in Zanzibar at 0915, leaving Zanzibar for the return at 1600. On Mon, Wed, Fri and Sun the ferry continues from Zanzibar (departing at 1000) to Pemba where it arrives at 1200, leaving Pemba at 1300 to return. Dar es Salaam to Pemba US$70.

Sea Star, T022-212 4988. Fast service to Zanzibar that takes 1 hr 30 mins, departs Dar at 1030. The return leaves Zanzibar at 0700. **Sepideh**, T0713-282365 (mob). Departs Dar at 0700, continuing on to Pemba at 0930 on Sat, Mon and Thu, arriving there at 1300.

Train

The **Central Railway Station** is off Sokoine Dr at the wharf end of the city at the corner of Railway St and Gerezani St, T022-211 7833, www.trctz.com. This station serves the passenger line that runs through the central zone to **Kigoma** on Lake Tanganyika and **Mwanza** on Lake Victoria.

TAZARA Railway Station is at the junction of Mandela Rd and Nyerere Rd, about 5 km from the city centre, T022-286 5187, www.tazara.co.tz. You can book train tickets online. It is well served by *dala-dala* and a taxi from the centre costs about US$5. This line runs southwest to **Iringa** and **Mbeya** and on to **Tunduma** at the Zambia border (24 hrs). It is a broader gauge than the Central and Northern Line.

To Zambia Express trains go all the way to **New Kapiri Mposhi** and this journey takes 40-50 hrs. The local trains, which stop at the Zambian border, are a little slower, and take approximately 23 hrs to get to **Mbeya**. First class cabins on both trains contain 4 berths and second class 6.

Directory

Dar es Salaam *p22, maps p26 and p32*
Banks
All banks listed have ATMs, though some may only accept Visa cards. **Standard Chartered**, in the Plaza on Sokoine Dr near Askari Monument, and at International House on corner of Garden Av and Shaaban Robert St. **Barclay's**, TDFL Building, Ohio St, and at The Slipway. **CitiBank**, Peugeot House, Bibi Titi Mohammed Rd. **National Bank of Commerce**, Samora Av and corner of Sokoine Dr and Azikiwe St. Bank hours are Mon-Fri 0830-1500, Sat 0830-1130.

Currency exchange Foreign exchange bureaux are to be found in almost every street, and are especially common in the area between Samora Av and Jamhuri St. They are usually open Mon-Fri 0900-1700 and Sat 0900-1300. Some are also open Sun morning. Rates vary and it is worth shopping around. Tanzania's sole agent for American Express is **Rickshaw Travel**, at the Royal Palm Hotel, T022-211 4094, www.rickshaw travels.com, open Mon-Fri all day, Sat-Sun mornings only, will issue TCs to card-holders.

Money transfers Western Union money transfer is available at the Tanzanian Postal Bank, on Samora Av, and at the General Post Office on Azikiwe St.

Embassies and consulates

You can usually be sure that diplomatic missions will be open between 0900 and 1200. Some have afternoon opening, and some do not open every day. Even when a mission is officially closed, the staff will usually be helpful if something has to be done in an emergency. **Austria**, Samora Av, T022-260 1492. **Belgium**, 5 Ocean Rd, T022-211 2688. **Burundi**, 1007 Lugalo Rd, T022-211 7615. **Canada**, 38 Mirambo St, Garden Av, T022-216 3300, dslam@ dfait-maeci.gc.ca. **Denmark**, Ghana Av, T022-2113 8878. **Egypt**, 24 Garden

Av, T022-211 3591. **Finland**, Mirambo St and Garden Av, T022-219 6565. **France**, 34 Ali Hassan Mwinyi Rd, T022-2666 0213. **Germany**, Umoja House, Garden Av and Mirambo St, T022-211 7409, www.dares salam.diplo.de. **Ireland**, 353 Toure Dr, T022-260 2355. **Italy**, 316 Lugalo Rd, T022-211 5935/6. **Japan**, 299 Ali Hassan Mwinyi Rd, T022-211 5827/9. **Kenya**, 127 Mafinga St, Kinondoni T022-266 8285. **Malawi**, 38 Ali Hassan Mwinyi Rd, T022-266 6248. **Mozambique**, 25 Garden Av, T022-211 6502. **Netherlands**, Umoja House 4th floor, Mirambo St T022-211 0000. **Norway**, 160 Mirambo St, T022-213 8852. **Rwanda**, 32 Ali Hassan Mwinyi Rd, T022-211 5889. **South Africa**, 1338 Mwaya Rd, Oyster Bay, T022- 260 1800. **Spain**, 99B Kinondoni Rd, T022- 266 6936. **Sudan**, 64 Ali Hassan Mwinyi Rd, T022-211 7641. **Sweden**, Extelcoms Bldg, Samora Av, T022-219 6500. **Switzerland**, 79 Kinondoni Rd, T022-266 6008/9. **Uganda**, Extelcom Bldg, Samora Av, T022-266 7391, daily 0830-1600. **UK**, Umoja House, Garden Av, T022-211 0101. **USA**, 686 Old Bagamayo Rd, Msasani, T022-266 8001. **Zambia**, Ohio St and Sokoine Dr, T022-2118 4812. **Zimbabwe**, Off Ali Hassan Mwinyi Rd, T022-211 6789.

Immigration

The immigration office is on the corner of Ohio St and Garden Av, T022-211 2174, open Mon-Fri 0730-1530.

Internet

There are hundreds of internet cafés all over the city centre and you will not have a problem accessing your email. The cost of internet access has fallen considerably over the last few years, and is available for less than US$0.50 per hour, although it is usually quite slow. Some places offer additional services such as printing or scanning.

Libraries

Alliance Française, behind Las Vegas Casino, T022-213 1406, offers library facilities, French TV news, occasional concerts and recitals, open Mon-Fri 1000-1800. **British Council**, on the corner of Ohio St and Samora Av, T022-2116 5746, has an excellent library, with reference, lending, newspapers and magazines. **National Central Library**, Bibi Titi Mohamed Rd, near the Maktaba St intersection, T022-215 0048/9.

Medical services

Hospitals The main hospital is **Muhimbili Hospital**, off United Nations Rd, northwest of the centre towards Msimbazi Creek, T022-215 1298. **Oyster Bay Medical Clinic**, follow the signs along Haile Selassie Rd, T022-266 7932, is an efficient and accessible small private medical centre. **Aga Khan Hospital**, Ocean Rd at the junction with Ufukoni Rd, T022-2115 1513. All these hospitals are well equipped and staffed. See also **Flying Doctors Society of Africa**, page 16.
Pharmacies In all shopping centres, and small dispensaries are also found in the main residential areas.

Police

The **main police station** is on Gerazani St near the railway station, T022-211 5507. There are also stations on Upanga Rd on the city side of Selander Bridge, T022-212 0818; on Ali Hassan Mwinyi Rd at the junction with Old Bagamoyo Rd (Oyster Bay), T022-266 7322/3; and at the port T022-211 6287.
Emergencies For police, ambulance and fire brigade, T112.

Post office

The **main post office** is on Azikiwe St, and it's here that you will find the poste restante. There's a small charge for letters collected. Other offices are on Sokoine Dr, behind the bus stand on Morogoro Rd; and Libya St. Post offices are generally crowded.
Courier services Several branches of the major courier companies around town which

will collect. **DHL** at DHL House, 12B Nyerere Rd, T022-286 1000/4, www.africa.dhl.com. **Fedex**, T022-270 1647. **TNT**, T022-212 4585.

Telephone
International calls and faxes can be made from the telecoms office near the main post office on Simu St. There are also many private telephone offices all over town. Hotels will usually charge up to 3 times the actual cost. There are mobile phone shops all over Dar and international calls may well be cheaper if you buy a local phone or pay-as-you-go SIM card.

North to Kilimanjaro & Moshi

Contents

- 54 *Map: North to Kilimanjaro and Moshi*

56 The road from Dar to Moshi
- 57 Usambara Mountains
- 58 *Map: Lushoto*
- 59 Back on the road to Moshi
- 60 Listings

64 Moshi and Marangu
- 65 Moshi
- 65 *Map: Moshi*
- 66 Machame
- 66 Marangu
- 67 Listings

74 Kilimanjaro National Park
- 74 Ins and outs
- 75 *Map: Kilimanjaro National Park*
- 77 Background
- 78 Routes up the mountain

Footprint features

- 54 Don't miss …
- 71 Kilimanjaro Marathon
- 76 Tipping on Kilimanjaro
- 78 The snow sepulchre of King Solomon
- 81 The meaning of Kilimanjaro

At a glance

◉ **Getting around** Buses regularly ply the Dar to Moshi road and there are connecting buses and *dala-dala* into the Usambara Mountains. Climbing operators include transfers to the ascent points of Kilimanjaro.

◐ **Time required** 2-3 days from Dar to Moshi with a night or 2 in Lushoto. A week to climb Kili, which includes a night on either side in Moshi or Marangu.

❄ **Weather** Temperate all year around the bottom of the mountain; icy conditions at the top.

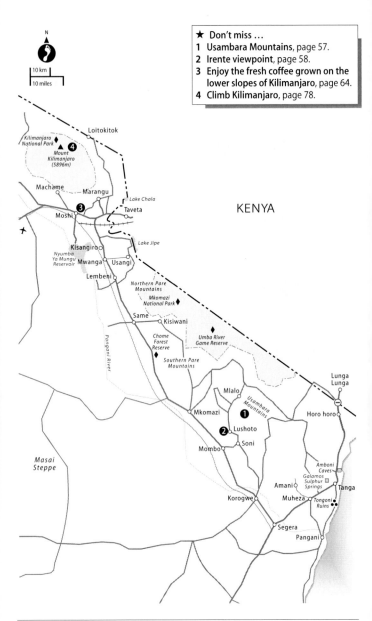

The main road out of Dar es Salaam travels inland and joins the highway that runs the length of Tanzania and effectively links Kenya to the north with Malawi to the south. Travelling north from Dar to Arusha is a scenic drive of some 650 km, through extensive farmland and sisal plantations with the ever-present backdrop of the Pare and Usambara mountain ranges to the east. The main road is very busy, with a steady stream of buses linking Dar with Arusha, and the small regional towns offer petrol stations and services for bus passengers and drivers wishing to take a break from their journey. Away from the main road is the small mountain town of Lushoto, which is very attractive and a recommended spot for some good hiking in the hills. The forests and mountain scenery of the Usambara are not what is normally expected by visitors to Tanzania. Moshi is the town at the foot of Kilimanjaro and climbs start just a few kilometres away at the entrance of the Kilimanjaro National Park. On the approach to Moshi you may well be rewarded with a glimpse of the snow-capped top of Kili when the mists lift off the summit in the late afternoon. Climbing Mount Kilimanjaro is an adventurous break from game viewing and reaching the 'Roof of Africa' is one of the continent's greatest challenges. It is the highest mountain in the world that can simply be walked up.

The road from Dar to Moshi

From Dar es Salaam, the main road goes 109 km to the west to Chalinzi and the junction with the main north-south road. North from Chalinzi it passes through the regional centres such as Karogwe, Mombo and Same before reaching Moshi at the foothills of Kilimanjaro. This is where climbers begin their ascent of the mountain. The road will not hold your attention long: the small towns that you pass through are fairly nondescript, but they do provide facilities such as petrol stations and shops and access to the Usambara Mountains to the east, which are worth a detour for the good hiking opportunities and country lodges, and the attractive town of Lushoto. Further north closer to Moshi are the Pare Mountains and Mkomazi National Park.

▸ *For listings, see pages 60-63.*

Ins and outs

The driving time between Dar and Moshi is roughly seven to eight hours and there are scores of buses each day that ply this route. From Moshi it is a further 80 km to Arusha. There are daily flights between Dar es Salaam and Zanzibar and **Kilimanjaro airport**, which lies roughly midway between Moshi and Arusha. ▸ *For further details, see Transport, page 63.*

Korogwe → *5°0'S 38°20'E. Phone code: 022.*

Korogwe is a small town that you pass through on the way from Tanga or Dar es Salaam north to Moshi. It lies at 52 m, on the north bank of Pangani/Ruvu Rivers, whose fertile valley, with its many settlements, stretches to the west. The local people are of the Zigua and Wasambaa tribes but call themselves Waluvu. It is a local administrative centre due to its position near the local sisal estates, the Dar es Salaam–Nairobi road and railway and its proximity to the Usambara and Pare Mountains. There are a few shops, a market, a hospital and a Christian mission. Most buses stop here at one of the many petrol stations in and around town, which also feature restaurants and shops catering for the bus passengers. There are a couple of reasonable places to stay and eat if you want to break the journey between Dar and Moshi but there's little reason to.

Mombo

Mombo is a small town on the Dar es Salaam to Moshi highway. There's little of interest here, its main activity is the provision of services for travellers and again lots of buses stop here at either the oddly named **Liverpool Hill Breeze**, 1.5 km north of Mombo, or the **Manchester Executive Inn** in town, which have petrol stations and serve fast food. It is worth a mention, however, as this is the junction with the road to Soni and Lushoto in the Usambara Mountains (see below). You can jump off the bus here and switch to one of the many *dala-dala* that climb the mountain road the 33 km from Mombo to Lushoto.

Usambara Mountains

The Usambara Mountains are approximately 110 km long, range 30-60 km in width and at their highest point at Mount Mgamba are 2440 m above sea level. They are accessible from Lushoto in the west and Amani in the east. The Usambaras are fairly unique in that they support tropical forests of the kind normally only found in West Africa forest and are home to euphorbias, acacias, giant ferns, palms, lobelias, camphors (Japanese and Usumbaru) eucalyptus and fig trees. Wildlife to be seen includes the elegant Colobus monkey, blue monkeys and a wide variety of birds. Several bird species are endemic, including the Usambara Eagle-owl and Usambara weaver. The views on the southern and western sides of the mountains are of spectacular vistas of the Masai plains below. Kilimanjaro can be seen on a clear day and at the end of the day the sun turns the land an unforgettable colour.

Lushoto is about 1½ hours or 33 km off the main Korogwe–Moshi road where the turn-off is at Mombo. The road up to Lushoto via the small town of **Soni** is spectacular as it twists and turns through the mountains, with glimpses of small waterfalls in Mlalo River. The tiny market town is reminiscent of an Indian hill station and the country lodges in the region have a charming colonial atmosphere. The climate changes quickly as you rise up into the mountains. Sunny days are warm, but cloudy and windy days get very cool and it is comfortable to sit around a fire in the evening throughout the year. The big pull here is exploring the Usambara Mountains, dotted with streams and waterfalls and rural villages. There is plenty of opportunity for hiking or mountain biking through the deep forests and green hillsides, and this part of Tanzania is a long way from the scorched plains of the game parks. From the hotels you can hire a guide for walks into the forest and up the peak of Kwa Mongo, a hike of three to four hours.

Lushoto → *Phone code: 027. Altitude: 1500 m.*

Lushoto, at an elevation of around 1500 m, was the town chosen by early German settlers to escape from the heat and dust of the plains for the holidays. Back then it was called Wilhemstal and the cool, fresh air and lush, green surroundings were greatly appealing. It was even once thought that it might develop into the capital of the colonial administration. It can get quite cold from June-September so take warm clothes.

Many of the surrounding farms and government buildings are originally German. There is a very fine Dutch-style **Governor's House**, just out of town on the road going north. Other reminders of the colonial connection are the horse riding arenas and the red tiles on some of the roofs of the buildings. There is a group of **German Alpine-style buildings** with flat red, rounded end tiles, chimney stacks and shutters on the east side of the main road near the Mission Hospital. The British changed the town very little. Their main contribution was to lay out a **cricket ground** just to the west of the town centre. Although football is played here now and not cricket, it is still possible to see the old weather-boarded cricket pavilion with a veranda, albeit in poor repair. East of the main road, near the Catholic church, is the **Parade Ground**. Horse riding was a favourite recreation of the Germans, and this was where the mounted officials were paraded, in front of the timber review stand. The **Lutheran church**, just west of the centre, is an attractive building, with blue window frames, black and white walls, Mangalore tile roof, a front stone arch and a free-standing bell in a wooden tower.

The **Tafori Arboretum** on the slope 1 km to the north of the town dates from the German colonial period and has thousands of pressed plants from all over Tanzania – ask for Mr Msangi or Mr Mabula if you would like to see the collection. The town also holds a fine **market** (close to the bus station) that is very colourful and lively with several small, inexpensive eating places, hair salons, tailors and a maize mill making *posho* (maize flour). Among the many products on sale is the locally produced pottery, with a variety of pots for cooking, storage or serving. One of the ancient beliefs of the Shambaa people is that Sheuta, their God or Supreme Being, made people from a handful of soil in the manner of a potter. In the Usambaras, potters are traditionally women, with the skills passed on from mother to daughter. Men are discouraged from participating in any stage of the potting process, as it is believed that to do so brings great misfortune including sterility. There is good fishing in the mountain streams, one of which runs through the centre of the town, but you'll need to be fully equipped.

This area is a place to enjoy the views and countryside. It is fertile and verdant and there are plenty of tracks to walk along. One such walk takes about 45 minutes from Lushoto to reach **Irente viewpoint** 5 km away, from where the view of the hills and the Masai Plain 1000 m below really is breathtaking. Take the road out of town towards Irente and head for the children's home. Ask around and you'll be shown the track. On the way is **Irente Farm**, where fresh fruit, vegetables, preserves, bread and cheese are sold – the large garden is an excellent picnic spot. There's now a hotel very near to the view point, aptly named **Irente View Cliff Lodge** (see page 61), with fantastic views from all the rooms.

Western Usambara Mountains Cultural Tourism Programme

ⓘ *Guides are available from the information centre just off the road opposite the bus station, open daily 0800-1800, which is run by the Friends of Usambara Society, T027-264 0132. Here there are details and photographs of each tour offered and you can discuss with the staff exactly what you would like to do. Further details from the Tanzanian Tourist Information Centre in Arusha, see page 89.*

This is a local tourism initiative advised and supported by the Dutch Development Organisation (SNV) and the Tanzanian Tourism Board. This has been one of the most successful of Tanzania's cultural tourism programmes and these days runs largely self-sufficiently. Local development projects benefiting from the scheme include maintaining traditional irrigation systems and soil erosion control for small farmers. It aims to involve and ultimately benefit the small local communities who organize tourist projects off the usual circuits. These include several one-day walking trips from Lushoto to the Irente viewpoint overlooking Mazinde village 1000 m below (see above), a walking tour of Usambara farms and flora, the increasingly popular rock tour from Soni and the Bangala River tour, which includes wading through the water. You can also visit and stay in **Carters Camp** at **Ndekia**. This is a hut precariously perched on a rocky outcrop, built by an American writer as his launch pad for hang-gliding. There are also longer three- to five-day excursions walking into the Western Usambara Mountains via the villages of **Lukozi**, **Manolo** and **Simga** to reach the former German settlement of **Mtae**, a small village perched high up on the western rim of the escarpment, and the tour to the **Masumbae Forest Reserve**. Another hike is to **Mlalo** and **Mount Seguruma** (2218 m) about 25 km north of Lushoto. One of the more ambitious tours offered is a seven-day bike ride from Lushoto to Moshi through the mountains. On overnight hikes and rides, you stay in local guesthouses and in some cases local homes, or the tourist office will supply tents and sleeping bags. The costs for all these trips varies greatly but expect to pay in the region of US$10-15 per day per group and US$3 per day per person for a guide. There are additional costs for accommodation and food. Most of the guides are former students of the Shambalai secondary school in Lushoto, speak fair to good English, and can give you information on the history of, and daily life in, the Usambara Mountains.

Back on the road to Moshi

Same

A small town 126 km north of Korogwe and 103 km south of Moshi, Same is a base for a visit to Mkomazi National Park (see below). The market has covered and open sections, with a good selection of earthenware pots and bowls, baskets and mats. The bus station is particularly well organized with bus shelters clearly displaying the destinations and routes of the various buses. A feature of the area is the hollowed-out honey-logs hanging from the trees. Every Friday there's a cattle market at Mgagau about 15 minutes drive away. Ask at the **Elephant Motel** (see page 63) for directions.

Mkomazi National Park

ⓘ *www.tanzaniaparks.com. Open daily sunrise to sunset. Entry into the park is US$20 per day per adult and US$5 per child (5-16). Access to the park is through the Zange Gate, 7 km east from Same. There is very little tourist development in the park, it is well off the normal safari circuit and there is only one camp (see page 63). The reason for this is it's primarily being kept as a conservation area (see below). There are 3 small airstrips inside the reserve used by chartered planes.*

This national park of 3600 sq km lies about 100 km north of Tanga and is contiguous with

Kenya's Tsavo National Park. In the rainy season herds of elephant, zebra and oryx migrate between the parks. The name means 'where the water comes from' in the local Pare language and refers to the Umba River on the south eastern border. Mkomazi Game Reserve was established in 1951, but by 1988 heavy poaching had destroyed its rhino and elephant populations, and overgrazing by pastorals who brought their cattle into the reserve had taken its toll. In 1989 the government gave Tony Fitzjohn, a conservationist with The George Adamson Trust a mandate to rehabilitate the wilderness. He set about building an infrastructure of roads, airfields, water pumps and dams, and recruited anti-poaching rangers. These efforts have proved successful and now Mkomazi is so well protected that the government upgraded it from a game reserve to a national park in 2005. In the 1980s, there were only 11 individual elephants; today there are over 1000.

The landscape is wide savannah dotted with baobab trees, which is an ideal environment for rhino. The **Mkomazi Rhinos Resettlement Project**, coordinated by the Tanzania Wildlife Protection fund, has taken a lead role in relocating black rhino from South Africa to Mkomazi Reserve and Ngorongoro. The eight released rhino here are kept in intensive protection zones and it is hoped that they will breed, after which they will be relocated within Tanzania to other traditional natural habitats. It is an expensive programme. The cost of transferring 10 rhinos is put at over US$1 million.

African hunting dogs, the endangered wild dog and other big mammals such as zebra, giraffes and gazelles have also been reintroduced. The reserve is home to about 400 bird species including falcons, eagles, hawks, hornbills, barbets, starlings, weavers and shrikes.

The road from Dar to Moshi listings

For Sleeping and Eating price codes and other relevant information, see pages 7-9.

Sleeping

Korogwe *p56*

$ Korogwe Transit Hotel, on the main road, T022-264 0640. Mosquito nets, private bath with hot water most of the time, some rooms have a/c, overpriced for what you get, front rooms have a balcony but are very noisy because of the traffic. With the number of people around security could be an issue.

$ Korogwe Travellers' Inn, main road opposite the bus station, T022-264 0564. Bar, restaurant, fans, very basic, only baths with cold water, no showers or toilet seats. Only stay if other places are full.

$ Motel White Parrot, from the bus stand turn left for 400m, T022-264 1068, motelwhiteparrot@yahoo.com. By far the best place to stay in Korogwe, and fairly new. The white double-storey building has 22 small but smart a/c rooms with hot showers, satellite TV and phones. You can also camp at the back for US$4 per person and there's a toilet and shower. There is a separate thatched restaurant and bar.

$ Segera Highway Motel, at Segera, the junction with the turn-off for Tanga, 17 km south of Korogwe, T022-264 0815. For motorists this is a useful stop en route to Tanga or Moshi, either overnight or just for a cup of tea at the Engen petrol station on this busy junction. The thatched roadside restaurant has a surprisingly large menu of steaks, salads, breakfasts, pizza and pastas, plus shakes and juices. Out back you can camp for US$5 or there are 23 very smart new motel-style chalets for US$25 a double.

$ Sunrise Guest House and Bar, Main Rd, 400 m from post office, T022-264 0967. Best of the budget options, clean with toilet and shower, fan and mosquito net, basic food available.

Usambara Mountains *p57*

$$-$ Maweni Farm, 2 km from Soni up a good dirt road, at the foot of a large rockface, T027-264 0427, www.maweni.com. This guesthouse on a farm has 1 single and 7 double rooms, 4 with en suite bathrooms. Lovely restaurant with veranda, organic locally grown food and home-made bread, bar serving local wine, lounge with fire place, established gardens, sauna and swimming pool, internet access. A very pretty setting next to a small lake, lots of nature trails through the forest, and they run 1-3 day guided hikes. En suite rooms are US$50, those with a shared bathroom are US$36. Rates are B&B, lunch is US$5 and dinner US$10. Pick ups can be arranged from the bus in Mombo.

$ Hotel Kimalube, on the hill coming up into Soni before reaching the bus stand, T0787-755385 (mob). There are 6 rooms with mosquito nets and warm bucket showers, very basic, warm beers and sporadic electricity, but cheap at US$4.

$ Soni Falls Hotel, about 1 km from Soni, a 5-min walk from the bus stand, T0787-765 378 (mob). Originally built in the 1930s and recently refurbished, there are 10 double rooms with nets and en suite bath, shower and flush toilet facilities and hot water. Restaurant has a mixed local and European menu (meals US$2-5), and the well-stocked bar offers wine made by the local Benedictine monks. From the veranda there are good views of the river and falls and the peak of Kwa Mongo. Space for parking. Excellent value, price includes breakfast. Camping in the grounds, from where you can hear the waterfall, US$3.50.

Lushoto *p57, map p58*

There are a number of basic guesthouses around the market in Lushoto itself, but by far the best places to stay to enjoy the mountain scenery are the country lodges on the outskirts.

$$$ Grant's Lodge, Mizambo, Lushoto, T027-264 2491, www.grantslodge.com. 15 km from Lushoto along a road that is rough in places; signposted from Lushoto, start by heading north on the road that passes the post office and district offices. Lovely brick house, 5 rooms, a welcoming atmosphere, open fireplace, games are organized on the lawn, lots of classic movies to watch. Generous helpings of tasty home- cooked food – soups are excellent as is the hot chocolate. Can organize short or long walking safaris with photocopied instructions. Car safaris can also be arranged. Range of bird reference books in the library. Highly recommended. Payment can be made in US$ or TSh.

$$$ Irente View Cliff Lodge, Irente Viewpoint, 5 km from Lushoto, T027-264 0026, www.itenteview.com. The newest and best positioned mid-range lodge in the region on a stunning cliff top location with 18 comfortable rooms with balconies, TV, phone, tea and coffee trays, hot water, spacious grounds with amazing views, restaurant and bar. Can organize guides for hikes. A single is US$50, a double US$65 and a triple US$95. Recommended. Adjacent to it is a campsite (US$3 per person) with hot showers and its own bar serving cheap meals.

$$$-$$ Lushoto Executive Lodge, 1.5 km from town T027-264 0076, www.lushotoexecutive lodge.co.tz. With comfortable self-contained rooms in single-storey brick buildings with TV and 4-poster beds, some have self- catering kitchens and thatched roofs, set in manicured gardens, restaurant and bar, meals are prepared from local farm produce. There's also a gym and sauna.

$$ Muller's Mountain Lodge, 13 km from town on the road to Migambo, on the same road as **Grant's Lodge**, so follow their signs, T027-264 0204, www.mullersmountain lodge.co.tz. Built in 1930 in the style of an English country home, it has brick gables, attractive gardens and orchards, and lovely views. 7 bedrooms, shared dining and living rooms with outsized fireplaces, large camping area on the hill above the house, plus very good food and service; they offer guided walks. Pick ups can be arranged from town.

$$-$ Irente Farm, 5 km from town southwest towards Irente viewpoint, T027-264 0000, murless@elect.org. Run by the Evangelical Lutheran Church. Has a wonderful cheese factory. You can buy a picnic lunch from the farm to take with you to climb to the viewpoint, including rich brown bread, several types of jam, fresh butter, cheese and fruit juice. Accommodation on offer is in a simply furnished self-catering house, sleeping up to 6 (US$83); doubles (US$16); or there's a campsite with an ablution block and watchman (US$4).

$$-$ Lawns Hotel, 1 km before town on Soni Rd, T027-264 0005, www.lawnshotel.com. Old colonial-style hotel, has wonderful views with fireplaces in the rooms plus a veranda, restaurant and lively bar. Rates include a very good breakfast. Some rooms are self- contained, the cheaper ones have shared facilities. Given that the building is over 100 years old, the quality of the rooms varies so look at a few. Run by a football-loving Cypriot who is quite a character and a good source of information about Tanzania. Camping possible, US$5 per person, with fairly new ablutions block with hot water.

$ Karibuni Lodge, 1 km south of town on a hill to the left of the road, T027-264 0104. A stone house with a wide veranda, set in a lush tract of vegetation with a lounge and bar, self-catering kitchen or meals can be organized. Accommodation is in a 6-bed dorm, in rooms with or without bathrooms or you can pitch a tent in the garden. Can organize local guided walks.

$ Lushoto Sun Hotel, Boma Rd near the police station, T027-264 0082. Popular, has a good restaurant and 10 large, but a little gloomy, double rooms with nets and hot water for US$12. Safe parking.

$ Mandarin Grand Hotel, 1 km on the hillside to the west of town, T027-264 0014. Best of the simple board and lodgings and cheap – from US$10 – and safe with good views over Lushoto. With 21 rooms there's a choice of singles with shared bathrooms or en suite spacious doubles with bath tubs and hot water, or you can negotiate to camp in the garden. There's also a restaurant and bar but service can be slow. The charismatic owner, Mr. Mandari is very helpful and has a 1951 Mercedes-Benz parked outside that he's owned that long.

$ St Eugene's Guesthouse, 2 km before Lushoto on the Soni Rd, T027-264 0055. Run by the Usambara Sisters, plain but comfortable, 14 self-contained rooms in a double-storey building decked with vines, hot water and phones. Check out the white starched bed linen and hand embroidered bed covers. Serves food, including delicious home-made ice cream, and in the farm shop you can buy home-made jam and marmalade made from various fruits such as passionfruit and grapefruit, herbed cheeses and rather potent banana wine. This is a convent and a Montessori teacher training centre with modern buildings in gardens well tended by the sisters.

$ Shooting Star Inn, Chakechake Rd to the south of town, T027-264 0192. Neat and modern with en suite bathrooms with showers and long drop toilets, in a bright white block with concrete patio and small restaurant serving basic meals. They plan to put TVs in the rooms, meaning the price of US$8 for a double will go up.

$ White House Annex, in town near the market, T0784-427471 (mob), whitehouse@raha.com. Self-contained singles and doubles in a tidy 1-storey white house near the tourist office and bus stand, TV room, bar and small restaurant, local food but good and big portions, sitting room. There is also an adjoining internet café here.

Same *p59*

$ Elephant Motel, T027-275 8193, www.elephantmotel.com. Simple but more than adequate, 16 double rooms with mosquito nets, bathroom with hot water, and TV with limited DSTV (BBC and CNN). Staff are helpful. Also has a good restaurant and bar serving Western and Oriental dishes. Set in well maintained gardens, you can also camp for US$5 per person and there's toilets and showers. You can organize a guide here to take you to some of the local farms or a cattle market.

Mkomazi National Park *p59*

$$$$ Babu's Camp, 11 km from the entrance gate of Zange, T027-254 8840, www.babus camp.com. Not as luxurious as the usual tented camps, but simple and comfortable, and the only accommodation within the park. The 6 tents are spacious and have attached bathrooms with shower and toilet. Activities include day and night game drives, game walks, and they can ask permission to take guests to see the rhino. Transport into the reserve is usually organized when you make a reservation.

Eating

Refer to Sleeping, above.

Lushoto *p57, map p58*
All guesthouses and lodges have restaurants and bars, and in town itself there are a number of cheap food stalls and local bars, again around the bus stand and market.

Transport

Lushoto *p57, map p58*
Bus, dala-dala and 4WD
The roads to Lushoto are excellent, all sealed, even the 33-km gradual climb up from Mombo, which was resurfaced by the Germans in 1989 and is still in fairly good repair. Public transport is frequent and hitching is possible as there are plenty of 4WDs who will give lifts in this area. Buses and *dala-dala* from **Mombo** take about 1½ hrs and cost US$2. You can also get a direct bus from **Tanga**, but it is slow, 6 hrs, and there are also slow buses between Lushoto and **Arusha** (6 hrs) and **Moshi** (5½ hrs). Direct buses from **Dar** leave the stand on Mafia St in the Kariakoo area throughout the morning and take 7 hrs.

Directory

Lushoto *p57, map p58*
Banks National Microfinance Bank (NMB), on the main road opposite the bus station, changes money but at poor exchange rates and although it has an ATM it doesn't take foreign cards. **Internet** There is internet access at **White House Annex** and some of the hotels offer access. **Post office** At the northern end of main street.

Moshi and Marangu

Moshi is the first staging post on the way to climbing Mount Kilimanjaro and a pleasant place to spend a few days organizing your trip. It's an unusual African town in that it has very few European or Asian residents, unlike Arusha. Climbing expeditions depart from the town into Kilimanjaro National Park early each morning. The two peaks of this shimmering snow- capped mountain can be seen from all over the town and it dominates the skyline except when the cloud descends and hides it from view. Moshi means 'smoke' – perhaps either a reference to the giant volcano that once smoked or the regular smoke-like cloud. Marangu is 23 km from Moshi and is the closest village to Kilimanjaro National Park, the entrance to which is 5 km away. Accommodation here is more expensive than Moshi, and if you're on a tight budget you should plan your assault on the mountain from Moshi. ►► *For listings, see pages 67-73.*

Background

The area around Moshi is particularly fertile due to the volcanic soils and there are lots of melt-water streams fed by the snow. This is where Arabica coffee, the premium quality of the two coffee varieties, is grown by the Chagga people, helping them to become one of the wealthiest of the Tanzanian groups. All around the town, and on the lower slopes of Kilimanjaro, vast plantations of coffee blanket the area. Notice that the low coffee bushes are grown with taller banana palms for shade. The first coffee grown in Tanzania was planted at the nearby Kilema Roman Catholic Mission in 1898. Growth was steady and, by 1925, 100 tons were being produced each year. The Chagga people are particularly enterprising and formed the Kilimanjaro Native Cooperative Union (KNCH) to collect and market the crop themselves.

Moshi is the centre of Tanzania's coffee industry; the Coffee Board is located here and coffee from all over Tanzania is sold at auction to international buyers. However, apart from the coffee produced in the immediate locality, the crop does not pass through Moshi, it is auctioned on the basis of certified type, quality and grade, and then shipped directly from the growing area to the buyer. Not all of the wealth generated by the sale of coffee makes its way back to the growing community. Local small farmers have been known to receive only half the Moshi export price. By the time the coffee is sold in London their purchase price amounts to only one-tenth of the London price. Interestingly, only 1-2% of the coffee grown in Tanzania is consumed in the country; simply because Tanzanians are traditionally chai (tea) drinkers. Moshi was the site of the signing of the Moshi Declaration after the war with Uganda in February 1979, which created the Uganda National Liberation Front (UNLF) government to replace Idi Amin.

Moshi

Moshi

Moshi is a pleasant town with the former European and administrative areas clustered around the clock tower, and the main commercial area southwest of the market. Despite being an attractive town, there are few places worth visiting in Moshi itself, and many visitors stay here just long enough to arrange their trek up the mountain and to enjoy a hot shower when they get back. The limited sights include the (non-operating) **Railway Station** southeast of the clock tower, a two-storey structure from the German period, with pleasing low arches, a gabled roof with Mangalore tiles and arched windows on the first floor. On the corner of Station Road and Ghalla Road is a fine **Indian shop building** dating from the colonial period, with wide curved steps leading up to the veranda, tapering fluted stone columns and a cupola adorning the roof. To the north of town on the roundabout marking the junction with the Dar–Arusha road, the **Askari Monument** is a soldier with a rifle and commemorates African members of the British Carrier Corps who lost their lives in the two World Wars. **Shah Industries Ltd** ⓘ *T027-275 2414*, employ many disabled

Sleeping
AMEG Lodge Kilimanjaro 11
Bristol Cottages 7
Buffalo Inn 10
Horombo Lodge 18
Keys 14
Kilemakyaro Mountain Lodge 15
Kilimanjaro Backpacker's 9
Kilimanjaro Crane 2
Kindoroko 8
Leopard 6
Mountain Inn 16
Mt Kilimanjaro View Lodge 4
Newcastle 5
Parkview Inn 1
Springlands 3
YMCA 13
Zebra 12

Eating
Aroma Coffee House 3
Chrisburger 1
Coffee Shop 7
Deli Chez 5
El Rancho 6
Golden Shower 2
Indoitaliano 9
Milan's 8
Panda 4
Tanzania Coffee Lounge 10

workers producing high-quality crafts like wood carvings, leatherwork, batiks and furniture. Their shop is on Karakana Street in the industrial area to the west of town.

Around Moshi

West Kilimanjaro The road running in a northerly direction from Boma ya Ngombe on the Moshi–Arusha road passes through Sanya Juu and Engare Nairobi to reach Olmolog. This was the main area for European farming in northern Tanzania prior to independence. After independence most estates were nationalized. These days while pockets of farmland still exist, most of the plains in this region are used by wildlife on a migratory route between Arusha National Park and Kenya's Amboseli National Park. In the dry season up to 600 elephant use this corridor and it's an important calving area for zebra, wildebeest, and Grant's and Thompson's gazelles. In addition to its diverse habitats and wildlife communities, West Kilimanjaro is also home to 12 Masai communities that depend on cattle grazing. Unfortunately, poaching for elephant ivory and bushmeat has been a problem in recent years, as this region is not protected by national park status. The Hifadhi Network is an African Wildlife Foundation (www.awf.org) initiative that has recruited local game scouts from the Masai communities who, with the rangers from Arusha and Kilimanjaro national parks, are involved in reporting and apprehending poachers. Since 2003, the Hifadhi Network has caught more than 50 poachers and this is an excellent example of how simple measures that involve local communities can be an effective conservation tool. There is a very good lodge in this region hosted by Hoopoe Safaris.

Machame

Machame is the village 30 km northwest of Moshi and the road turns off the Arusha-Dar road 12 km from Moshi. This is the start of the second most popular route up Kilimanjaro, the Machame Trail (see page 83), which is tougher than the Marangu Trail but is considered one of the most beautiful routes up. Machame itself lies in a fertile valley of farmland on the lower slopes of the mountain and the park gate is 4 km beyond the village. Accommodation is presently limited to the **Protea Hotel Aishi** (see page 69), but climb operators will transport you to the park gate from Moshi.

Marangu

Most people visit Marangu only to attempt the climb to the summit of Mount Kilimanjaro. However, Marangu is an excellent base for hiking, birdwatching and observing rural Africa. Marangu is 11 km north of Himo, a village 27 km east of Moshi on the road to the Kenya border.

The Ordnance Survey map of Kilimanjaro (1:100,000) is an essential guide for walks. The main tracks in the region radiate from the forest boundary, through the cultivated belt of coffee and bananas, to the road that rings the mountain. Other maps are less accurate but widely available at about US$10. For full details of climbing Kilimanjaro, see page 78.

Foothill walks

The **Marangu/Mamba Cultural Tourism Programme** ⓘ *further details from the Tanzanian tourist information in Arusha, see page 89, www.infojep.com/culturaltours,* supported by the

Dutch Development Organisation SNV, arranges guided walks through the attractive scenery of the valleys near Marangu and Mamba. **Mamba** is a small village 3 km from Marangu. From here you can also visit caves where women and children hid during ancient Masai-Chagga wars or see a blacksmith at work, using traditional methods to make Masai spears and tools. From Marangu there is an easy walk up Ngangu hill, a visit to a traditional Chagga home, or a visit to the home and memorial of the late Yohano Lawro, a local man who accompanied Dr Hans Meyer and Ludwig Purtscheller on the first recorded climb of Mount Kilimanjaro in 1889. He is reputed to have guided Kilimanjaro climbs until he was 70 and lived to the age of 115. Profits from the programme are used to improve local primary schools. Any of the Marangu hotels can organize guides from the programme.

Moshi and Marangu listings

For Sleeping and Eating price codes and other relevant information, see pages 7-9.

Sleeping

Most of the hotels offer arrangements to climb Kili, or at the least will recommend a tour operator. Without exception they all offer a base from which to begin your climb. Ensure that the hotel will store your luggage safely whilst you are on the mountain. Facilities to consider include hot water and a comfortable bed, and of course cold beer and a good hot meal on your return from the climb. Some establishments also offer saunas and massages. The Marangu hotels are better located on the lower slopes of Kilimanjaro but are considerably more expensive. Almost all hotels have restaurants.

Moshi *p65, map p65*
$$$ Kilemakyaro Mountain Lodge, 7 km from Moshi, take the Sokoine road out of town, T027-2754925, www.kilimanjaro safari.com. Perched on a hill above Moshi, set in a 240-ha coffee plantation at an altitude of 1450 m, a stay here will very much help climbers with acclimatization. The reception, bar and dining room are in the main house, a restored 1920s farmhouse, while rooms are in chalets dotted throughout the garden. Can organize climbs of Kilimanjaro and also Meru, and quite uniquely organize weddings at Uhuru Peak at the top of Kili.
$$$ Mt Kilimanjaro View Lodge, 16 km from Moshi, follow the unpaved road out of town north of the **YMCA** or arrange a pick up, bookings through the website, www.mtkilimanjaroviewlodge.com. A country retreat in the Kilimanjaro foothills with great views and accommodation in colourful stone and thatch Chagga huts with bathrooms and home-made chunky wooden furniture. There's a restaurant and bar serving authentic African food, jacuzzi, lots of local walks to nearby waterfalls and in the evenings traditional dancing and storytelling. An excellent opportunity to interact with the local Chagga people. They'll pick up 1-3 people from Moshi for US$40, and from Kilimanjaro International Airport for US$90.
$$ AMEG Lodge Kilimanjaro, off Lema Rd, near the Moshi International School, Shantytown, T027-275 0175, www.ameglodge.com. Very new, set in 1.5-ha garden, 20 rooms with en suite bathrooms and lovely modern, bright furniture, satellite TV, phone and fan. The more expensive suites have a/c and internet access for laptops. Good value in this price range with the cheapest double only US$55. Swimming pool and pool bar, good restaurant, gym and business centre.
$$ Bristol Cottages, Rindi Lane, T027-275 0175, www.bristolcottages.com. Within walking distance from the bus stand, this is

set in a pretty garden compound with parking. The 8 cottages, including 3 family ones, are spacious and have TV, hot water and Wi-Fi. The pleasant restaurant and bar serves continental and Indian food, and rates include an English breakfast.

$$ Mountain Inn, 6 km from Moshi on the road to Marangu, T027-275 2370, www.kilimanjaro-shah.com. 35 basic but comfortable rooms, a dining room with a veranda, set meals and an à la carte menu, Indian food at the pool bar, lush gardens, swimming pool, sauna. This is the base for **Shah Tours**, see page 72, a quality operator for Kilimanjaro climbs.

$$ Parkview Inn, Aga Khan Rd, T027-275 0711, www.pvim.com. Local business hotel with little character but nevertheless spacious rooms with modern bathrooms, TV, a/c, internet, secure parking in a compound, spotless swimming pool and a restaurant serving continental and Indian food and can make up lunch boxes to takeaway.

$$ Springlands Hotel, Tembo Rd, Pasua area towards the industrial area, T027-275 3581, www.springlandshotel.com. Set in large, attractive gardens, this place offers all sorts of treats that are ideal to recover from a Kili climb. 37 rooms with bathrooms. Restaurant, bar, swimming pool, TV room, massages, sauna, manicures and pedicures, bicycle hire, internet. Double room is US$60 with breakfast. Base for **Zara Travel**, see page 72, a recommended operator for climbs.

$$ Zebra Hotel, New St, T027-275 0611, www.zebrahotelstz.com. A 7-storey block with 70 neat rooms with TV and fridge (and rather garish flowery bedspreads), plus fans or pay a little more for a/c. Spacious lobby, internet café, restaurant, lounge and bar. A good buffet breakfast is included in the rates. Increasingly becoming popular with overseas visitors.

$$-$ Keys, Uru Rd, just north of the town centre, T027-275 2250, www.keys-hotels.com. This hotel functions primarily as a base for budget climb operations. Accommodation is in the main building or simple round huts and there is a restaurant and bar. The location itself is not particularly interesting and probably not as pleasant as basing yourself out in the more rural locations, but nevertheless a firm favourite. Special rates for residents, food and rooms OK, but some rooms over the rear entrance can be noisy at night because of late returners or early starters for climbing. Single/double/triple are US$30/40/50, with breakfast, and camping is available in the grounds for US$5 per person.

$$-$ Kilimanjaro Crane, Kaunda St, T027-275 1114, www.kilimanjarocranehotels.com. 30 simple but neat rooms with mosquito nets and TV, en suite bathrooms. Facilities include swimming pool, sauna, fitness centre, gardens, good views, pizza kitchen, several bars including one on the roof with fantastic views of the mountain. There is a very good bookshop in the lobby. A good mid-range option; single/double/triple US$40/50/60. Can organize transfers from Kilimanjaro International Airport.

$ Buffalo Inn, 2 blocks south and east of the bus station, T027-275 0270. Clean budget hotel, very friendly, hot water with/without bathroom. Good restaurant and bar. Will store your luggage if you are going on safari. Rates include breakfast.

$ Horombo Lodge, Old Moshi Rd, above the Tanzania Postal Bank, T027-275 0134, www.eliamensontours.com/horombo_lodge. This has 33 rooms with en suite bathroom, TV and phone, a small restaurant downstairs serving drinks and affordable meals for guests only. It's reasonably new so still fairly smart but with garish furnishings, hot water all day, doubles from US$25.

$ Kilimanjaro Backpacker's Hotel, Mawenzi Rd, T027-275 5159, www.kilimanjarobackpackers.com. Here there are 10 rooms, which are small but comfortable with fans and shared bathrooms. There's a small restaurant and bar with TV showing sports, or guests can also use the facilities at the

Kindoroko next door, which has the same owner. You can't argue with the price here; just US$4 for a single and US$6 for a double.

$ Kindoroko, Mawenzi Rd, close to market, T027-275 4054, www.kindorokohotels.com. One of the best mid-range options in the middle of town, very organized and friendly, and fantastically decorated. 46 rooms which are on the small side but have satellite TV, some also have fridges and bathrooms have plenty of hot water. Rates include a hot breakfast. Downstairs is a restaurant and bar, internet café and tour booking office, upstairs is the rooftop restaurant and bar with excellent views of Kili. The menu's very good and includes authentic Indian dishes and 3-course set meals. A great place to meet other travellers even if you are not staying here. They operate their own Kili climbs on all routes, prices include a night before and after the climb in the hotel. Recommended.

$ Leopard Hotel, Market St, T027-275 0884, www.leopardhotel.com. This small centrally located hotel claims to have received an award for good service from Bill Clinton when he visited Tanzania … a fact which makes the mind boggle. 16 clean but cramped rooms, with balconies, a/c, satellite TV and en suite bathrooms, half of which have a view of Kilimanjaro. Reasonable bar and restaurant downstairs, and a bar with nice views on the roof.

$ Newcastle, close to the market on Mawenzi St, T027-275 0853. Offers 51 rooms on 5 floors, 36 with bathrooms, the rest with shared bathrooms, good views from the top, hot water, rooms are well kept though all the dark wood makes the place a little gloomy. Rooftop bar.

$ YMCA, Uhuru Highway, to the north of the clock tower, T027-275 1734. Facilities include gym, shop, several tour desks, bar, restaurant and swimming pool (non-guests can use the pool for US$2). Mostly used by local people, this has 60 bare rooms with communal showers with hot water. Nevertheless, it's secure and clean with spotless sheets and mosquito nets and has recently been repainted. A double is US$15.

Camping There is camping at the **Golden Shower Restaurant**, 2 km from Moshi on the road to Marangu (see Eating). It is also possible to camp at the **Keys Hotel**.

West Kilimanjaro

$$$$ West Kilimanjaro Tented Camp, reservations, Hoopoe Safaris, Arusha T027-250 7011, T027-250 7541, www.kiru rumu.com. The 5 tents are spacious with en suite bathrooms and fully and tastefully furnished, set under the spreading branches of an acacia tree. Views of Kilimanjaro are superb and there is game in this region. Game drives, night drives, walks with the Masai and fly camping away from camp are possible. High season rates are US$540 per person full board and there's a conservancy fee of US$30 per day and minimum stay is 2 nights.

Machame *p66*

$$$ Protea Hotel Aishi, 30 km from Moshi in Machame Village, T027-275 6941, www.proteahotels.com. This is one of the most luxurious hotels in the region run by South African chain Protea, and is an ideal base to conquer Kili on the Machame Trail (see page 83). The hotel arranges mountain climbing, safaris and also nature trails in the area. The 30 rooms, with private facilities, have recently been completely refurbished to the highest standard. Set in well-kept gardens, there's also a restaurant, bar and gym.

Marangu *p66*

$$$ Marangu Hotel, 5 km back from Marangu towards Moshi, T027-275 6594, www.maranguhotel.com. Long-established, family-owned and run country-style hotel, warm and friendly atmosphere, self-contained cottages with private baths and showers, hot water, set in 5 ha of gardens offering stunning views of Kilimanjaro, swimming pool, croquet lawn, one of the original operators of Kilimanjaro climbs with over 60 years' experience. Can arrange treks on all the routes. Also has a pretty campsite and will safely look after vehicles for overlanders doing the climb. Partnered with the Kilimanjaro Porters Assistance Project.

$$ Ashanti Lodge, close to the Marangu Gate, T027-275 6443, www.ashanti-lodge.com. Old-style country hotel. Spacious but rather plain rooms with en suite bathrooms, in thatched bungalows in the garden. Bar, restaurant, can organize local cultural tours and safaris. There is ample parking so if in your own vehicle, and climbing Kili, you could negotiate to leave your car here.

$$ Babylon Lodge, 500 m from the post office on the Jarakea Rd, T027-275 6355, www.babylonlodge.com. Clean and comfortable, sited in well kept gardens, built into the hillside, all 30 slightly small rooms have private facilities, and there's a bar and restaurant with a set 4-course meal each evening and a swimming pool with sun deck.

$$ Kibo Hotel, about 1 km from Marangu Village towards the park gate, T027-275 1308, www.kibohotel.com. Old German building with 45 old fashioned but adequate rooms, restaurant, bar, swimming pool and fine gardens. Evelyn Waugh stayed here in 1959 and found it "so comfortable" with its "cool verandah". You can also camp here for US$5 and 3 course dinners cost US$16. Climbs can be organized.

$ Coffee Tree Campsite, 2 km before the park gate, T027-275 6604, www.coffeetree campsite.com. Grassy lawns for camping (US$8 per person), you can hire 2-man tents for US$8 and they sell beers, soft drinks, firewood and charcoal. Cook for yourself in the kitchen hut or they can provide basic meals with notice. There's also a cabin that sleeps 5 for US$12 per bed with a toilet and guests can use the camper's hot showers and wooden sauna – a godsend after the Kili climb.

Eating

Moshi p65, map p65

♉ El Rancho, off Lema Rd, Shanty Town, T027-275 5115. Tue-Sun 1230-2300. Northern Indian food, good choice for vegetarians, very authentic and full range of curries, each dish is prepared from scratch so it can take a while. However, there are plenty of diversions in the garden to keep you occupied, including table football, a crazy golf course and a pool table. There's a full bar with 16 brands of whisky.

♉ Golden Shower, 2 km from Moshi on the road to Dar, T027-275 1990. Daily 1200-1500, 1700-2300. The owner, John Bennet, is the son of the legendary character 'Chagga' Bennet, ex-First World War Royal Flying Corps ace, and economic adviser to the former Kilimanjaro Native Co-operative Union. He is a wonderful source of local information. Excellent restaurant serving continental food and friendly bar. Disco at weekends that goes on until the early hours. You can also camp here.

♉ Indoitaliano, New St, T027-275 2195. Daily 1200-2230. A wide selection of Indian and Italian food with main dishes for around US$6, the outside veranda is popular and serves a good choice of wine, including a bottle of Moet for US$80 a pop.

♉ Panda, off Lema Rd, Shanty Town, just south of the Impala Hotel, T0744-838193 (mob). Daily 1200-1500, 1800-2200. Good Chinese food served by ladies in Chinese clothes, tables set up in a house, very good seafood, including king size prawns and sizzling dishes.

♈ Aroma Coffee House, Boma Rd, T027-275 134. Daily 0800-2100. Pleasant café selling a good range of coffee from the region, including creamy cappuccinos and lattes and iced coffee, plus snacks and ice cream.

♈ Chrisburger, Kibo Rd, close to the clock tower, T027-275 0419. Mon-Sat 0830-1630, Sat 0830-1400. Has a small veranda at the front and sells cold drinks and snacks,

Kilimanjaro Marathon

Now in its fifth year, a fairly new event in Moshi is the Kilimanjaro Marathon, held in March and run on a 42.2 km route around the town and in the foothills of the mountain. The route is at an altitude of 800 to 1100 m and passes along a stretch of the Moshi-Dar road before crossing a countryside of banana plantations and smallholder farms, with Africa's highest mountain as a backdrop. It's open to professionals, many of which are famed Tanzanian, Kenyan and Ethiopian long-distance runners, as well as amateurs. In 2009 it attracted some 1500 for the full- and half-marathon and 5 km fun run.

A new event started in 2009 is the Kili(man)jaro Adventure Challenge, which is a seven-day climb to the top of Kili, a two-day mountain bike race around the mountain, followed by the marathon. Visit www.kilimanjaromarathon.com.

---

including burgers and very good fruit juice and sometimes home-made soup, closes mid-afternoon though.

Coffee Shop, Hill St, near the bus station, T027-275 2707. Mon-Fri 0800-2000, Sat 0800-1630. Lovely food using fresh produce from Irente Farm in Lushoto – cakes, home-made jam, cheese and tea. Healthy breakfasts, and light meals include omelettes, carrot and lentil soup and quiche. Try the cheese platter with apple, pickle and brown bread. Garden to sit in at the back. Outlet of St Margaret's Anglican Church. It also sells Tanzanian coffee beans.

Deli Chez, Hill St, T027-275 1144. Daily 1000-2200. Popular white tiled restaurant with a/c and decorated with mirrors and plants. Comprehensive menu of good Indian and Chinese food, plus lighter meals and shakes and ice cream desserts. No alcohol though.

Milan's, Double Rd, T027-275 1841. Daily 0830-2300. With bright pink walls, clean plastic tables and a TV in the corner, this serves a large range of vegetarian Indian dishes and snacks like bhajis and samosas from the takeaway counter.

Tanzania Coffee Lounge, Chagga St, opposite the fruit and vegetable market, T027-275 1006. Mon-Sat 0800-2000, Sun 0800-1800. A Western-style café serving good coffees, milkshakes, juices, muffins, bagels, waffles and cakes. Also has 8 terminals for high speed internet and is consistently popular with travellers.

▲ Activities and tours

Moshi *p65, map p65*
Tour operators

It is cheaper to book tours for Kilimanjaro from Moshi than it is from either Arusha or Marangu. Like booking an organized safari in Arusha for the game parks (see box, page 111) give yourself a day or 2 in Moshi to talk to a couple of the tour operators that arrange Kilimanjaro climbs. Find one that you like, does not pressure you too much, and accepts the method of payment of your choice. Ignore the touts on the street. You may find if it is quiet that the tour companies will get together and put clients on the same tour to make up numbers. All tour operators below offer Kili climbs on most of the routes, some offer additional tours. This is a far from comprehensive list. A good place to start looking for a registered tour operator is on the Kilimanjaro Association of Tour Operator's website (www.kiato.or.tz). Some of the hotels also organize climbs and packages usually include a night's accommodation before and after the climb. The **Keys** (see page 68) and **Marangu Hotel** (see page 69) have long established reputations. Also consider

Hoopoe Safaris (see page 111, and **Tropical Trails** (see page 113) in Arusha.
Akaro Tours Co Ltd, ground floor of NSSF House on Old Moshi Rd, T027-275 2986, www.akarotours.com. Kilimanjaro climbs and northern circuit tours.
Kilimanjaro Crown Birds Agency, based in the **Kindoroka**, see page 69, T027-275 1162, www.kilicrown.com. Offers a good, friendly service, and offers Kili climbs, Mt Meru climbs and road safaris to the parks.
Kilimanjaro Serengeti Tours & Travel Ltd, Old CCM Building, Mawenzi Rd, T027-275 1287, www.kilimanjaroserengeti.com. All Kili routes plus a day trip to Mandara Hut and back.
Kilimanjaro Travel Services Ltd, THB Building, Boma Rd, T027-275 2124, www.kilimanjarotravels-tz.com. Meru and Kilimanjaro climbs, budget camping safaris to Ngorongoro, Serengeti and Manyara.
Mauly Tours & Safaris, Mawenzi Rd, opposite Moshi post office, T027-275 0730, www.mauly-tours.com. Well established operator.
MJ Safaris International, CCM Building, Taifa Rd, T027-275 2017, www.mjsafarisafrica. com. Climbing and trekking and tailor-made safaris to the northern and southern circuit parks.
Moshi Expedition & Mountaineering (MEM), Kaunda St, T027-275 4234, www.memtours.com. A professional company with experience of the lesser used routes.
Shah Tours and Travel, Mawenzi Rd, T027-275 2998, www.kilimanjaro-shah.com. There is also an office at the **Mountain Inn Hotel** (see Sleeping, page 68), where all tours start. A recommended operator with lots of experience.
Snow Cap, CCM Building, Taifa Rd, T027-275 4826, www.snowcap.co.tz. Also has French speaking guides.
Summit Expeditions and Nomadic Experiences, based in Marangu, T027-275 3233, www.nomadicexperience.com. Well regarded company owned by Simon Mtuy who currently holds the fastest ascent-descent record for climbing Kili – 8 hrs 27 mins – and he's been to the top of the mountain more than 300 times. Trekkers stay in cottages on his family farm before and after the climb.
Trans-Kibo Travels Ltd, YMCA Building, T027-275 1754/275 2017, www.transkibo. com. All Kilimanjaro routes, one of the oldest operators in existence, also Meru and Mt Kenya.
Zara Tanzania Adventure, at Springlands Hotel, see page 68, T027-2753581, www. zara.co.tz, www.kilimanjaro.co.tz. Kilimanjaro climb US$1172 for 5-day 'Coca-Cola route' or Marangu route, US$1447 for Machame and the Umbwe route, the safari charges are from US$240 per person per day for a tour of Serengeti/Ngorongoro but these drop considerably for 4 or more people, as does the Kili climb. Recommended for groups as prices are very good. There are also discounts of up to US$50 per day in low season (Apr-Jun). Zara takes thousands of people up the mountain each year, recommended as one of Tanzania's best budget operators.

Transport

Moshi *p65, map p65*
Air
Kilimanjaro International Airport is halfway between Moshi and Arusha, for flight details, see **Arusha** page 114. A taxi between Moshi and the airport should cost around US$40-50 or arrange for one of the tour operators or your hotel to organize a shuttle. **Kilimanjaro Aero Club**, based at Moshi Airport, T027-275 0555, www.kilimanjaroaeroclub.com, can arrange charter flights, sightseeing flights and flying lessons.

Bus and dala-dala
Moshi is 580 km from Dar, 79 km from Arusha and 349 km from Nairobi. Local buses and *dala-dala* to nearby destinations like

Marangu and **Arusha** cost little more than US$1 and go from the stand just to the south of the main bus stand, which are both on Market St. There are daily buses to and from **Dar**, US$18 'luxury', US$12 'semi-luxury' and US$9 'ordinary' which take about 7 hrs and stop for 20 mins at one of the roadside restaurants en route. The road has improved considerably. For **Tanga** the bus takes 4-6 hrs and costs US$10. It is possible to get a direct bus to **Mombasa**, cost approximately US$13, 7-8 hrs. These go through the Taveta border, on to **Voi** in Kenya where they join the main road from Nairobi to Mombasa. Take lots of care at the bus stands as pick pocketing is rife and you need to protect your belongings. On arrival its best just to jump straight in a taxi as soon as you get off the bus. The hustlers, who try to get people on to their buses can be particularly annoying too.

Regular *dala-dala* to **Marangu**, 45 mins, US$3. A taxi will cost in the region of US$25, whilst those who organize a climb in Moshi will be transferred to the park gate by their tour operator.

To Kenya There are private shuttle services to **Nairobi** via Arusha and the Namanga border. **Impala Shuttle**, Kibo Rd, T027-275 1786, departs daily for Nairobi at 0630 and 1130, US$40. **Riverside Shuttle**, THB House, T027-275 0093, www.riverside-shuttle.com, departs daily at 0630 and 1100, US$40. **AA Shuttles**, www.aashuttles.com, picks up and drops off at the hotels and leaves Moshi at 1100, US$40, and on request it will pick up/drop off at the Marangu Hotel at 0800, US$70.

Taxi
A taxi to **Marangu** will cost in the region of US$25, whilst those who organize a climb in Moshi will be transferred to the park gate by their tour operator.

Directory

Moshi *p65, map p65*
Banks **Standard Chartered Bank** on Rindi Lane and opposite the Kindoroko Hotel on Mawenzi Rd, and the **National Bank of Commerce** on the clock tower roundabout both have ATM facilities and will advance money on Visa and MasterCard. **Internet** There are several places around Moshi to check email. These include **Dot Café**, Rengua Rd; **Duma** and **Fahari**, both on Hill St, next door to the Coffee Shop; and **Tanzania Coffee Lounge** near the market (page 71). **Medical services** Moshi is home to what is said to be the best hospital in Tanzania, the **Kilimanjaro Christian Medical Centre** (**KCMC**), which is 6 km out of town beyond Shantytown, T027-275 4377, www.kcm c.ac.tz. **Mawenzi Moshi District Hospital**, in town. **Police** Market St, T027-275 5055. **Post office** In the centre of town near the clock tower. **Courier services**, DHL, Kahawa House on the clock tower roundabout, T027-275 4030, www.dhl.com. **Telephone** International calls can be made from the post office.

Kilimanjaro National Park

In *The Snows of Kilimanjaro*, Ernest Hemingway described the mountain: "as wide as all the world, great, high, and unbelievably white in the sun, was the square top of Kilimanjaro". It is one of the most impressive sights in Africa, visible from as far away as Tsavo National Park in Kenya. Just 80 km east of the eastern branch of the Rift Valley, it is Africa's highest mountain with snow-capped peaks rising from a relatively flat plain, the largest freestanding mountain worldwide, measuring 80 x 40 km and one of earth's highest dormant volcanoes. At lower altitudes, the mountain is covered in lush rainforest, which gives way to scrub – there is no bamboo zone on Kilimanjaro – followed by alpine moorland until you get to the icefields. Try to see it in the early morning before the clouds mask it. Despite its altitude even inexperienced climbers can climb it, provided they are reasonably fit and allow themselves sufficient time to acclimatize to the elevation.

Ins and outs
Getting there
There are a number of ways of getting to Mount Kilimanjaro. The easiest is to fly to **Kilimanjaro International Airport** – during your approach you will get a magnificent view of the mountain if it is not covered by cloud. The park entrance is about 90 km from the airport, which takes about 1½ hours by road. Alternatively by road go to Moshi and from there to Marangu, the village at the park entrance at the base of the mountain. Many *dala-dala* go from Moshi to Marangu each day; they take 45 minutes and cost US$2. It is also cheap and easy to get to Kilimanjaro from Kenya by taking a shuttle. Alternatively, for the Machame Trail, there are regular *dala-dala* from the bus stand in Moshi the 30 km to the village of Machame taking about an hour and again cost around US$2.

Climate
Kilimanjaro can be climbed throughout the year but it is worth avoiding the two rainy seasons (late Mar to mid-May and October to the beginning of December) when the routes become slippery. The best time to visit is January-February and September-October when there is usually no cloud.

Information
Anyone planning to climb Mount Kilimanjaro is advised to buy the *Trekking Guide to Africa's Highest Mountain* by Henry Steadman (Trailblazer Guides). It is full of practical information and

covers preparing and equipping for the climb, much of the book's information is available on Henry's website, www.climbmountkilimanjaro.com; *Kilimanjaro & East Africa; a Climbing and Trekking Guide* by Cameron M Burns (Mountaineers Books), is also a useful guidebook. There are plenty of maps on the market, many of which now list GPS coordinates, and other locally produced maps and coffee-table books are available in both Moshi and Arusha. The tour operators that offer climbs have comprehensive information about the climbs on their websites and visit Tanzania National Parks, www.tanzaniaparks.com.

Altitude sickness

Altitude sickness is often a problem while climbing Kilimanjaro. If you know you are susceptible to it you are advised not to attempt the climb. Symptoms include bad headache, nausea, vomiting and severe fatigue. It can be avoided by ascending slowly – if at all possible, spend an extra day half-way up to help your body acclimatize. Mountain sickness symptoms can often be alleviated by descending to a lower altitude. The drug Diamox helps if taken before the ascent. Other more serious conditions include acute pulmonary oedema and/or cerebral oedema. In the former, the sufferer becomes breath-

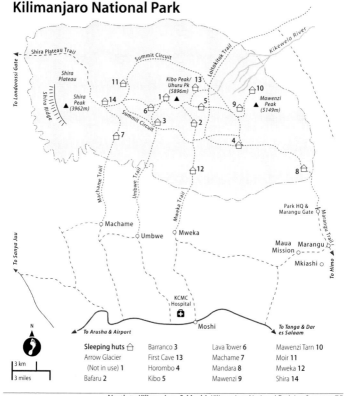

Kilimanjaro National Park

Sleeping huts	Barranco 3	Lava Tower 6	Mawenzi Tarn 10
Arrow Glacier	First Cave 13	Machame 7	Moir 11
(Not in use) 1	Horombo 4	Mandara 8	Mweka 12
Bafaru 2	Kibo 5	Mawenzi 9	Shira 14

Tipping on Kilimanjaro

On the last day of the tour your guide will request a tip for himself and his cook and porters. Tipping is more or less mandatory, as a way of supplementing the low incomes of people who essentially have a remarkably physically demanding job. Porters in particular are very poorly paid (as little as US$8 a day) and cannot always afford the right equipment/clothes needed on the mountain. A good tour operator will have a fair tipping procedure in place. One method that is popular with groups is for everybody to contribute 10% of the total cost of their trek towards tips. So if you paid US$1200 for your trek, you should pay US$120 into the tip kitty. Another approach is for each member of the trekking staff to receive a set amount; roughly US$5 per porter per day, US$7 for the cook or assistant guide per day, and US$10 for the guide per day. However if you feel your climb was particularly difficult or a certain person went out of his way to help you, or, on the flipside the staff were surly or weren't as helpful as they should have been, then this should reflect in the tipping. Give tips out to the trekking team individually, and don't give a lump sum to the guide as the money may not always go to who it's intended for. You may want to have the right denomination US$/TSh notes to be able to do this. For more information about tipping on Kilimanjaro (and why you should do it) visit the website for the Kilimanjaro Porters Assistance Project; www.kili porters.org. Something else to consider, is that you won't need much 'stuff' on the mountain – you'll be wearing most of it anyway – and porters are limited to 15 kg of trekkers' packs and 5 kg of their own things. Kili is a hard slog for anyone – imagine what it's like climbing it over and over again with 20 kg on your back? Keep it light and leave the bulk of your luggage at a hotel. Finally, if you're never going to climb a big mountain again, think about making gifts of your specialist clothing and gear to your trekking team; it is after all these people who were responsible for your welfare on the mountain and (hopefully) got you to the top.

---

less, turns blue in the face and coughs up froth. The latter is even more serious – symptoms are intense headache, hallucinations, confusion and disorientation and staggering gait. It is caused by the accumulation of fluid on the brain and can cause death or serious brain damage. If either of these conditions are suspected the sufferer should immediately be taken down to a lower altitude to receive medical care. It is, however, normal to feel breathless and fatigued at high altitudes and these are not always precursors to the more serious conditions.

Guides

A guide is compulsory on all routes and it essential to go with a tour operator who will supply not only guides but porters and relevant equipment (see Moshi tour operators, page 71). Marangu is the usual route for tourists and only fit and experienced hikers or climbers should use the other routes.

Equipment

Being well equipped will increase your chances of reaching the summit. In particular be sure you have a warm sleeping bag, insulating mat, warm rainproof jacket, thermal underwear, gloves, wool hat, sunglasses or snow goggles, sun cream, large water bottle and first-aid kit. Some of these are available to buy or hire in Moshi from the tour operators; at the park gate for example is a shop that sells thick socks amongst other items. However, the quality is variable and it is best to come fully prepared. As regards clothing, it is important to wear layers as they provide better insulation than bulkier items, and sturdy waterproof hiking boots should be well worn-in. Other essential items include a small daypack for things you'll need during the day – porters carry your main pack but tend to go on ahead by some distance – a head torch and spare batteries (essential for the final midnight ascent), toilet roll, and you may want to consider a light weight trekking pole. Energy snacks are also a good idea.

Costs

Climbing Mount Kilimanjaro is an expensive business, though everyone who makes it to the summit agrees that it is well worth it. The costs are much higher than those in the Alps or the Andes. Park fees alone, charged by Tanzania National Parks, are US$60 per person per 24 hours, camping or hut fees US$50 per person per day (whether you use the huts or not), a rescue fee insurance of US$20 per person, and guides at US$20 per day, cooks US$15 per day and porters US$10 per day per 15 kg of luggage. These are the set fees that the tour operator must pay on your behalf to Tanzania National Parks and can amount to over US$900 for a six-day trip, though while everyone needs a porter, costs come down if a group are sharing a guide and cook. On top of this, other costs for the tour operators include the salaries of the guides and porters, the additional 20% VAT on the total invoice, 10% commission if booking through a third party travel agent, transport to the start of the trail, food and the costs of equipment. The absolute cheapest you will probably manage to do it for will be around US$1175 for the five-day Marangu Route. An extra day on this route (recommended) is about US$200 per person. The other more technical or longer climbs are US$1400 or more.

Background

Formation

Kilimanjaro was formed about 1 million years ago by a series of volcanic movements along the Great Rift Valley. Until this point, the area was a flat plain at about 600-900 m above sea level. About 750,000 years ago volcanic activity forced three points above 4800 m – Shira, Kibo and Mawenzi. Some 250,000 years later Shira became inactive and collapsed into itself forming the crater. Kibo and Mawenzi continued their volcanic activity and it was their lava flow that forms the 11-km saddle between the two peaks. When Mawenzi died out, its northeast wall collapsed in a huge explosion creating a massive gorge. The last major eruptions occurred about 200 years ago and Kibo now lies dormant but not extinct. Although Kibo appears to be a snow-clad dome, it contains a caldera 2.5 km across and 180 m deep at the deepest point in the south. Within the depression is an inner ash cone that rises to within 60 m of the summit height and is evidence of former volcanic activity. On the southern slopes the glaciers reach down to about 4200 m, while on the north slopes they only descend a little below the summit.

Vegetation and wildlife

Kilimanjaro has well-defined altitudinal vegetation zones. From the base to the summit

The snow sepulchre of King Solomon

Legend has it that the last military adventure of King Solomon was an expedition down the eastern side of Africa. Exhausted by his battles the aged king was trekking home with his army when they passed the snow-covered Mount Kilimanjaro. Solomon decided this was to be his resting place. The next day he was carried by bearers until they reached the snows. As they steadily trudged up to the summit they saw a cave glittering in the sunlight, frost sparkling in the interior, icicles hanging down to close off the entrance. As they watched, two icicles, warmed by the sun, crashed to the ground. They carried the old king inside and placed him on his throne, wrapped in his robes, facing out down the mountain. Solomon raised a frail hand to bid farewell. The bearers left with heavy hearts. The weather began to change and there was a gentle fall of snow. As they looked back they saw that icicles had reformed over the entrance.

these are: plateau, semi-arid scrub; cultivated, well-watered southern slopes; dense cloud forest; open moorland; alpine desert; moss and lichen. The lower slopes are home to elephant, rhino, buffalo, leopard, monkey and eland. Birdlife includes the enormous lammergeyer, the scarlet-tufted malachite sunbird as well as various species of starlings, sunbirds, the silvery-cheeked hornbill and the rufous-breasted sparrowhawk.

History

When, in 1848, the first reports by the German missionary Johannes Rebmann of a snow-capped mountain on the equator arrived in Europe, the idea was ridiculed by the Royal Geographical Society of Britain. In 1889 the report was confirmed by the German geographer Hans Meyer and the Austrian alpine mountaineer Ludwig Purtscheller, who climbed Kibo and managed to reach the snows on Kilimanjaro's summit. At the centenary of this climb in 1989, the Tanzanian guide was still alive and 115 years old. Mawenzi was first climbed by the German Fritz Klute in 1912.

The mountain was originally in a part of British East Africa (now Kenya). However, the mountain was 'given' by Queen Victoria as a gift to her cousin, and so the border was moved and the mountain included within German Tanganyika. This is why if you look at a map of the border between Tanzania and Kenya, Tanzania juts into Kenya to include Kilimanjaro on the otherwise dead straight border drawn up by the colonialists. The national park was established in 1973 and covers an area of 756 sq km.

Routes up the mountain

About 22,000 climbers attempt to get to the top of Kilimanjaro each year. The altitude at Marangu Gate is 1829 m and at Kibo Peak 5895 m – that's a long way up. Officially anyone aged over 12 may attempt the climb. The youngest person to climb the mountain was a 10 year old, while the oldest was 79. However, it is not that easy and estimates of the number of people who attempt the climb and do not make it to the top vary from 20-50%. The important things to remember are to come prepared and to take it slowly – if you have the chance, spend an extra day half-way up to give you the chance to acclimatize.

There are a number of different trails. The most popular is the Marangu trail, which is the recommended route for older persons or younger people who are not in peak physical condition. The climbing tends to be much more strenuous than anticipated, which when combined with lower oxygen levels accounts for the 20-50% failure rate to reach the summit.

The Marangu trail is the only one that uses hutted dorm accommodation. On the other routes, even though the campsites are called huts this actually refers to the green shacks. Some of these have fallen into disuse or are usually inhabited by the park rangers on the lower slopes, they are also sometimes used by the guides and porters. Trekkers are accommodated in tents carried and set up by the porters.

Marangu trail

This is probably the least scenic of the routes but by being the gentlest climb and by having a crop of hotels at the beginning in Marangu and hutted accommodation on the way up, this is the most popular.

Day 1 The national park gate (1830 m) is about 8 km from the **Kibo Hotel**. This is as far as vehicles are allowed. From here to the first night's stop at **Mandara Hut** (2700 m) is a walk of three to four hours. It is through *shambas* – small farms growing coffee – as well as some lush rainforest, and is an enjoyable walk although it can be quite muddy. On the walk you can admire the moss and lichens and the vines and flowers, including orchids. There is an alternative forest trail, which branches left from the main track a few minutes after the gate and follows the side of a stream. It is a little slower than the main track, which it rejoins after about three hours. The Mandara Hut, near the Maundi Crater, is actually a group of A-frame huts that can sleep about 60 people. Mattresses, solar lighting and stoves are provided but nothing else. The complex was built by the Norwegians as part of an aid programme. There is piped water, flushing toilets and firewood available, and a dining area in the main cabin.

Day 2 The second day will start off as a steep walk through the last of the rainforest and out into tussock grassland, giant heather and then on to the moorlands, crossing several ravines on the way. There are occasional clearings through which you will get wonderful views of Mawenzi and Moshi far below. You can also enjoy the views by making a short detour up to the rim of Maundi Crater. You will also probably see some of the exceptional vegetation that is found on Kilimanjaro, including the giant lobelia, Kilimanjaro's 'everlasting flowers' and other uncommon alpine plants. The walk to **Horombo Hut** (3720 m) is about 14 km with an altitude gain of about 1000 m and will take you five to seven hours. This hut is again a collection of huts that can accommodate up to 120 people. There are flushing toilets and plenty of water but firewood is scarce. Some people spend an extra day here to help get acclimatized and if you are doing this there are a number of short walks in the area but remember to move slowly, drink plenty of water and get lots of sleep. It is a very good idea to spend the extra day here – but there is the extra cost to be considered.

Day 3/4 On the next day of walking you will climb to the **Kibo Hut** (4703 m), which is 13 km from Horombo. As you climb, the vegetation thins to grass and heather and eventually to bare scree. You will feel the air thinning and it is at this altitude that altitude sickness may kick in. The most direct route is the right fork from Horombo Hut. It is stony and eroded, a climb of six-seven hours up the valley behind the huts, past **Last Water** and on to the **saddle**. This is the wide, fairly flat, U-shaped desert between the two peaks of Mawenzi and Kibo and from here you will get some awe-inspiring views of the mountain. After **Zebra Rocks** and at the beginning of the saddle, the track forks. To the right, about three hours from Horombo Hut, is Mawenzi Hut and to the left across the saddle is Kibo Hut. The left fork from Horombo Hut is gentler, and comes out on to the saddle 1 km from Kibo Hut. Kibo Hut is where the porters stay and from here on you should just take the absolute bare essentials with you. It is a good idea to bring some biscuits or chocolate for the final ascent to the peak, as a lunch pack is not always provided. Mawenzi Hut sleeps about 60 people. There is a stone-built main block with a small dining room and several dormitory rooms with bunks and mattresses. There is no vegetation in the area and no water unless there has been snow recently, so it has to be carried up from Last Water. However, the camp does sell bottled water and soft drinks but they are understandably expensive. Some people decide to try and get as much sleep as possible before the early start, while others decide not to sleep at all. You are unlikely to sleep very well because of the altitude and the temperatures anyway.

Day 4/5 On the final day of the climb, in order to be at the summit at sunrise, and before the cloud comes down, you will have to get up at about midnight. One advantage of beginning at this time is that if you saw what you were about to attempt you would probably give up before you had even begun. You can expect to feel pretty awful during this final five-hour ascent and many climbers are physically sick. You may find that this climb is extremely slippery and hard going. The first part of the climb is over an uneven trail to **Hans Meyer Cave**. As the sun rises you will reach **Gillman's Point** (5680 m) – it is a wonderful sight. From here you have to decide whether you want to keep going another couple of hours to get to **Kibo Peak** (5896 m). The walk around the crater rim to Kibo Peak is only an extra 200 m but at this altitude it is a strenuous 200 m. At the peak there is a fair amount of litter left by previous climbers. You will return to **Horombo Hut** the same day and the next day (**Day 5/6**) return to Marangu where you will be presented with a certificate.

Umbwe trail

Note This route is presently closed because of four fatalities in 2005 after a serious rock fall but check locally. The climb is hard, short and steep but is a wonderfully scenic route to take to reach **Uhuru Peak**. However, it is not recommended for inexperienced climbers. Many climbers descend this way after climbing up by a different route. To get to the start of the trail take the turning off the Arusha road about 2 km down on the right. From there it's 14 km down the Lyamungu Road, right at the T-junction towards Mango and soon after crossing the Sere River you get to **Umbwe** Village (1400 m).

Day 1 ⓘ *Umbwe to Bivouac I, 4-6 hrs' walk*. From the mission the former forestry track continues through rainforest for about 3 km up to **Kifuni Village**. From there it's another 6 km before you get to the start of the trail proper. There is a sign here and the trail branches to the left and climbs quite steeply through the forest along the ridge between the Lonzo River to the west and Umbwe River to the east. In several places it is necessary to use branches to pull yourself up. You will reach the first shelter, a cave, about six to eight hours' walk from Umbwe. This is **Bivouac I** (2940 m), an all-weather rock shelter formed from the rock overhangs. It will shelter about six or seven people. There is firewood nearby and a spring about 15 m below under a rock face.

The meaning of Kilimanjaro

Since the earliest explorers visited East Africa, people have been intrigued by the name Kilimanjaro and its meaning. The Chagga people do not have a name for the whole mountain, just the two peaks: *Kibo* (or kipoo) means 'spotted' and refers to the rock that can be seen standing out against the snow on this peak; *Mawenzi* (or Kimawenze) means 'having a broken top' and again describes its appearance.

Most theories as to the origin of the name Kilimanjaro for the whole mountain break the word down into two elements: *kilima* and *njaro*. In Swahili the word for mountain is *mlima* while *kilima* means hill – so it is possible that an early European visitor incorrectly used *kilima* because of the analogy to the two Chagga words Kibo and Kimawenzi.

The explorer Krapf said that the Swahili of the coast knew it as Kilimanjaro 'mountain of greatness', but he does not explain why. He also suggests it could mean 'mountain of caravans' (*kilima* = mountain, *jaro* = caravans), but while *kilima* is a Swahili word, *jaro* is a Chagga word. Other observers have suggested that *njaro* once meant 'whiteness' and therefore this was the 'mountain of whiteness'. Alternatively, *njaro* could be the name of an evil spirit, or a demon. The first-known European to climb Mount Kilimanjaro mentions 'Njaro, the guardian spirit of the mountain' and there are many stories in Chagga folklore about spirits living here – though there is no evidence of a spirit called Njaro, either from the Chagga or from the coastal peoples.

Another explanation suggests that the mountain was known as 'mountain of water', because of the Masai word *njore* for springs or water and because all the rivers in the area rose from here. However, this theory does not explain the use of the Swahili word for 'hill' rather than 'mountain', and also assumes that a Swahili word and a Masai word have been put together.

The final explanation is from a Kichagga term *kilelema* meaning that 'which has become difficult or impossible' or 'which has defeated'. Njaro can be derived from the Kichagga words *njaare*, a bird, or else *jyaro*, a caravan. Thus the mountain became *kilemanjaare*, *kilemajyaro* or *kilelemanjaare*, meaning that which defeats or is impossible for the bird or the caravan. This theory has the advantage of being composed entirely of Chagga elements.

It seems possible either that this was the name given to the mountain by the Chagga themselves, or by people passing through the area, who heard the Chagga say *kilemanjaare* or *kile- majyaro*, meaning that the mountain was impossible to climb. Over time the name was standardized to Kilimanjaro.

If you made an early start and are fit you can continue on to Bivouac II on the same day. However, most climbers take an overnight break here, camping in the forest caves.

Day 2 ⓘ *Bivouac I to Barranco Hut, 5 km, 4-5 hrs' walk*. From the caves, continue up, past the moorland and along the ridge. It is a steep walk with deep valleys on each side of the ridge and this walk is magnificent with the strange 'Old Man's Beard' – a type of moss – covering most of the vegetation. The second set of caves is **Bivouac II** (3800 m), three to four hours from Bivouac I. There are two caves – one about five minutes further down the track – and this is where you will camp. There is a spring down the ravine about 15 minutes to the west.

From the second set of caves the path continues less steeply up the ridge beyond the tree line before reaching **Barranco** or **Umbwe Hut** (3900 m). Barranco Hut is about five hours away from the first caves or two hours from Bivouac II. The path is well marked. About 200 m beyond the hut is a rock overhang, which can be used for camping. There is one pit latrine, water is available about 250 m to the east and firewood is available in the area. Some people may choose to spend an extra day at Barranco Hut to acclimatize to the altitude.

Day 3/4 ⓘ *Barranco Hut to Lava Tower Hut, 3-4 hrs' walk*. Just before reaching Barranco Hut the path splits in two. To the left, the path goes west towards Shira Hut (five to six hours) and the northern circuit, or you can climb the west lateral ridge to the **Arrow Glacier Hut** (now defunct after it was buried in an avalanche) towards the **Lava Tower Hut** (4600 m) about three to four hours away. Up this path the vegetation thins before disappearing completely on reaching the scree slopes. The campsite at Lava Tower Hut is very barren and there is no shelter so you need to be prepared for the extreme cold. No toilets, but water is available in a nearby stream.

Day 4/5 ⓘ *Lava Tower Hut to Uhuru Peak, 4-6 hrs' walk*. Having spent the night at Lava Tower Hut you will want to leave very early for the final ascent. Head torches are imperative and if there is no moonlight the walk can be quite difficult. Climb up between **Arrow Glacier** (which may have disappeared completely if you are there towards the end of the dry season) and **Little Breach Glacier** until you get to a few small cliffs. At this stage the course follows the Western Breach summit route and turns to the right heading for the lowest part of the crater rim that you can see. This part of the walk is really steep on scree and snow, and parts of it are quite a scramble. From December to February, crampons and ice axes are recommended. Having reached the crater floor, cross the **Furtwangler Glacier** snout to a steep gully that reaches the summit plateau about another 500 m west of **Uhuru Peak** (5895 m), returning to **Mweka Hut**, among the giant heathers, for an overnight stop.

Day 5/6 ⓘ *Descent from Mweka Hut to Mweka Gate, 14 km, 5-7 hrs' walk*. The return journey can be achieved in approximately half the ascending time.

Umbwe trail – alternative route

Day 3/4 ⓘ *Barranco Hut to Bafaru Hut, 5 km, 4-5 hrs' walk*. The route is well marked at lower levels but not at higher altitudes. If you take the path to the right from **Barranco Hut** (eastwards on the southern circuit) you will cross one small stream and then another larger one as you contour the mountain to join the **Mweka trail**. The path then climbs steeply through a gap in the **West Breach**. From here you can turn left to join the routes over the south glaciers. Alternatively, continue along the marked path across screes, ridges and a valley until you reach the **Karangu Campsite**, which is a further two to three hours on from the top of the Breach. A further couple of hours up the **Karangu valley** (4000 m) will come out at the **Mweka-Barafu Hut** path. If you go left down along this you will get to the **Barafu Hut** after 1-1½ hours. If you go straight on for about three hours you will join the Marangu trail just above the **Horombo Hut**.

Day 4/5 ⓘ *Barafu Hut to Uhuru Peak to Mweka Hut, 5-6 hrs' walk to crater rim plus another hour to Uhuru Peak*. Parties heading for the summit set off around midnight to 0100, reaching the crater at Stella Point. If the weather conditions are favourable, **Uhuru Peak**

(5895 m) is normally reached by first light. From here it is often possible to see the summit of Mount Meru to the west. Descend to **Mweka Hut** for an overnight stop.

Day 5/6 ⓘ *Descent from Mweka Hut to Mweka Gate, 14 km, 5-7 hrs' walk.*

Machame trail
This trail is considered by some to be the most attractive of the routes up Kilimanjaro. It is between Umbwe trail and Shira trail and joins the latter route at Shira Hut. The turn-off to the trail and the village of Machame is to the west of Umbwe off the main Arusha–Moshi road.

Day 1 From the village to the first huts takes about nine hours so be sure to start early. Take the track through the *shambas* and the forest to the park entrance (about 4 km), from where you will see a clear track that climbs gently through the forest and along a ridge that is between the Weru Weru and Makoa streams. It is about 7 km to the edge of the forest, and then four to five hours up to the **Machame Huts** (3000 m), where you camp. There are pit latrines and plenty of water down in the valley below the huts and firewood available close by.

Day 2 From the Machame Huts go across the valley, over a stream, then up a steep ridge for three to four hours. The path then goes west and drops into the river gorge before climbing more gradually up the other side and on to the moorland of the Shira Plateau to join the Shira Plateau trail near the **Shira Hut** (3800 m). This takes about five hours. From the Shira Plateau you will get some magnificent views of Kibo Peak and the Western Breach. The area is home to a variety of game including buffalo. The campsite at the Shira Hut is used by people on the Shira Plateau trail as well as those on the Machame trail. There is plenty of water available 50 m to the north and firewood nearby, but no toilets.

Day 3 onwards From here there are a number of choices. You can go on to the **Barranco Hut** (five to six hours, 3900 m) or the **Lava Tower Hut** (four hours, 4600 m). The path to **Arrow Glacier Hut** is well marked. The ascent includes scrambling over scree, rocks and snow fields – tough at times and probably only suited to experienced hikers. It goes east from Shira Hut until it reaches a junction where the North Circuit route leads off to the left. The path continues east, crossing a wide valley before turning southeast towards the Lava Tower. Shortly before the tower a route goes off to the right to Barranco Hut and the South Circuit route. To the left the path goes to Arrow Glacier Hut and the Western Breach.

Shira Plateau trail
This route needs a 4WD vehicle and so for this reason is little used. The road can be impassable during wet periods. However, if you do have access to such a vehicle and are acclimatized you can get to the **Arrow Glacier Hut** in one day.

The drive is a complex one and you may need to stop and ask the way frequently. Pass through West Kilimanjaro, drive for 5 km and turn right. At 13 km you will pass a small trading centre on the left. At 16 km you will cross a stream followed by a hard left. At 21 km you will enter a coniferous forest which soon becomes a natural forest. The plateau rim is reached at 39 km. Here the track continues upwards gently and crosses the plateau to the roadhead at 55 km. Just before the roadhead, about 19 km from **Londorossi Gate**, is a rock shelter. This site is suitable for camping and there is a stream nearby. From the roadhead you will have to walk. It is about 1½ hours to **Shira Hut** (3800 m). From here you continue east to join the Umbwe trail to the **Lava Tower Hut**. The walk is fairly gentle and has magnificent views.

Mweka trail

This trail is the most direct route up the mountain. It is the steepest and the fastest. It begins at Mweka Village, 13 km north of Moshi.

Day 1 The first day's walk takes six to eight hours. The trail follows an old logging road, which you can drive up in good weather, through the *shambas* and the forest, for about 5 km. It is a slippery track that deteriorates into a rough path after a couple of hours. From here it is about 6 km up a ridge to the **Mweka Huts** (3100 m) where you camp, which are some 500 m beyond the tree line in the giant heather zone. Water is available nearby from a stream in a small valley below the huts five minutes to the southeast and there is plenty of firewood. No toilets.

Day 2 From the Mweka Huts follow the ridge east of the Msoo River through heathland, open tussock grassland and then on through alpine desert to the **Barafu Huts** (4400 m), a walk of six to eight hours. There are no toilets, and no water or firewood available – you will need to bring it up from Mweka Huts.

Day 3 From the Barafu Huts the final ascent on a ridge between **Rebmann** and **Ratzel** glaciers takes about six hours up to the rim of the crater between **Stella** and **Hans Meyer Points**. From here it is a further hour to **Uhuru Peak**. At the lower levels the path is clearly marked, but it becomes obscured further up. It is steep, being the most direct non-technical route. Although specialized climbing equipment is not needed, be prepared for a scramble. To catch the sunrise you will have to set off no later than 0200 from Barafu Huts. You return to the huts the same day, and (**Day 4**) make the final descent the next day.

Loitokitok trail

This, and the Shira Plateau trail, both come in from the north unlike the other trails. It used to start on the Kenya border and was known as the Rongai trail (and is still today confusingly referred to as that) but the start has been shifted eastward to start in Tanzania from the village of Loitokitok and has been renamed. You register at the Marangu Gate and then operators transfer you to the village and the trail head which takes about 2½ hours.

The first part of the trail crosses maize fields and then a pine plantation and is not very steep. Beyond is heather and moorlands until you reach First Cave (2600 m) where you camp. It is a total of approximately five to six hours or 8 km to the caves from the trail head.

From these caves follow the path that heads towards a point just to the right of the lowest point on the saddle. You will pass **Bread Rock** after about 1½ hours. The track then divides. To the right is the **Outward Bound Hut** that you will almost certainly find locked. The path continues upwards to the saddle towards the **Kibo Huts** – a climb of three to four hours. To the left another path crosses towards the **Mawenzi Hut**.

The Summit Circuit

A route around the base of Kibo, the Summit Circuit links Horombo, Barranco, Shira and Moir Huts. The southern section of the circuit is most spectacular, as it cuts across moorland, in and out of valleys and under the southern glaciers.

Contents

86 *Map: Arusha region*

87 Arusha

- 88 Ins and outs
- 89 Sights
- 90 *Map: Arusha*
- 93 Around Arusha
- 96 Arusha National Park
- 96 *Map: Arusha National Park*
- 100 Listings

Footprint features

- 86 Don't miss ...
- 99 Climbing Mount Meru
- 111 How to organize a safari

At a glance

⊖ Getting around The centre's easily walkable (but not at night), and *dala-dalas*, buses and taxis are all over the town. Tour operators can help you trek Mt Meru or explore Arusha National Park.

⌚ Time required 1-2 days to sort out safari arrangements and see the town, another day for a trip around the National Park, 3 days to climb Mt Meru and 1 day to recover.

☁ Weather Mostly warm and sunny, but Mt Meru can be tough in the rainy season from end of Mar-May and the summit, at over 4000 m, can be cold at any time of year.

✖ When not to go The city is accessible all year. You may want to avoid Mt Meru in rainy season, when the climb can hard-going, slippery and sometimes dangerous.

Arusha

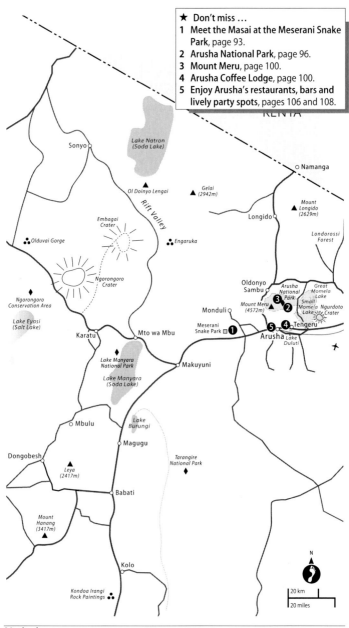

In the northern highlands of Tanzania, beneath the twin peaks of Mount Meru and Mount Kilimanjaro, Arusha is the safari capital of the country. It is a pleasant town set at an altitude of 1380 m above sea level, and is the halfway point between Cairo and Cape Town (the actual point is in a field 20 km or so to the south of town). The drive up from Dar es Salaam to Arusha passes through the semi-arid grass plains, gradually becoming greener, more cultivated and more heavily populated; Mount Meru, in the Arusha National Park appears on the right with its fertile, cultivated slopes. Built by the Germans as a centre of colonial administration in the early 20th century, Arusha was a sleepy town with a garrison stationed at the old boma and a few shops around a grassy roundabout. But from its backwater status amidst the farmlands and plantations of northern Tanzania, Arusha has today been transformed into one of the busiest Tanzanian towns after Dar es Salaam. Its prominence has particularly increased in recent years since becoming the headquarters of the East African Community and being the host town for the Rwandan War Crimes Tribunals. The International Conference Centre has witnessed the signing of some of the most important peace treaties and international agreements in modern African history. Arusha is also the starting point for safaris in the north of Tanzania – the Serengeti, Ngorongoro, Lake Manyara, Tarangire, Olduvai Gorge and Arusha national parks. It can be very busy with tourists, mostly either in transit to, or returning from, these attractions. The dusty streets are filled with 4WD game-viewing vehicles negotiating potholed roads, and Masai warriors in full regalia mingling with tourists clad in crisp khaki. There are lots of good hotels and restaurants, and tourism has made Arusha a very prosperous town.

Ins and outs
→ *Phone code: 027. Population: 400,000. Altitude: 1380 m.*

Getting there
Arusha is 50 km from Kilimanjaro International Airport, which is well served by international flights, 79 km from Moshi, and 650 km from Dar es Salaam. If you fly into Kilimanjaro International Airport with Air Tanzania or Precision Air, shuttle buses will meet the incoming flights. Passengers travelling with other airlines will have to get a taxi for about US$40, or can arrange to be picked up by one of the hotels, lodges or safari companies. Closer to town is Arusha Airport, 10 km west along the road to Dodoma. This is mostly used for charter flights and scheduled services operated by Coastal Air.

The road between Dar es Salaam and Arusha has recently been upgraded and is now smooth tar all the way. The journey by bus takes eight to nine hours. It is also only 273 km south of Nairobi, with the Namanga border with Kenya being roughly halfway. The two cities are linked by regular shuttle buses and the journey normally takes around four hours. At the time of writing, however, extensive road repairs were being carried out on this road, almost doubling journey times. ⇾ *For further details, see Transport, page 114.*

Getting around
The town is in two parts, separated by a small valley through which the Naura River runs. The upper part, to the east, contains the government buildings, post office, immigration, most of the top-range hotels, safari companies, airline offices, curio and craft shops, and the huge Arusha International Conference Center (AICC), which is on East Africa Community Road (Barabara ya Afrika Mashariki). This road used to be called Simeon Road and the name Simeon Road has now been given to the road further east that links Old Moshi Road and the Nairobi–Moshi Road, near the Impala Hotel (formerly Nyerere Road). This can be quite confusing when reading local maps. Further down the hill and across the valley to the east are the commercial and industrial areas, the market, small shops, many of the budget hotels and the bus stations. In the middle of the centre is the clock tower and roundabout. From here, Sokoine Road neatly bisects the town to the west and continues further out of town to become the main road that goes to both Dodoma and the parks of the northern circuit. To the southeast of the clock tower is Old Moshi Road, along which some of the better hotels are located. *Dala-dala* run frequently up and down the main throroughfares, costing US$0.30, taxis are everywhere and should cost little more than US$3-4 for a short journey around town.

Safety
Alas safety is becoming an increasing concern in Arusha. Muggings have become more common, and in 2004 there was a serious attack just outside Arusha when a group of 32 tourists were ambushed and robbed. Sokoine Road and Moshi Road towards the Impala Hotel are unsafe at night, unless you are in a big group, and the area around the bridge crossing River Themi on Old Moshi Road has seen increasingly higher numbers of muggings recently – if you have to carry a laptop make sure it's not in an obvious laptop bag and be discreet with cameras, valuables, etc. Taxis are advised at night, and extra caution should be taken around the market and bus station where pickpockets (especially street children) are common. If you are in a vehicle, ensure that it is securely locked.

Tourist information

Information for tourists in Arusha, with displays on the surrounding attractions, can be obtained from the following places. The **Tanzanian Tourist Board** ⓘ *Information Centre, 47E Boma Rd, T027-250 38402/3, www.tanzaniatouristboard.com, Mon-Fri 0800-1600, Sat 0830-1330, this office does not arrange bookings or hotel reservations*, a useful source of local information, including details of the excellent Cultural Tourism Programmes that were set up in conjunction with SNV, the Netherlands Development Agency. In the office are all the leaflets outlining these tours, which directly involve and benefit the local people. It is best to make reservations and arrangements here before going out to the individual locations. To date, this initative has involved 32 villages around Arusha, Kilimanjaro, Iringa, Pangani, Mbeya and other regions. These programmes are an excellent way to experience traditional customs, music and dance, and modern ways of life in rural areas. They tend to be off the beaten track, giving a very different tourist experience. An example is the Usambara Mountains Cultural Tourism Programme (see page 58). The tours offered by each programme have been described by one traveller as relatively expensive but worth the cost. More information can be found at www.tanzaniacultural tourism.com, from which you can download each of the programme's brochures. See Around Arusha, below, for the ones in the immediate region. The Tanzanian Tourist Board office also holds a list of registered tour companies as well as a 'blacklist' of rogue travel agencies (see page 113). They also provide copies of "The official Arusha City Map" which has the latest street names (see above).

Ngorongoro Information Office ⓘ *Boma Rd, T027-254 4625*, is a couple of doors along from the tourist information office. There's not much to pick up here in the way of leaflets, but it does sell some books and maps of the national parks, and there is an interesting painting on the wall that shows all the parks in the northern circuit, which gives a good idea where they all are in relation to each other. There is also a model showing the topography of the Ngorongoro Crater. **Tanzania National Parks (TANAPA)** head office ⓘ *Dodoma Rd, T027-250 3471, www.tanzaniaparks.com*, stocks booklets on the national parks at much more competitive prices than elsewhere, and is a useful resource if you require specialist information. It also provides information about the accommodation options in the more remote national parks.

There are also a couple of noticeboards with feedback bulletins from travellers at **Dolly's Patisserie** on Sokoine Road (see page 107) and the **Jambo Makuti Garden** on Boma Road (see page 106). There is a superb colour map of Arusha and the Road to Moshi by Giovanni Tombazzi, which can be obtained from bookshops (see page 108) or **Hoopoe Safaris** on India Street (see page 111).

Sights

Centre

The centre of town is the **clock tower**, which was donated in 1945 by a Greek resident, Christos Galanos, to commemorate the Allied victory in the Second World War. The German Boma now houses the **National Natural History Museum** ⓘ *north end of Boma Rd, www. houseofculture.or.tz/natural_history_museum, daily 0900-1700, entry US$5*, opened in 1987. The building was built by the Germans in 1886 and it has an outer wall, with block towers at each corner. Inside the fortifications are a central administrative

Arusha

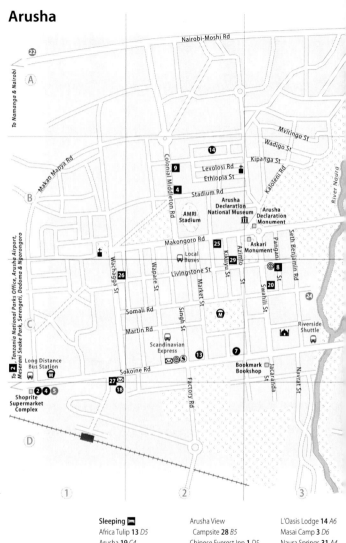

Sleeping

Africa Tulip **13** *D5*
Arusha **19** *C4*
Arusha Backpackers **27** *C1*
Arusha by Night Annexe **4** *B2*
Arusha Coffee Lodge **2** *C1*
Arusha Crown **25** *B2*
Arusha Naaz **18** *C4*
Arusha Tourist Centre
Arusha View
  Campsite **28** *B5*
Chinese Everest Inn **1** *D5*
Flamingo **29** *C2*
Golden Rose **9** *B2*
Ilboru Safari Lodge **7** *A6*
Impala **11** *D6*
Karama Lodge **5** *D6*
Klub Afriko **16** *A6*
L'Oasis Lodge **14** *A6*
Masai Camp **3** *D6*
Naura Springs **31** *A4*
New Safari **21** *C4*
Outpost **23** *D5*
Pamoje Expeditions **3**
Palm Court **26** *C1*
Pepe One & Pepe's
  Restaurant **32** *C5*

90 • Arusha Sights

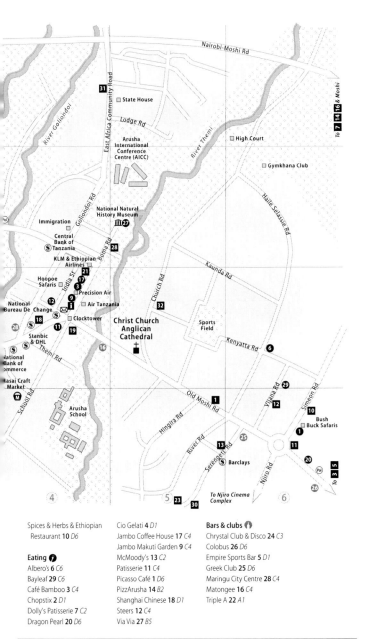

building, a captain's mess, a soldiers' mess, a guard house and a large armoury. A laboratory has been established for paleoanthropological research (study of man's evolution through the record of fossils).

The museum contains the celebrated **Laetoli Footprints**, dating back 3,500,000 years, set in solidified volcanic grey ash. Three hominids walking on two legs have left their tracks. The discovery was made at Laetoli, about 30 km southwest of Olduvai Gorge, by Andrew Hill, who was visiting Mary Leakey's fossil camp in 1978. Another display of interest is the tracing of the evolution of man based on the findings at Olduvai Gorge (see page 139).

The new **Tanzanite Museum** ⓘ *on the 3rd floor of the Blue Plaza Building, India St, T027-250 5101, www.tanzaniteexperience.com, Mon-Fri 0900-1600, Sat 0900-1300*, is nearby and explains about the history, mining and processing of tanzanite, found only in Tanzania, on the foothills of Kilimanjaro. There's a shop here where you can buy certified gems.

North of the museum, the huge **Arusha International Conference Centre (AICC)** ⓘ *T027-250 3161, www.aicc.co.tz*, is made up of three main blocks – the Kilimanjaro, Ngorongoro and Serengeti wings. It has been an important centre for international deliberations, with recent events such as the Rwandan War Crimes Tribunal and the Burundi peace negotiations taking place here. The centre also has a bank, post office, foreign exchange bureau and cafeteria, as well as various tour operators and travel agents.

On the east side of East Africa Raod, just north of the AICC complex, is the former **State House**, a small but handsome building with double gables and a green tin roof. This was the residence of the provincial commissioner in the colonial period. Nowadays it houses the Nyere Centre for Peace Research.

Old Moshi Road

In the colonial period Europeans settled in the area adjacent to the River Themi, along Old Moshi Road, and to the north and south of it. The Asian community lived near their commercial premises, often over them, in the area between Boma Road and Goliondoi Road. Africans lived further to the west on the far side of the Naura River. On the north side of the Old Moshi Road is **Christ Church Anglican Cathedral**, built in the 1930s in traditional English style of grey stone with a tiled roof and a pleasant interior. The cathedral is surrounded by a vicarage and church offices. Further along the road there are several bungalows with red tile roofs and substantial gardens. These housed government servants. One building in particular, the **Hellenic Club** (or Greek Club), stands out with its classical porticos, on the corner of Old Moshi Road and Njiro Road.

Makongoro Road

The **Arusha Declaration Monument** is set on a roundabout past the police station on the Makongoro Road. Also commonly referred to as the Uhuru (Freedom) Monument, it has four concrete legs that support a brass torch at the top of a 10-m column. Around the base are seven uplifting scenes in plaster. The Declaration of 1967 outlined a socialist economic and political strategy for Tanzania. The nearby **Arusha Declaration National Museum** is dedicated to this landmark in Tanzania's history, outlining the evolution of Tanzania's political and economic development. It also has historic photographs of the

German period and a display of traditional weapons including clubs, spears and swords. South of the museum is a small park containing the **Askari Monument**, dedicated to African soldiers who died in the Second World War. On the east side of Azimio Street is an interesting **temple** with a portico, fretworked masonry and a moulded coping.

Arusha School

Arusha School dominates the area on the left bank of the Themi River. It is sited on sloping ground, has huge eucalyptus trees and is surrounded by a large swathe of playing fields. Nyerere's two sons were taught there. It also hosted the meeting of the Organization of African Unity (OAU) Heads of State in 1966, which included Nyerere, Obote, Kaunda, Moi (as vice president), Haile Selassie and Nasser. Sadly, the school and grounds are now very neglected. On the opposite side of School Road near Arusha School is the recently relocated **Masai and Crafts Market**, which has a good selection of crafts and souvenirs.

Around Arusha

Meserani Snake Park

ⓘ 25 km from Arusha on road to the Ngorongoro Crater and Serengeti, T027-253 8282, www.meseranisnakepark.com. US$1. See also Camping, page 105.

Meserani houses mostly local snake species with the non-venomous snakes housed in open pits, though the spitting cobras, green and black mambas and boomslangs are kept behind glass. There are other reptiles including monitor lizards, chameleons, tortoises and crocodiles, and also a few species of birds that are orphaned or injured for whom a temporary home is provided at the park. There are gardens, a campsite, a restaurant and a bar. Run by Barry and Lynn Bale from South Africa, this project works very well with the local community and the local Masai village. Some of the snakes in the park were brought in by the local Masai who instead of killing snakes that may harm livestock, captured and took them to the park. The Bales also provide antidote treatment for snake-bites and other basic health services for the Masai and other local communities free of charge, as well as providing antivenom for most of Tanzania. Barry has recently established an excellent museum of the local Masai culture, which has mock-ups of Masai huts and models wearing various clothing and jewellery, and a Masai guide will explain the day-to-day life of the Masai. Local craftspeople sell their goods, and camel rides and treks can be arranged to meet the people in the Masai village.

Lake Duluti

Just south of **Mountain Village Hotel**, about 15 km from Arusha along the Moshi road, this small crater lake, fringed by forest, provides a sanctuary for approximately 130 species of birds, including pied and pygmy kingfishers, anhinga, osprey, and several species of buzzards, eagles, sandpipers, doves, herons, cormorants, storks, kingfishers and barbets. Reptiles including snakes and lizards are plentiful too. The pathway around the lake starts off broad and level, but later on it narrows and becomes more difficult to negotiate. There are wonderful views of Mount Meru and occasionally the cloud breaks to reveal Mount Kilimanjaro. 'Ethno-botanical' walks are available, starting from the hotel through the coffee plantation and circumnavigating the lake. The walks are accompanied by guides who are knowledgeable about the flora and birds.

Cultural tourism programmes

Several villages on the lower slopes of Mount Meru, north of Arusha, have started cultural tourism programmes with help from the Dutch development organization, SNV, and the Tanzanian Tourist Board. Profits from each are used to improve the local primary schools. Further details of the programmes described below can be obtained from the Tanzanian tourist information centre in Arusha (see page 89), www.tanzaniaculturaltourism.com.

Ng'iresi Village ⓘ *7 km from Arusha north of the Moshi Rd, transportation by pickup truck can be arranged at the Arusha tourist centre.* Offers half-day guided tours of farms and local development projects such as irrigation, soil terracing, cross breeding, bio gas and fish nurseries. Longer tours can involve camping at a farm and a climb of **Kivesi**, a small volcano with forests where baboons and gazelle live. The Wa-arusha women will prepare traditional meals or a limited choice of Western food. Profits go towards enlarging the local school.

Ilkiding'a Village ⓘ *7 km north of Arusha along the road signposted to Ilboru Safari Lodge from Moshi Rd.* You will be welcomed in a traditional boma, be able to visit craftsmen and a traditional healer, and walk through farms to one of several viewpoints or into **Njeche canyon**. A three-day hike is also available, stopping at various villages and culminating in a visit to a Masai market. The guides of both this and the Ng'iresi programme are knowledgeable and have a reasonable standard of English. Funds go towards improving the local primary school.

Mulala Village ⓘ *1450 m above sea level on the slopes of Mt Meru about 30 km from Arusha, the turn-off is just before Usa River, follow signs for the Dik Dik Hotel, after the hotel the road climbs for about 10 km.* This programme is organized by the Agape women's group. There are walks through the coffee and banana farms to Marisha River, or to the top of Lemeka hill for views of mounts Meru and Kilimanjaro, and on to the home of the village's traditional healer. You can visit farms where cheese- and bread-making and flower-growing activities have been initiated. The women speak only a little English but interpreters can be arranged.

Mkuru camel safari ⓘ *North side of Mt Meru, the camp is 5 km from Ngarenanyuki Village, which is 5 km beyond the Momela gate of Arusha National Park.* The Masai of this area began keeping camels in the early 1990s and there are now over 100 animals. Camel safaris of half a day or up to one week, towards Kilimanjaro, to Mount Longido, or even further to Lake Natron can be arranged. Alternatively, there are walks through the acacia woodland looking for birds, or up the pyramid-shaped peak of Ol Doinyo Landaree. In the camel camp itself, it is possible to see the Masai carry the new-born camels to their overnight shelters and watch them milk the camels. The guides are local Masai who have limited knowledge of English, communicating largely by hand signals – another guide to act as translator can be arranged with advance notice. There are three cottages at the camel camp, meals can be prepared if notice is given. Profits are used to support the village kindergarten, which was established because the nearest schools are too far for young children to walk to.

Mount Longido ➔ *Altitude: 2629 m.*

ⓘ *100 km north of Arusha on the road to Namanga on the border with Kenya. The town of Longido lies on the main road, at the foot of the mountain. To get here by public transport from Arusha take one of the shuttle buses or* dala-dala *that go to Namanga or on to Nairobi; the journey to Longido should take about 1½ hrs. The tours are co-ordinated locally by Mzee Mollel, a local Masai who studied in Zambia and Australia. Mzee is happy to answer any enquiries about the Masai way of life.*

Mount Longido rises up steeply from the plains 100 km north of Arusha on the border with Kenya and forms an important point of orientation over a wide area. To climb Mount Longido is useful preparation for Mount Meru or Mount Kilimanjaro. The **Longido Cultural Tourism programme** is an excellent way of supporting the local Masai people and learning about their lifestyle and culture. There are several walking tours of the environs, including a half-day 'bird walk' from the town of Longido across the Masai plains to the bomas of Ol Tepesi, the Masai word for acacia tree. On your return to Longido you can enjoy a meal cooked by the FARAJA women's group. The one-day walking tour extends from Ol Tepesi to Kimokonwa along a narrow Masai cattle trail that winds over the slopes of Mount Longido. On clear days there are views of Kilimanjaro and Mount Meru and from the north side there are extensive views of the plains into Kenya. The tour includes a visit to a historic German grave. There is also a more strenuous two-day tour climbing to the top of the steep Longido peak, following buffalo trails guarded by Masai warriors armed with knives and spears to protect you. Accommodation is in local guesthouses or at campsites. Part of the money generated by this cultural tourism project goes to the upkeep of the cattle dip in Longido. The Masai lose about 1500 head of cattle per annum, mainly because of tick-borne disease. Since Masai life is centred around their livestock this creates serious problems as reduced herd size means less work, income and food. Regular cattle dipping eradicates tick-borne diseases.

Babati and Mount Hanang

ⓘ *There are regular bus services from Arusha to Babati (172 km) starting from 0730. Once there ask for Kahembe's Guest House, a 5-min walk from the main bus stand.*

Mount Hanang is the ninth-highest peak in East Africa and the fourth highest in Tanzania, with an altitude of 3417 m, and a challenge for more adventurous trekkers. It lies to the southwest of Babati, a small town approximately 170 km southwest of Arusha on the road to Dodoma. Here, ethnic commercial and farming groups co-exist with conservative cattle herders and provide a distinguished cultural contrast. Amongst these people the Barbaig's traditional culture is still unchanged and unspoiled. The women wear traditional goatskin dresses and the men walk around with spears. English-speaking guides who know the area will help you around, and a Barbaig-born guide will tell you about Barbaig culture. **Kahembe's Trekking and Cultural Safaris** (see page 113) offers a two-day trek up Mount Hanang along the Katesh route for US$128 per person. The Katesh route can be completed in one day with the ascent and descent taking up to 12 hours in total. They also have a number of imaginative local tours for US$45 per person per day (US$40 each for three or more people). Independent exploration of the area is possible but not common.

Arusha National Park

The compact Arusha National Park is remarkable for its range of habitats. It encompasses three varied zones: the highland montane forest of Mount Meru to the west, where black and white colobus and blue monkeys can be spotted; Ngurdoto Crater, a small volcanic crater inhabited by a variety of mammals in the southeast of the park; and, to the northeast, Momela Lakes, a series of seven alkaline crater lakes, home to a large number of water birds. On a clear day it is possible to see the summits of both Mount Kilimanjaro and Mount Meru from Ngurdoto Crater rim. There are numerous hides and picnic sites throughout the park, giving travellers an opportunity to leave their vehicles and this is

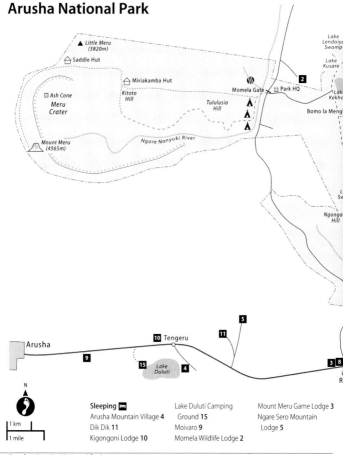

Sleeping
Arusha Mountain Village **4**
Dik Dik **11**
Kigongoni Lodge **10**
Lake Duluti Camping Ground **15**
Moivaro **9**
Momela Wildlife Lodge **2**
Mount Meru Game Lodge **3**
Ngare Sero Mountain Lodge **5**

one of the few of the country's parks where walking is permitted. Climbing Mount Meru or enjoying the smaller trails that criss-cross its lower slopes is a popular activity for visitors to the park. Although only taking three days to reach the crater's summit, it's something of a short, sharp shock – a quieter, but some say more challenging, alternative to the famous peak of nearby Mount Kilimanjaro. Along the lower slopes, paths through ancient fig tree forests, and crystal clear cascading rivers and waterfalls make a relaxing day's hike for visitors who don't want to attempt the longer and more arduous climb. Canoeing on Small Momella Lake, where there are several hippos and interesting birdlife, is also an option for the active and allows you the chance to see wildlife from a slower, quieter perspective. **Green Footprint Adventures** operate these canoeing safaris (see page 111). Park fees for canoeing are US$20 per person for a half day and US$40 for a full day.

» *For more information on national parks and safaris, see page 9.*

Ins and outs

Getting there Arusha National Park is about 25 km east of Arusha and 58 km from Moshi. The road is a good one and the turning off the main road between Arusha and Moshi, about 35 km from Kilimanjaro International Airport, is at Usa River and is clearly signposted. From the airport the landscape changes from the flat dry and dusty Sanya Plain, gradually becoming greener, more fertile and more cultivated. Take the turning (on the right if you are heading towards Arusha) and follow the gravel road for about 10 km until you reach the **Ngurdoto Gate**. This is coffee country and you will see the farms on each side of the road. On reaching the park entrance this changes to dense forest.

There's a second gate, **Momela Gate**, from which you access Mount Meru, to the north of the park. There are two routes leading to Momela Gate, starting near the village of Usa River, close by the Arusha/Moshi road. From here it is 8 km to Ngurdoto Gate. A single road enters the park, dividing near Serengeti Ndogo. The road to the northwest is known as the Outer Road (25 km) and National Park fees are not payable if in transit. The only available transport is pickup trucks, which walk this route too. The right fork takes you to the road that runs northeast towards

Ngurdoto Mountain
Lodge **14**
Rivertrees Country Inn **13**
Tanzanite **8**

Ngurdoto Crater, before turning north (18 km) beside the Momela Crater Lakes, and this route attracts the National Park fee. These roads through the park meet up again at the Momela Gate. If you don't have your own vehicle many safari companies offer day trips to Arusha National Park.

The best time to visit is October-February. There are several excellent lodges around Usa River and on the lower slopes of Meru. Entry to the park is US$35.

Park information

At the main entrance a small museum provides information for the visitor on the bird, animal and plant life of the park. Park accommodation can be booked in advance through Tanzania National Parks (TANAPA) head office, see page 89.

Background

The Arusha National Park, which contains Mount Meru, was established in 1960. The Howard Hawks film *Hatari* was made here in 1962, starring John Wayne, Elsa Martinelli, Red Buttons and Hardy Kruger. The park has changed its name a number of times from Ngurdoto Crater National Park to Mount Meru National Park and finally to Arusha National Park. It covers an area of 137 sq km and rises from 1524 m at the Momela Lakes (also spelt Momella) to 4565 m at the peak of Mount Meru. Although it is only small, because of this gradation there is a variety of landscapes, a variety of eco-systems and therefore a wide variety of flora and fauna. Within the park are the Ngurdoto Crater and the Momela Lakes.

Mount Meru is believed to have been formed at around the time of the great earth movements that created the Rift Valley, about 20 million years ago. The crater was formed about 250,000 years ago when a massive explosion blew away the eastern side of the volcano. A subsidiary vent produced the volcano of Ngurdoto, which built up over thousands of years. In a way similar to Ngorongoro, when the cone collapsed the caldera was left as it is today. Ngurdoto is now extinct, while Meru is only dormant, having last erupted about 100 years ago. The lava flow from this eruption can be seen on the northwest side of the mountain. It was at around this time in 1872 that the first European, Count Teleki, a Hungarian, saw the mountain.

Arusha National Park contains many animals including giraffe, elephant, hippo, buffalo, rhino (if you're lucky), colobus monkey, bush buck, red forest duiker, reed buck, waterbuck and warthog and reportedly the highest density of giraffes in the world. There are no lions but you may see leopard. Birds include cormorants, pelicans, ibis, flamingos and grebes.

Ngurdoto Crater

Within the park there are over 50 km of tracks but no roads have been built into the Ngurdoto Crater in order to protect and preserve it. From the Ngurdoto Gate a road leads off towards the Ngurdoto Crater. This area is known as the 'connoisseur's park' – rightly so. The road climbs up through the forest until it reaches the rim. At the top you can go left or right, either going around the crater clockwise or anti-clockwise. The track does not go all the way round the rim of the crater so you will have to turn round and retrace your tracks back to the main road. You will be able to look down on to the animals in the crater below but will not be able to drive down. The crater is about 3 km in diameter and there are a number of viewing points around the rim from which you can view the crater floor,

Climbing Mount Meru

The walk up Mount Meru involves a 3500-m altitude hike, frequently climbed up and down within three days. The last section of the walk to the summit is very steep. It is easy to underestimate what are common problems associated with this walk – altitude sickness and frostbite. Snow is not unknown at the summit. On the ascent you will pass through the changing vegetation. The first change is to lower montane forest at about 2000 m, then to higher montane forest. The road climbs up the mountain up to the heath zone at about 2439 m from where you can climb to the peak. From the road and the park headquarters a track leads up to the Miriakamba Hut, which takes about three hours. The trail continues as a steady climb through montane forest, where there is an abundance of birds and black and white colobus monkeys. The first mountain hut sleeps about 48 people, while the second, Saddle Hut, sleeps about 24. Both huts provide firewood. It is a three-hour walk between the two huts but is a steep climb and having reached Saddle Hut you can spend the afternoon climbing Little Meru (3820 m), which takes about 1½ hours. From Saddle Hut the climb up to the rim of the mountain and around to the summit usually starts at 0200 in order to see the sunrise from the top. It's a steep climb to Rhino Point (3800 m), before continuing along an undulating ridge of ash and rock to reach Cobra Point (4350 m). The final ascent from Saddle Hut is difficult, cold and can be dangerous, but the views of the cliffs and crater rim are stunning: you can see the ash cone rising from the crater floor and Kilimanjaro floating on the morning clouds. Most of the tour operators in Arusha, and some in Moshi, can arrange climbs. Like the Kilimanjaro climb there are a number of park fees to climb the mountain that are paid to the Tanzania National Parks. Though these are not quite as expensive as for Kili, nevertheless expect to pay in the region of US$400 for a package including park fees, guide, porters, food and accommodation in mountain huts.

known as the 'park within the park'. These include Leitong Point (the highest at 1850 m), Glades Point, Rock Point, Leopard Hill, Rhino Crest and Mikindani Point. From this latter point you will be able to see Mount Kilimanjaro in the distance.

Momela Lakes route

From Ngurdoto Gate, if you take the left track you will reach the Momela Lakes. This track goes past the Ngongongare Springs, Lokie Swamp, the Senato Pools and the two lakes, Jembamba and Longil. At the peak of the dry season they may dry up but otherwise they are a good place to watch the animals and in particular the birdlife. At various spots there are observation hides. At **Lake Longil** there is a camping and picnic site in a lovely setting.

From here the track continues through the forest, which gradually thins out and through the more open vegetation you will be able to see Mount Meru. The Hyena Camp (Kambi ya Fisi) is reached at the point where you will probably see a pack of spotted hyenas. Beyond this there is a small track leading off the main track to **Bomo la Mengi** – a lovely place from which to view the lakes. Unless the cloud is down you will also be able to see Kilimanjaro from here. The main track continues past two more lakes – **Lake El**

Kekhotoito and **Lake Kusare** – before reaching the Momela Lakes.

The **Momela Lakes** are shallow alkaline lakes fed by underground streams. Because they have different mineral contents and different algae their colours are also different. They contain few fish but the algae attracts lots of birdlife. What you see will vary with the time of year. Flamingos tend to move in huge flocks around the lakes of East Africa and are a fairly common sight at Momela Lakes. Between October and April the lakes are also home to the migrating waterfowl, which are spending the European winter in these warmer climes.

The track goes around the lakes reaching the **Small Momela Lake** first. This lake often has a group of hippos wallowing in it. Follow the road anti-clockwise and you will pass **Lake Rishetani**, which is a fantastic emerald green colour. Along this route you will be able to stop off at the various observation sites. The next lake that you will get to is the **Great Momela Lake**, which has a huge variety of birdlife and is a lovely spot. The last two lakes are **Tulusia** and **Lekandiro** where you may see animals grazing.

Mount Meru

The other major attraction of Arusha National Park is Mount Meru (4565 m), the second highest mountain in Tanzania and also the fifth highest in all Africa. The mountain lies to the west of the Ngare Nanyuki road in the western half of the park. There is a road that leads up the mountain to about 2439 m from the **Momela Gate**, passing through an open space called **Kitoto** from where there are good views of the mountain, but vehicles are no longer allowed to pass this way.

Arusha listings

For Sleeping and Eating price codes and other relevant information, see pages 7-9.

Sleeping

The best hotels in the Arusha area are out of town in the foothills of Mt Meru. They have fine gardens, good standards and charming atmosphere. They are recommended above similar priced hotels in Arusha or its outskirts. If you do not have your own transport most will offer transfers from town and many are used as part of a safari package. At the budget end of the market there are a number of cheap hotels around the stadium and market that cost as little as US$10 and are good value. If using a hotel's 'safe', you are advised to check your money when deposited and on collection, or seal it in a bag with tape. There are reports of false receipts being issued and less money being returned on collection.

Arusha *p88, map p90*

$$$$ Arusha Coffee Lodge, a few kilometres from town on the road to the crater on a working coffee estate, T027-250 06309, www.arushacoffeelodge.com, www.elewana.com. One of the most luxurious options in Arusha, with 23 stunning spacious chalets with balconies, fireplaces, facilities to make coffee, enormous beds with mosquito nets, hardwood floors and wooden decks, Zanzibar-style furniture and Persian rugs. Very elegant lounge, and a restaurant for fine dining (see Eating, page 106) with dressed up tables and leather sofas. Swimming pool.

$$$$ The Arusha Hotel, previously the New Arusha, near the clock tower, T027-250 7777, www.thearushahotel.com. Formerly the site of the old German hotel built in 1903, of which the splendid restaurant is the only surviving feature. 86 elegantly decorated rooms, with a/c, phone and internet access. Behind the hotel is a beautiful garden running down to the Themi River. Swimming pool, gym (open to non-residents), snack bar, restaurant serving international food, Italian and Indian dishes, and the bar downstairs leads to the garden. Also a good bookshop, gift/craft shop and a foreign exchange bureau.

$$$$ Onsea Country Inn and Guest Cottage, Baraa Rd, about 5 km outside Arusha off Moshi Rd, T0784-833207 (mob), www.on seahouse.com. In a beautiful location over-looking the hills and Mt Meru, this stylish boutique hotel owned by Belgians Dirk and Inneke Janssens has 5 rooms, 3 in the main house and 2 in the guest cottage across the road, which can be used as one huge family suite. All rooms are elegantly furnished and there's a swimming pool in tranquil gardens. Excellent restaurant, on the terrace of the main house with stunning views, see Eating, page 106. Massages are available either in the guest rooms or in the private jacuzzi area. Rates are US$360 for a double room full board, including wines.

$$$ African Tulip, 44/1 Serengeti Rd, T027-254 3004, www.theafricantulip.com. A new boutique hotel, owned by **Roy Safaris**. 29 rooms decorated in smart contemporary style with an African safari theme, all with window seats overlooking the grounds or the roof garden that appropriately is full of African tulips. Rooms have a/c, flat screen TV, Wi-Fi and minibar. There's a chic Zanzibar bar, a Baobab themed restaurant and a pool in lawned gardens. Rates include breakfast.

$$$ Impala Hotel, 500 m down Old Moshi Rd from the clock tower, T027-254 3082/7, www.impalahotel.com. 160 rooms in an ultra modern block with TV and phone, pleasant garden and patio, and swimming pool. Rates include breakfast, several good restaurants, including an excellent Indian one, and coffee shops, 24-hr room service, gift shop and bureau de change. Arranges tours and safaris through **Classic Tours** (see page 110). Run their own shuttle bus to and from Kilimanjaro airport and Nairobi. A useful hotel with several amenities but somewhat impersonal service.

$$$ Karama Lodge & Spa, 3 km from town off the Old Moshi Rd, turn off just past Masai Camp, T027-250 0359, www.karama-lodge.com. 22 thatched stilted log cabins built on the hillside in a pretty tract of forest. Close enough to town but a very peaceful with good views of Meru and Kilimanjaro. Colourful rooms have hanging chairs on the balcony. Rustic bar on a deck, and the restaurant uses ingredients from the garden. A popular choice for a rest after climbing Kilimanjaro or Meru, a spa is currently being built.

$$$ Naura Springs Hotel, East Africa Community Rd, about 500m from AICC on the opposite side of the road, T027-205 0001/8, www.nauraspringshotel.com. You can't miss the tall, blue-glass building housing Arusha's newest hotel. Beautifully crafted wooden carvings decorate the communal areas but beyond that, the place has little character. The bar and main restaurant are by the main cavernous reception lobby and there's a pool and lawns at the rear, with another bar and restaurant. The salon and gym are still being built. The 124 rooms are spacious but soulless, with flat screen TVs and fridges; some are more attractive than others.

$$$-$ Ilboru Safari Lodge, 2 km west from town towards Mt Meru off the Nairobi Rd, T0754-270357 (mob), www.ilborusafarilodge.com. Well managed by Aad, a Dutchman and his Tanzanian wife, this popular lodge has 30 en suite rooms in thatched rondavaals with a Masai theme, which were about to be upgraded at the time of our visit. There's an excellent restaurant (see Eating, page 106) with a Dutch pancake place due to open and a German beer garden at weekends. The large swimming pool is open to non-residents. Nearby is the campsite (US$10) with good facilities. Various activities offered, from traditional tingatinga painting to cookery classes. Friendly lodge which is excellent value for money. Highly recommended.

$$ Arusha Crown Hotel, Makongoro Rd, T027-254 4161, www.arushacrownhotel.com. A modern hotel and very centrally located. 38 rooms on 6 floors, stylish decor throughout (though very much a business travellers' hotel with 24 single rooms), internet access, CCTV security cameras. Very good restaurant open to non-residents (see Eating, page 106). A single is US$60, a twin or a double US$74, excellent value in this price range. The rooms facing north overlook Meru and directly into the stadium – if there's a match on you can watch the football from bed.

$$ Arusha Naaz Hotel, near clock tower on Sokoine Rd, T027-250 2087, www.arusha naaz.net. Once you get through the bizarre shopping centre entrance and head up the small staircase, the 21 rooms are centred around a little internal courtyard. Clean, en suite bathrooms, 24 hr hot water, fans and mosquito nets, restaurant with good food (closed in evening), internet access. You can also hire cars from here.

$$ New Safari, Boma Rd, T027-250 3261, www.thenewsafarihotel.com. Friendly hotel, conveniently located in the New Safari Complex, which also houses businesses such as internet cafés and bureaux de change. Very smart modern building, nice terrace restauranton the 1st floor with good views of Meru, 48 rooms with TV, internet connection for laptops, and minibar with soft drinks.

$$ Outpost, Serengeti Rd, off the Old Moshi Rd, near **Impala Hotel**, T027-254 8405, www.outposttanzania.com. Run by a Zimbabwe couple, Kathy and Steve Atwell, the staff are superb and very welcoming. Popular with expats. Accommodation either in spacious rooms in the main house or in bandas, the family unit can sleep 6, full English breakfast included. Manicures, pedicures and massages also on offer. A new swimming pool has recently been added together with Café Mambo, a cheerful bakery, café and bar, with chilled music, around the pool area. Highly recommended.

$$-$ Golden Rose, Colonel Middleton Rd, T027-250 7959, www.hotelgoldenrose.net. Comfortable, good value, self-contained rooms with hot water, telephones, balconies. Bar and restaurant, internet café and bureau de change. Accept Visa and MasterCard but charge 10% more. Reported to have rather noisy generator at back. Can arrange car hire.

$$-$ Hotel Pepe One, just off Church Rd, T0784-365515 (mob), www.hotelpepeone.co.tz. This popular restaurant now has 5 rooms, all off the main reception area. Rooms are newly decorated with good bathrooms, nets and TV. Tidy and clean but a bit cramped. Lively restaurant serving a varied menu (see Eating, page 107) and is in a quiet location in pretty grounds. Good value at US$45 for a double, breakfast is an extra US$5.

$$-$ Klub Afriko Hotel and Safaris, Kimandolu, 3 km from town on the Moshi Rd, T027-254 8878, www.klubafriko.com. Set in tropical gardens in a quiet neighbourhood just outside Arusha town. 7 airy en suite bungalows, decorated with local artwork. Excellent food, friendly bar with satellite TV.

$$-$ L'Oasis Lodge, 2 km out of town, in the quiet residential area of Sekei, T027-250 7089, www.loasislodge.com. 22 rooms, some on stilts and some in the main building, have en suite facilities, and there are 13 smaller twin budget rooms with shared bathrooms. Good food, extensive menu including Thai, Indonesian, Greek, seafood and vegetarian dishes. There's also a more casual lounge bar by the pool which serves burgers and pizzas. Pool with fish and wading birds, a dining area, bar, internet services. Highly recommended.

$$-$ Le Jacaranda, Vijana Rd, T027-254 4624, www.chez.com/jacaranda. 23 African themed rooms, small but clean with private bath-rooms and Masai artwork. Some rooms are in the main building, others are dotted around the gardens. Internet access, comfortable bar area with sofas on terrace overlooking gardens. Crazy golf. Restaurant serves everything from Chinese to Swahili with plenty of vegetarian options (see Eating, page 107).

$$-$ Pamoja Expeditions, Serengeti Rd, T027-250 6136, www.pamojaexpeditions lodge.com. Rooms are in bungalows in the garden, simply furnished with white-washed walls, nets and TV. There's a small pool in the gardens with plastic chairs and sunbeds. Internet café. Lacking in character compared to its neighbour, the **Outpost**.

$$-$ Sinka Court, near the market, T027-250 4961, sinkacourthotel@hotmail.com. In a very modern block, 29 rooms with built-for-hotel furniture and excellent bathrooms, a/c, cable TV, mosquito nets, the larger rooms have fridges and floor to ceiling windows, though the view is not up to much as the hotel overlooks an ugly block of flats. Under-ground parking, restaurant and bar.

$ Arusha Backpackers, Sokoine Rd, T027-250 4474, www.arushabackpackers.co.tz. This is a popular low budget option with good facilities, including a lively bar and restaurant on the top floor. Free internet for residents. The 34 rooms are sparsely furnished and some are like windowless cells with nothing but bunk-beds and a chair. But they're still good value at US$16 for a double including breakfast. There are also some dormitories with 2 sets of bunk beds for US$7 per person. Communal toilets and showers.

$ Arusha by Night Annexe, on corner of Col Middleton Rd and Stadium Rd, T027-250 6894 . Very basic rooms with bathrooms and hot water, though the plumbing is leaky, and mosquito nets. Small restaurant and courtyard bar, where friendly ladies cook up Tanzania staples plus a stab at something international such as spag bol.

$ Arusha Tourist Centre Inn, Livingstone St, next to **Hotel Fort des Moins**, T027-250 0421, icerestaurant@yahoo.com. The reception area for the hotel is through the **Ice Restaurant and bar** at the front. All 18 rooms are en suite and have TV, phone and mosquito nets. Simple but clean. The owners also run **Arusha Tourist Inn** on Sokoine Rd near Meru House.

$ Chinese Everest, Old Moshi Rd, near the **Impala**, T0732-975274 (mob), everesttzus@ yahoo.com. 7 clean and comfortable rooms in the gardens at the back of this popular Chinese restaurant, with friendly and helpful hosts. There are also pleasant gardens at the front of the restaurant, which serves excellent Sechuan food. Internet access. Room rate includes an English or Chinese breakfast. Single, double and triple rooms available. Recommended.

$ Hotel Flamingo, Kikuyu St, by the market area, T027-254 8812, flamingoarusha@ yahoo.com A good low budget option. 9 clean, light and airy rooms with mosquito nets and own bathrooms. Friendly staff and a pleasant bar area that serves soft drinks only.

$ Palm Court Hotel, 500 m from the bus station off Wachagga St, T0754-975468 (mob). A friendly low-budget option with rooms around the restaurant. Rates include breakfast and are more expensive if you want your own bathroom. Basic but clean, nets, shared hot showers, laundry service, small restaurant, bar, tea and coffee, lounge with satellite TV, exceptionally good value.

$ Spices & Herbs, a few metres north of the **Impala Hotel** off Old Moshi Rd, T027-254 2279, axum_spices@hotmail.com. Well appointed, with a garden and veranda leading to the restaurant which specializes in Ethiopian cuisine (see Eating, page 107). The 19 rooms are set around a courtyard to the rear, small but comfortable with hot showers, some are adjoining for families. In the middle of the courtyard are some chairs and a satellite TV.

Camping

$ Arusha View Campsite, next to **Equator Hotel**, Boma Rd. Very central and very basic camping. Only US$3. It's possible to hire tents but you will need a sleeping bag. Grassy sites next to a small river, mosquitoes love it.

$ Masai Camp, 3 km along Old Moshi Rd T027-250 0358, www.masaicamp.tripod.com. Fantastic restaurant, serving Tex Mex, burgers, pizzas and the best nachos in East Africa. Spotless ablutions with steaming hot water, shady camping spots on grassy terraces, some budget rooms in huts, internet, lively bar with frequent party nights and live music, also new cocktail bar. Highly recommended for backpackers. The excellent safari company, **Tropical Trails** (see page 113) is based here.

Around Arusha *p93*
Mountain lodges

$$$$ Dik Dik, 20 km from Arusha off the Moshi Rd near Usa River, T027-255 3499, www.dik dik.ch. Swimming pool, good restaurant, pleasant grounds, set on the slopes of Meru, very proficiently run by Swiss owners, though lacks African atmosphere, concentrates on running upmarket Kilimanjaro climbs. More reasonable rates are available if you are buying accommodation as part of a climb package.

$$$ Arusha Mountain Village, 20 km out of town along the Moshi Rd, T027-255 3313 (lodge number), for reservations www.serena hotels.com. Quality lodge in an old colonial homestead. 42 thatched bomas, with hand-carved African animals on the doors, nestled within a coffee plantation. Excellent gardens, splendid location overlooking the Lake Duluti. Very good restaurant, relaxed open bar and impeccable service.

$$$ Kigongoni Lodge, 10 km east of Arusha, 1 km before Tengeru, 1 km off the Moshi Rd, T027-255 3087, www.kigongoni.net. On a 28-ha coffee farm with good views of Kilimanjaro and Meru, the lodge has 18 cottages, built with local materials, with fireplaces and verandas, 4-poster beds with mosquito nets and en suite bathrooms. Some rooms have internet access, the restaurant serves a set 3-course meal each night and there's a cocktail lounge and a swimming pool on top of a hill with fantastic views. Revenues from the lodge support a local foundation for mentally disabled children and their families. Guided walks available.

$$$ Mount Meru Game Lodge, 20 km from Arusha off Moshi Rd near Usa River, T027-255 3643, www.mountmerugamelodge.com. Small, well run, high-standard establishment in garden setting with charming atmosphere and very good restaurant. 4-poster beds swathed in nets. Impressive animal sanctuary, which includes baboons, vervet monkeys and probably the only Sanje mangabey, *Cercocebus sanjei*, in captivity. A large paddock is home to zebra, waterbuck and eland, as well as saddle-billed and yellow-billed storks, sacred ibis and ostrich. Rates differ by US$100 per room between high and low seasons.

$$$ Ngare Sero Mountain Lodge, 20 km east of Arusha on the Moshi Rd, T027-255 3638, www.ngare-sero-lodge.com. Just 1.5 km from the main road is a jacaranda avenue leading to a footbridge. You reach the lodge by crossing the lake by the footbridge and climbing steps up through the gardens or by driving around the forest reserve to reach the car park. 10 garden rooms and 2 suites, pool and sauna in the garden, horse riding, yoga classes, trout fishing and trekking on Mt Meru can all be arranged, and you can play croquet on the lawn. Formerly the farm of Haupt-mann Leue, a colonial administrator from the German period, the name means 'sweet waters' and there are magnificent gardens with an estimated 200 species of birds.

$$$ Ngurdoto Mountain Lodge, 27 km from Arusha, 3 km off Moshi Rd, T027-254

2217/26, www.thengurdotomountain lodge.com. Very smart lodge in beautiful grounds with a range of facilities on a 57-ha coffee estate. 60 rooms in double-storey thatched rondavaals, 72 rooms in the main building, and 7 suites, some rooms have disabled access, satellite TV, most with bathtubs with jacuzzis. Good views of Kilimanjaro and Meru, 3 restaurants, 2 bars, a coffee shop, 18-hole golf course, health club and fully equipped gym, 2 tennis courts, badminton court, swimming pool, toddlers' pool, children's play area and tour desk that can arrange all safaris. An excellent base in the region especially for families.

$$$ Rivertrees Country Inn, 20 km from Arusha, off the Moshi Rd, near Usa River, T027-255 3894, www.rivertrees.com. Set in natural gardens along the picturesque Usa River, this is a very elegant country lodge with excellent farm cuisine and personal service. There are 8 individually decorated rooms with bathrooms in the farmhouse and 2 garden cottages with additional decks and fireplaces. Swimming pool, and horse riding village visits and walking trips can be arranged with notice.

$$$-$$ Moivaro, 7 km from Arusha off the Moshi Rd, T027-255 3243, www.moivaro.com. 42 lovely double- or triple-bed cottages with verandas and en suite bathrooms. Set in gardens in a coffee plantation, swimming pool, good restaurant and bar, children's playground, massages, jogging or walking trail through the plantation. Internet access.

$$-$ Tanzanite, about 22 km along the road to Moshi, near Usa River, T027-257 3038. Popular with locals at the weekend, chalets set in verdant gardens, swimming pool, tennis, restaurant, small animal sanctuary, child friendly, nature trail, lovely surroundings, good value. Camp for US$5.

Camping

$ Lake Duluti camping ground, 11 km from town toward Moshi, turn right at the sign and follow the road through a coffee plantation. Secure camping and parking is in a grassy yard around the jetty and bar, though ablutions are basic. There is a basic restaurant with a limited choice of food and you may have to wait. Cold beers and sodas available and you can pay to get your laundry done.

$ Meserani Snake Park, 25 km out of town on the road towards the Ngorongoro Crater and Serengeti, T027-253 8282, www.meseranisnakepark.com. A hugely popular spot with backpackers, independent overlanders and overland trucks, and just about any safari company on the way to the parks will stop here. Lively atmosphere and friendly, the bar serves very cold beers. The campsite has hot showers and vehicles are guarded by Masai warriors. Meals from simple hamburgers to spit roast impala are on offer (see also page 93).

Arusha National Park *p96, map p96*
Mountain lodges

$$$ Momela Wildlife Lodge, about 50 km from Arusha, just outside Arusha National Park, 3 km to the northeast of the Momela Gate, T027-250 8104, www.lions-safari-intl.com/momella.html. Made famous by the 1960 movie *Hatari* starring John Wayne, which was filmed in the area. The formidable actor stayed here and the hotel was the production base. The lodge will screen the film on request for guests. Beautiful gardens, with a swimming pool, 55 rondavaals with private bathrooms, excellent views of Meru and Kilimanjaro. The lodge is well placed for visits to the Momela Lakes, and nearby are many plains animals and a huge variety of birds.

Camping

$ Arusha National Park Campsites, there are 4 sites in the park, 3 are at the base of Tululusia Hill, the other in the forest near Ngurdoto Gate; another is proposed at the edge of Lake Kusare. All have water, toilets and provide firewood. Book through Tanzania National Parks head office, see page 89.

Eating

Arusha *p88, map p90*

In addition to those listed below, there are also several cafés and restaurants in the new Njiro Cinema Complex, 3 km out of town on the Njiro Rd, including the **Tanzania Coffee Lounge** and the **Oriental Shisha Lounge**, the first Shisha lounge in Arusha.

₸₸₸ Arusha Coffee Lodge, see Sleeping, above. Fabulous setting in a luxurious lodge, lovely wooden building surrounded by decks and overlooking the swimming pool, fine china and crystal, very elegant, big fireplace in the bar area, superb service. At lunch there are set menus with at least 4 main courses to choose from, plus a snack menu. At dinner choose steak, pork, chicken or fish, and then pick a marinade and accompanying sauce, with a wide choice of veg and salad. Wines are from South Africa and Chile. Recommended.

₸₸₸ Arusha Crown Hotel, see Sleeping, above. The downstairs restaurant in this smart hotel is very modern with excellent service and prices are surprisingly cheap for what you get. Dishes include asparagus with crispy bacon and poached egg, pizza, steaks, seafood and fish including red snapper and king fish, lamb chops, curries and schnitzels, and a full Indian menu, good choice of wine and flavoured coffees. Recommended.

₸₸₸ Bayleaf Restaurant, 102 Vijana Rd, T027- 254 3055. A stylish new restaurant near **Le Jacarandra**. Excellent quality food, including the quartet starter – a sample of 4 of the starter dishes, *poisson extraordinaire* and fresh ravioli. Expensive and portions are sometimes small. The restaurant is also a boutique hotel with 2 bedrooms. Reports welcome.

₸₸₸ Jambo Makuti Garden, Boma Rd just south of the **New Safari Hotel**, T027-250 3261. Superb breakfasts, baguettes and stuffed chapatis, burgers, juices and shakes during the day, and afternoon tea from 1400-1700 with cakes and muffins. Dinner from 1930, fish, steaks, ribs and vegetarian dishes and a good wine list. The art on the walls is for sale.

₸₸₸ Onsea Country Inn, see Sleeping, above. Stunning views overlooking the Monduli Mountains and Mt Meru. The Belgian chef prepares brasserie dishes which are Belgian/ French with an African influence, accompanied by fine wines. The restaurant has received excellent reports and bookings are essential – this is fast gaining a reputation as the best place to eat in Arusha.

₸₸ Albero, Haile Sellassie Rd, T0762-248779 (mob), air@yahoo.com. A popular Italian restaurant with an Italian chef and a pleasant bar around a huge fig tree. Reasonable prices and generous portions. Pastas range from US$7-9 and pizzas cooked on a wood fired stove from US$6-8.

₸ Chopstix, in the shopping centre to the left of Shoprite, T027-254 8366. Quality Chinese takeaway and pizzas. Same chain as **Dragon Pearl**, below.

₸ Dragon Pearl, just off the roundabout near **Impala**, T027-2544107. Mon-Fri 1100-1500, 1800-2230, Sat-Sun 1230-2245. Newer sister restaurant of **Shanghai**, different menu, good food and pleasant outdoor setting in lovely gardens. Wines from South Africa, very good vegetarian dishes, full range of Chinese, some Thai, specialities include fried wonton and sizzling dishes, try the crispy chilli prawns. A Korean chef will grill meat at your table and serve it with sauces, similar to a fondue.

₸ Ilboru Safari Lodge, see Sleeping, above. This restaurant has become increasingly popular – and deservedly so – since changing ownership recently. It serves a mix of international and Swahili cuisine, along with some Dutch dishes, and a pancake restaurant should be open by the time this book is published. There's a relaxed atmosphere in the Masai-inspired restaurant and if you're lucky, the staff choir will demonstrate their singing talents. Try the Swahili stews, which include a delicious veggie option.

¶¶ Le Jacaranda, see Sleeping, above. Restaurant and bar on an attractive upstairs wooden deck, lounge area downstairs, surrounded by pretty gardens. Continental, Indian, Chinese and Swahili meals, grills and steaks, and a wide selection of vegetarian options. BBQs at weekends.

¶¶ Masai Camp, 3 km west on Old Moshi Rd, T027-254 8299. Good food and bar, excellent place to meet other travellers, frequent party nights, cocktail bar, serves hamburgers, chips, pizzas and Mexican food on tables in a boma around a roaring fire. Recommended.

¶¶ Pepe's, just off Church Rd, T0784-365515 (mob), www.hotelpepeone.co.tz. A lively Italian and Indian restaurant, well known for its pizzas. Tables are set in pretty gardens or in the restaurant with Masai artwork.

¶¶ Shanghai Chinese Restaurant, Sokoine Rd near the bridge, beside Meru Post Office, T027-250 3224. Daily 1200-1500, 1830-2230. Extensive menu, fairly authentic, quick, the hot and sour soup is highly recommended.

¶¶ Spices & Herbs Ethiopian Restaurant, see Sleeping, above. Open daily 1100-2300. Simple, informal, Ethiopian place with good vegetarian options made from lentils, peas and beans, very good lamb, and continental food (steaks, chops and ribs). Set in a beautifully landscaped garden full of birds. Good service, full bar and live music Thu-Sat. Some accommodation at the back.

¶ Café Bamboo, Boma Rd, near the main post office, T027-250 6451. Very pleasant, bright and airy atmosphere, light pine tables and chairs, blue tablecloths, wicker-shaded lights over each table. Serves good value tasty food, including excellent salads, burgers, juices, fruit salad and ice cream. Fairly busy at lunchtime, closed evenings.

¶ Cio Gelati, Shoprite complex, Sokoine Rd. Snacks, samosas, cold orange juice, 14 flavours of ice cream, sundaes, milkshakes, cappuccino, espresso. Uses fresh ingredients and no eggs.

¶ Dolly's Patisserie, Sokoine Rd, south of the market. Daily from early morning to 1930. Very smart with modern counters and spotless tiles, fantastic freshly baked French bread, cakes and sweets, excellent biryanis, kormas and masalas, hot and cold drinks.

¶ Jambo Coffee House, Boma Rd just south of **New Safari Hotel**. Reasonable snacks and grills, toasted sandwiches, cakes, and excellent coffee (you can also buy coffee beans here).

¶ McMoody's, on the corner of Sokoine and Market St, T027-250 3791/2. McDonald's-inspired fast food for those hankering after fries and milkshakes. It has a peculiar circular staircase and mirrored walkway that goes absolutely nowhere. There is an internet café next door and you can take your drinks in.

¶ Naaz, Sokoine Rd, 150 m from the clock tower. Snack bar at the end of an arcade serving meat chop, egg chop, samosas, kebabs, tea and coffee, excellent juices, buffet lunches with lots of options for vegetarians. Spotless surroundings.

¶ Patisserie, Sokoine Rd, just down the hill from the clock tower. Mon-Fri 0715-1930, Sun 0800-1400. Freshly baked breads, pies, cakes, cookies, croissants, Indian snacks, fresh juices, cappuccino, espresso and hot chocolate. Also internet café.

¶ Picasso Café, by Kijenge Supermarket, Simeon Rd, T0756-448585 (mob). Not open in the evenings or on Sun. A great place for an upmarket breakfast or brunch, with a full English for US$7. Popular lunch spot serving sandwiches, crêpes, burgers and delicious cakes. Wine and beer served too.

¶ PizzArusha, Levolosi Rd to the north of the market. Superb pizzas, curries and steaks, big cheap portions, one of the best budget places to eat in town. Superb service too.

¶ Steers, near the clock tower. South African fast food chain selling ribs and burgers, sodas and shakes, in a/c and spotless environment.

Bars and clubs

Arusha *p88, map p90*
Bars

There are a number of popular places in town and almost all the hotels and many of the restaurants have bars. There are also several in the new Njiro Cinema Complex, 3 km out of town on the Njiro Rd,

Empire Sports Bar, in the arcade behind the Shoprite, off Sokoine Rd. A large modern bar, with high ceiling and mezzanine floor, pool tables, dart board, long bar, large Tvs for watching sport and some tables outside in the courtyard. Popular with expats.

Greek Club, Old Moshi Rd. Set back from the road in a large white house with Grecian pillars out front. Sports bar with large TVs for football, darts board and pool table. Outdoor tables on a terrace or in the garden.

Matongee, Old Moshi Rd. Outside tables in a spacious garden with *nyama choma* barbecues and plenty of cold beer. Relaxed and good value. Popular with local people.

Via Via, in the gardens of the Natural History Museum on Boma Rd. A popular bar with occasional live bands.

Nightclubs

Chrystal Club & Disco, Seth Benjamin Rd. Open most nights from 2200. Large dance floors with 2 rooms (techno and African/trance) and pool tables. Very lively at weekends, has a wide selection of drinks.

Colobus, Old Moshi Rd just past the Impala Hotel. Popular disco in town, open every night.

Maringu City Centre, just opposite Exim Bank in the town centre. Another popular and quite new nightclub.

Triple A, Nairobi Rd. Open Wed, Fri and Sat, 2100-0500 . Also open on Sun afternoons to allow the kids to get down and boogie. This is easily the largest and most popular nightclub in Arusha with a big range of music including R&B and hip hop. Enormous dance floor, pool tables, 2 bars, gets completely packed, also runs its own FM radio station.

Around Arusha *p93*

if you are looking for a party with other travellers the best places to go are the **Meserani Snake Park** and the **Masai Camp**.

Shopping

Arusha *p88, map p90*
Bookshops

Arusha Hotel bookshop sells international newspapers and magazines as well as books.

Bookmark, just off Sokoine Rd behind the BP garage. The best bookshop in Arusha. Stocks a wide range of up to date novels, coffee table books on Africa, guide books, maps, intelligent Africana titles, as well as wrapping paper and greeting cards. Prices are steep as everything is imported, but never theless one of the best ranges of books in Tanzania. Small juice bar and internet access.

Kase Stores, Boma Rd. Has a good selection of books, stationery and postcards.

Crafts

There are some craft shops on Goliondoi Rd and near the clock tower with some very good examples of carvings. The curio markets crammed between the clock tower and India Rd are brimming with carvings, masks, beads and some unusual antique Masai crafts including masks, drums, headrests, and beaded jewellery, and similar items are available at the **Masai Craft Market** on School Rd. Tingatinga paintings are for sale at various outlets, including the **Il Boru Safari Lodge** and at a gallery opposite the **Meserani Snake Park**.

Cultural Heritage Centre, 3 km out on the road towards Dodoma and the crater. A massive structure show-casing some of the finest of African art, though of course it is very expensive. The items are of very high quality and there are carvings, musical instruments, cloth, beads, and leatherwork from all over the continent. They can arrange shipping back to your home country and there is a DHL branch office on site. Many of the safari companies stop here en route to the parks.

Markets and shops

The main market is behind the bus station along Market St and Somali Rd. It is very good for fruit, locally made basketware, wooden kitchenware and spices, and is very colourful. The range of fresh produce is very varied and you can buy just about every imaginable fruit and vegetable. If you are shopping, then be prepared to haggle hard and visit a variety of stalls before deciding on the price. Market boys will help carry goods for a fee. In the rainy season watch where you are stepping – it becomes a bit of a quagmire. There are lots of shops along Sokoine Rd. Small supermarkets are found along Sokoine Rd, Moshi Rd and Swahili St. These sell imported food and booze as well as household goods.

Next door to Shoprite is a wholesale food outlet, and outside towards the back on the left is a small arcade of shops, including a jeweller's, a massage place, a Western-style hairdresser and 3 coffee shops.

Kijenge Supermarket, Simeon Rd. Smaller than Shoprite but useful and near the Impala.
Shoprite, at the end of Sokoine Rd, beyond Meru Post Office and opposite the long distance bus station. A South African chain which is beginning to feature in most African cities. An enormous supermarket selling just about anything you might be looking for.

▲ Activities and tours

Arusha *p88, map p90*
Golf
Gymkhana Club, Haile Selassie Rd out towards the High Court. 9-hole golf course. Temporary membership available. Also has facilities for tennis and squash.

Horse and camel riding
Horse safaris are increasingly popular and can be arranged through the tour operators in Arusha. Most of these begin from Usa River, which is 22 km from Arusha on the Moshi road. For camel rides guided by a local Masai, see **Mkuru Camel Sarfari**, page 94.
Equestrian Safaris, based on a farm on the slopes of Mt Meru, www.safaririding.com. Offer day rides, and 3-14 day horse safaris around Kilimanjaro, Meru and Lake Natron. These are for experienced riders as several hours a day are spent in the saddle. A real opportunity to explore terrain where vehicles cannot go. Full board rates inclusive of meals and fly camping are around US$300 per day.
Meserani Snake Park (see page 93). Ride a camel to a nearby Masai village.

Running
Mt Meru Marathon is held yearly and attracts competitors from all around the world.

Swimming
Available at the pool at the **Il Boru Safari Lodge**, open to non-residents.

Tour operators
Note The cost of taking foreign-registered cars into the national parks in Tanzania means that it is usually cheaper to go on a safari in a Tanzania-registered vehicle.

There are over 100 tour operators and safari companies based in Arusha who organize safaris to the different national parks in the northern circuit (see next chapter). Most also offer Mt Kilimanjaro and Meru treks, holidays in Zanzibar, hotel and lodge reservations, vehicle hire, charter flights, cultural tours, and safaris to the other parks. The list below is far from comprehensive. It is just a matter of finding one you like and discussing what you would like to do. See box opposite, for further information. Many have also adopted cultural or environmental policies – supporting local communities, schools or empowerment projects – which are worth thinking about when choosing a safari operator. On the downside, travellers have reported that rival tour companies sometimes double up, with 2 or 3 groups sharing the same cars and other facilities – all paying different amounts. As a result, itineraries are changed without agreement. It is a good idea to draw up a written contract of exactly what is included in the price agreed before handing over any money. Sometimes touts for rival tour companies are very persistent and this can be very frustrating. To get them off your back, tell them you have already booked a safari even if you haven't. Once in Arusha, give yourself at least a day or 2 to shop around and organize everything. Likewise, allow for at least 1 night in Arusha on the final day of your safari as you will usually return late.

Aardvark Expeditions, Old Moshi Rd, Kijenge, T0754-759120 (mob). Good reports about this company, which operates mostly mid-upper range safaris and treks. As well as Meru and Kilimanjaro, they also offer treks to Ol Donyo Lengai and to Olmeti and Empakai Craters, and safaris across the country.

Abercrombie & Kent, Njiro Hill, T027-250 8347, www.akdmc.com. Quality operator with years of experience, not cheap but they use the best local guides and have a variety of tours in the region, online reservations.

Adventureland Safaris, Sokoine Rd, T0744-886339 (mob), www.adventurelandsafari.com. All safaris, Kili and Meru climbs, cultural tours to the Lake Natron and Lake Eyasi regions, trips to Zanzibar. Budget operator.

Africa Royal Trekking, based at **Arusha View Campsite**, see Sleeping, page 104, T027-246 3391, www.africa-royal-trekking.com. Safaris, Meru and Kilimanjaro climbs.

Africa Walking Company, awc-richard@habari.co.tz. Specialist Kilimanjaro operator with fixed weekly departures through various tour operators on the quieter routes for Kilimanjaro, the Rongai and Shira routes. Excellent value. Highly recommended.

African Adventures, AICC, Suite 10527, T0744-263147 (mob), www.africanadventures.com. Camping and lodge safaris to the northern circuit, climbing, Zanzibar add-ons.

African Trails Ltd, New Safari Hotel Complex, Boma Rd, 2nd floor, T027-250 4406, www. africantrails.com. Mid-range and budget tours to the major parks.

Angoni Safaris, AICC, www.angoni.com. Safaris throughout Tanzania, cultural tours including trekking and donkey rides. Car hire.

Bobby Tours, Goliondoi Rd, T027-250 3490, www.bobbytours.com. Good value camping safaris, expect to pay around US$300 for a 3 day/2 night safari to the crater and Serengeti. Established operator but reports of poor camping equipment.

Bush Buck Safaris, Simeon Rd, T027-250 7779, www.bushbuckltd.com. An established operator with 20 years experience, all safaris, hotel reservations, special arrangements for honeymooners, all the vehicles are 4WD landrovers, not minibuses.

Classic Tours and Safaris, Impala Hotel, see Sleeping, page 101, T027-2508448, www.theclassictours.com. Safaris to northern circuit plus mountain climbs, Gombe, Usambara Mountains, all budgets. Recommended.

Duma Safaris, Njiro Rd, T027-250 0115, www.dumasafari.com. Consistently good feedback from readers for this company. Kilimanjaro climb US$850, 6-day northern circuit US$900, some of their profits support a local school, excellent guides and food.

Easy Travel & Tours Ltd, New Safari, see Sleeping, page 102, T027-250 3929. In Dar, see page 46, www.easy travel.co.tz. Budget tours to all the Tanzanian parks, mountain trekking for Kili and Meru, travel agent with representation of Air Zimbabwe and Air Mauritius.

Fly-Catcher Safaris, Serengeti Rd, T027- 254 4109, www.flycat.com. Safaris to Rubondo, Serengeti, Kitavi and Mahale. Dutch speaking.

Fortes Safaris, Nairobi Rd, T027-254 4887, www.fortes-safaris.com. Trips to Lake Eyasi,

How to organize a safari

→ Figure out how much money you are willing to spend, how many days you would like to go for, which parks you want to visit and when you want to go.

→ If you have the time before arriving in Arusha, check out the websites and contact the safari operators with questions and ideas. Decide which ones you prefer from the quality of the feedback you get.

→ Go to the Tanzania Tourist Board at the clock tower and ask to see the list of licensed tour operators. Also ask to have a copy of the companies that are blacklisted and that are not licensed to operate tours.

→ Pick 3-4 tour operators in your price range.

→ Shop around. Talk to the companies. Notice if they are asking you questions in order to gain an understanding of what you are looking for, or if they are just trying to book you on their next safari (regardless of what would be the best for you). Also, are they open about answering your questions and interested in helping you get the information you need. Avoid the ones that are pressuring you.

→ Make sure you understand what is included in the price, and what is not. Normally, breakfast on the first day and dinner/accommodation on the last day is not included.

→ Listen to the salesperson and guide. They have current news about which parks are best at the moment. If they recommend you a different itinerary than you originally planned, it is probably the best itinerary for game viewing. They know the best areas to visit depending on the time of year and where the animals are in their yearly migrations.

→ Get a contract with all details regarding itinerary, conditions and payment.

→ Ask what kind of meals you can expect. If you are on a special diet, confirm that they can accommodate your needs.

→ Ask how many people will be on the safari. Make sure there is enough room in the vehicle for people and equipment.

→ Talk to the guide. Make sure that he is able to communicate with you, and that he is knowledgeable.

→ If possible, inspect the vehicle you will be using beforehand. If you are going on a camping safari or trek, ask to see the equipment (tents, sleeping bags, etc).

---

where they have an upmarket tented camp.
Good Earth Tours and Safaris, T027-250 8334, www.goodearthtours.com. Toll free (USA) T877-265 9003. Kili climbs, safaris, beach holidays, standard and luxury lodges.
Green Footprint Adventures, Sekei Village Rd, T0784-330495 (mob), www.greenfootprint.co.tz. Offer more adventurous activities such as canoeing in Manyara and Arusha national parks, night game drives in Manyara, and mid- to high-budget safaris (from US$350 a day) specializing in small camps and lodges.
Hima Tours & Travel, Shule Rd, T0784-211 131 (mob), www.himatours.com. A variety of tours, helpful staff.
Hoopoe Safaris, India St, T027-250 7011, UK address: PO Box 278, Watford WD19 4WH, T+44-(0)1923-255462, www.hoopoe.com. Consistently recommended by travellers. Excellent commitment to local communities and conservation. Range of safaris and climbs,

and unusual trekking itineraries including a 5-day trek with donkeys and the Masai. Run exclusive safaris using their **Kirurumu Tented Camps and Lodges**. Highly recommended.

JMT African Heart, just outside town, not far from **Iboru Safari Lodge**, T027-250 8414, www.africanheart.com. Luxury and budget safaris. Horseback, motorbike and mountain bike safaris, cultural treks, Kili climbs, Zanzibar.

JM Tours Ltd, Plot 15, Olorien, T027-250 1034, www.jmtours.co.tz. Specializing in travel planning for disabled travellers, school exchange programs and cultural tourism.

Kearsley Travel & Tours, next to **Golden Rose Hotel**, T027-2508 043/4, www.kearsley.net. Established safari operator with over 50 years experience.

Klub Afriko Safaris, at the **Klub Afriko Hotel**, see page 102, T027-254 8878, www.klub afriko.com. Various safaris, specializing in Serengeti, Tarangire, Zanzibar and Kilimanjaro.

Laitolya Tours and Safaris, Meru Plaza, Esso Rd, T027-250 9536, www.laitolya.com. Northern circuit, Mikumi, Udzungwa and Bagamoyo. Scheduled and custom-made.

Leopard Tours, Old Moshi Rd, Kijenge, T027-250 3603, www.leopard-tours.com. One of the bigger tour operators offering safaris in the northern circuit, Kilimanjaro climbs, cultural and historical tours, and beach trips.

Lions Safari International, Sakina/Nairobi Rd, T027-250 6423, www.lions-safari-intl.com. Good, professional company operating camping and lodge 3-11 day safaris.

Moon Adventure Tours & Safaris, Seth Benjamin Rd, opposite Meru School, T027-250 4462, www.moon-adventure.com. Low cost camping safaris, Ngorongoro Highlands trekking, birdwatching safaris.

Nature Beauties, Old Moshi Rd, T027-250 4083, www.nature-beauties.com. Alternative routes and trekking safaris. Strong focus on sustainability of environment.

Nature Discovery, Box 10574, T027-254 4063/8406, T0754-400003 (mob), www.naturediscovery.com. Tailor their trips, including Kilimajaro and Oldonyo Lengai climbs, to the traveller and their budget.

Predators Safari Club, Namanga Rd, Sakina, T027-250 6471, www.predators-safaris.com. Wide range of safaris from luxury lodges to camping all over Kenya and Tanzania, good national park combination packages, professionally run. Recommended.

Ranger Safaris, Wachagga St, T027-250 3023, www.rangersafaris.com. Easily one of the biggest safari operators in Tanzania with a wide choice of lodge and camping safaris from 3-10 days and regular departure dates.

Roy Safaris Ltd, 44 Serengeti Rd, T027-250 2115, T027-250 8010, www.roysafaris.com. Good value and experienced operator offering both luxury lodge and camping safaris to the northern circuit game parks and Kili and Meru treks, as well as treks in the Ngorongoro highlands, trips to Zanzibar and cultural tours.

Shidolya Safaris, AICC, T027-254 8506, www.shidolya-safaris.com. Drivers, cooks and guides are excellent, recommended for lodge or camping safaris but not the Kili climb. Birdwatching safaris in Arusha National Park.

Simba Safaris, between Goliondoi Rd and India St, T027-250 1504, www.simbasafaris.com. Kili climbs, reservations for Pemba and Mafia, safari packages, lots of departure dates.

Skylink Travel & Tours, Bushbuck Building, T027-211 5381, www.skylinktanzania.com. Quality travel agent for flights, also has offices in Dar and Mwanza, agent for Avis Rent-a-Car.

Sunny Safaris Ltd, Col Middleton Rd, opposite **Golden Rose Hotel**, T027-250 8184, www.sunnysafaris.com. A very good fleet of game viewing vehicles, lodge and camping safaris, mountain trekking, mountain bike and walking safaris.

Tanganyika Film & Safari Outfitters, T027-250 2713, www.tanzania-safari.com. Top-of-the-range tailor-made safaris for individuals, private groups, professional photographers and filmmakers.

Takims Holidays Tours and Safaris, Uhuru Rd, T027-250 8026, www.takimsholidays.com. An established operator with over 20 years' experience. Photographic safaris to all the national parks, including Serengeti, Kilimanjaro, Selous and Ruaha. Recommended.

Tanzania Serengeti Adventure, Sokoine Rd, T027-250 8475, T027-250 4069 www.about tanzania.com. Range of tented lodge or budget camping safaris and lodge bookings.

Tanzania Travel Company, AICC, Ngorongoro wing, T027-250 9938, T0754-294365 (mob), www.tanzaniatravelcompany.com. Experienced and reliable, offering a range of classic and budget safaris, Kilimanjaro and Meru climbs, cultural tours, trekking with Masai and trips to Zanzibar. Friendly and helpful, knowledgeable staff. Highly recommended.

Tropical Trails, Masai Camp on Old Moshi Rd, T027-250 0358, www.tropicaltrails.com. Experienced operator offering northern circuit safaris aimed at the budget and mid-range traveller, Lengani, Meru and Kilimanjaro climbs, cultural tours and crater highland trekking. Recommended.

Victoria Expeditions Safaris & Travels, Meru House Inn, Sokoine Rd, T027-250 0444, T0754-288740 (mob), www.victoriatz.com. Professionally run safaris and trekking, northern circuit from 2-7 days camping, Zanzibar beach holidays, Kili climbs. Can accommodate disabled clients.

Wild Frontiers, reservations Johannesburg, T+27-117 022 035, www.wildfrontiers.com. Excellent tour operator offering safaris across Tanzania, particularly northern circuit and southern national parks, and Kilimanjaro treks. They also run lovely mobile camps in the Serengeti and Ngorongoro. One of the few operators approved to undertake walking safaris in the Serengeti (see box page 150). Highly recommended.

Wildersun Safaris and Tours, Joel Maeda Rd, T027-254 8847, www.wildersun.com. Standard safaris and an unusual half-day trip to Lake Manyara National Park for canoeing.

WS Safaris Ltd, Moshono Village, near Baraa Primary School, Box 2288, T027-250 4004, www.wssafari.com. Offering a range of safaris, and tours for US$150 per person per day to the Serengeti and Ngorongoro.

Blacklist At the tourist office there is a blacklist of rogue travel agencies, unlicensed agents and the names of people who have convictions for cheating tourists. It is recommended that you cross-check before paying for a safari. In addition, when going on safari check at the park gate that all the fees have been paid, especially if you plan to stay for more than a day in the park. Also check that the name of the tour company is written on the permit. Sadly there is a lot of cheating at present, and many tourists have fallen victim to well-organized scams. The tourist office also has a list of accredited tour companies.

Babati and Mount Hanang *p95*
Cultural safaris

Kahembe's Trekking and Cultural Safaris, T0784-397477 (mob), www.kahembecultural safaris.com. A local company whose owner, Joas Kahembe, has been the pioneer for tourism in this rarely visited but rewarding area. Offers a 2-day trek up Mt Hanang along the Katesh route for US$128 per person. The Katesh route can be completed in 1 day with the ascent and descent taking up to 12 hrs in total. They also have a number of imaginative local tours for US$45 per person per day (US$40 each for 3 or more people). These include 3- to 5-day walking safaris that explore the still largely intact traditional culture of the semi-nomadic pastoralist Barbaig people, and other longer cultural safaris, which have visits to, and stays with, several different local ethnic groups. There is the chance to participate in local brick- and pottery-making and beer brewing, and visit development projects like cattle, dairy farming, or piped water projects. Arranges full board accommodation in local guesthouses and in selected family homes.

Transport

Arusha p88, map p90
Air
Kilimanjaro International Airport, T027-250 2223, is half way between Arusha and Moshi. To get to the airport you can get the Air Tanzania or Precision Air shuttle buses, which leave about 2 hrs before flight departure. **Air Tanzania** fly to **Dar** daily (booking in advance is essential), Mon-Wed, Fri 0800, 1550 and 1930, Thu, Sat-Sun at 1615 (55 mins). Some flights have connections in Dar for **Zanzibar**. **Precision Air** fly daily flight to **Dar** at 0915; and to **Nairobi** at 0835, 1615 and 1940. There are flights to **Mombasa** Mon-Wed, Sat-Sun 1440 (1 hr). Also a daily flight to **Shinyanga** (1½ hrs) and **Mwanza** at 1120 (2 hrs).

Closer to town is **Arusha Airport**, 10 km west along the road to Dodoma. This is mostly used for charter flights and scheduled services operated by **Coastal Air**. To **Dar** daily at 1215 via Zanzibar (2 hrs). To **Mwanza** daily 1230 via **Grumeti** (3½ hrs), **Manyara** and the other airstrips in the **Serengeti** (2½ hrs). To **Ruaha** 0800 (3½ hrs) via Manyara (25 mins), Tarangire and Dodoma.

Airline offices Air Tanzania, Boma Rd, T027-250 3201, www.airtanzania.com. **Coastal Air**, T027-211 7969, T027-211 7960, T0713-530730 (mob), www.coastal.cc. **Ethiopian Airlines**, New Safari Hotel Complex, Boma Rd, T027-250 6167, www.flyethiopia.com. **KLM**, New Safari Hote Complexl, Boma Rd, T027-250 8062/3, www.klm.com. **Precision Air**, New Safari Hotel Complex, Boma Rd T027-250 6903, T027-250 2836, www.precisionairtz.com.

Bus, dala-dala and shared taxi
There are now 2 bus stations in Arusha. The first is on Zaramo St just to the north of the market and buses from here mostly go to places not too far away. Buy your ticket from the driver on the day of travel. There are regular buses and dala-dala to **Moshi**, 1½ hrs, US$1.50. You can also get a shared taxi, which will be more expensive.

Long distance buses go from the new bus station opposite the Shoprite Supermarket at the western end of Sokoine Rd. There are reported to be thieves operating around the Arusha bus stations and there are certainly many persistent touts. Go directly to the bus companies' offices and make sure there is the company's stamp on the ticket. There are daily departures to **Tanga** and **Mwanza**: via both the **Serengeti** and **Singida**. There are countless departures each day to **Dar**, 8-9 hrs, around US$30 'luxury', US$20 'semi-luxury' and US$12 'ordinary'. The road has improved considerably and journey times are shortening. **Taqwa** offers a fast, reliable service; **Fresh ya Shamba** and **Royale** are also very good; **Scandinavia Express Services Ltd**, Kituoni St near the police mess, south of the bus station, T027-250 0153, www.scandinaviagroup.com, are recommended for reliability and safety.

To Kenya Dala-dala take 4 or 5 hrs from here, depart regularly through the day, and the border crossing is efficient. There are several through shuttle services to **Nairobi**, including **Riverside Shuttle**, ACU Building, Sokoine Rd, T027-250 2639, www.riverside-shuttle.com, which departs at 0800 and 1400 daily, US$25.

Car hire
Available from most tour companies and **Angoni**, AICC, T027-250 8498, www.angoni.com, which offers car hire and shuttle services; **Avis**, Bushbuck Building, T027-250 9108, www.avis.com.

Cars can also be hired at the **Arusha Naaz Hotel**, **Golden Rose Hotel** and **Meru House Inn**.

Directory

Arusha *p88, map p90*
Banks Barclays, Sopa Plaza, Serengeti Rd; **Central Bank of Tanzania**, Makongoro Rd near the roundabout with Goliondoi Rd; **CRDB**, further west along Sokoine Rd, on the corner with Singh St; **Exim**, at the Shoprite Centre; **National Bank of Commerce**, Sokoine Rd down towards the bridge; **Stanbic Bank**, next to the National Bank of Commerce; **Standard Chartered**, Goliondoi Rd. Almost all the town centre banks now have ATMs. **Currency exchange** There are many **forex** offices in town. Some will change both cash and TCs as well as give cash advances in local currency against credit cards. Others will not change TCs – cash only. Most of the bureaux are open Mon-Sun 0900-1700. Good exchange rates at **National Bureau de Change** opposite the post office at the clock tower. **Impala Hotel** will give cash advances but there is a large fee – approximately 25%.
Immigration Immigration office, East Africa Rd, T027-250 3569, Mon-Fri 0730-1530 for visa extensions. **Internet** Places to check email are all over town. **The Patisserie**, near the clock tower; an internet café next to Meru House Inn on Sokoine Rd; and **McMoody's**, Sokoine Rd. Typical cost US$0.50 per hr. Worth looking around as there are differences in charges. **Medical services AICC Hospital**, Old Moshi Rd, T027-250 2329; **Mount Meru Hospital**, opposite AICC, East Africa Rd, T027-250 3352/4; **X-Ray Centre**, near the tourist office, T027-250 2345.
Police Makongoro Rd, T111/112. **Post office** The main post office is by the clock tower opposite the Arusha Hotel, Mon-Fri, 0800-1230, 1400-1630, Sat 0800-1230. Meru Post Office is at the other end of Sokoine Rd beyond the market. There are 3 other post offices around town. **Courier Services** DHL, Sokoine Rd next to the Stanbic Bank, T027-250 6749. **Telephone** The cheapest place to make calls is from the **Telephone House** on Boma Rd, opposite the tourist office. Very efficient service, Mon-Sat 0800-2200, Sun 0900-2000. There are also mobile phone shops all over town if you plan to buy a local SIM card. The main networks are Vodacom, Zain, Tigi and Zantec.

Northern Circuit Game Parks

Contents

- 118 *Map: Northern Circuit game parks*
- 120 Ins and outs

121 Tarangire National Park

- 122 *Map: Tarangire National Park*
- 123 Routes
- 123 *Map: Tarangire migrations*
- 124 Listings

127 Mto wa Mbu to Lake Natron

- 127 Mto wa Mbu
- 128 Lake Manyara National Park
- 128 *Map: Lake Manyara National Park*
- 130 North of Mto wa Mbu
- 132 Listings

135 Ngorongoro Conservation Area

- 136 Karatu
- 136 Ngorongoro Crater
- 138 *Map: Ngorongoro Conservation Area*
- 139 Embagai Crater
- 139 Olduvai Gorge
- 140 Lake Eyasi
- 142 Listings

146 Serengeti National Park

- 147 *Map: Serengeti National Park*
- 148 *Map: Serengeti migrations*
- 152 Listings

Footprint features

- 118 Don't miss …
- 150 Take a walk on the wild side

At a glance

◉ **Getting around** The best option is local tour operators, they cater for every budget. There is some public transport to towns near park borders, then you'll need to book day trips into parks.

◐ **Time required** At least 3 days for the Serengeti and a day for Ngorongoro Crater. If you want to go off the beaten track, a couple of days for Manyara or Tarangire – both are worth exploring.

☁ **Weather** Warm and sunny for most of the year, although evenings can be cool, especially during Jun-Oct. Light rains Nov-Dec and heavy rains end of Mar-May. Hot and sticky before the rains.

✖ **When not to go** Roads in the parks can be challeging and often impassable during the rainy season (Apr-May), with access to the crater floor sometimes restricted.

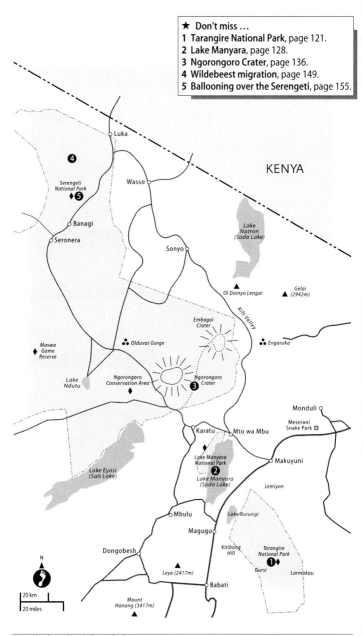

Everything you imagine Africa to be is here in the Northern Circuit Game Parks, from the soaring masses of wildebeest galloping across the plains of the Serengeti, to the iconic image of a lone acacia tree at sunset, to exclusive *Out of Africa*-style lodges deep in the bush. By now, the area's extremely experienced in catering for tourists – it's the most visited area of Tanzania – and it's able to provide for most budgets from the uber-luxurious to the camping backpackers.

Despite it's popularity, it's still easy to escape the crowds. Tarangire National Park, famous for its elephants and quirky baobab trees, is overlooked by many travellers wanting to head for the big names in game parks, and yet it has a gentle beauty and varied landscape with tremendous bird life as well as game. Then there's Lake Manyara National Park, where the lake becomes a blanket of pink, as flamingos come here to feed on their migratory route. Also in this region are the little visited Lake Natron and Ol Doinyo Lengai volcano – a challenging climb for robust walkers – which offer a glimpse into the rural lives of the local Masai.

Ngorongoro Crater never disappoints and because of its steep sides down into the crater, it has almost captive wildlife. Even if you see nothing, the stunning landscapes in this 265 sq km caldera plunged 600 m from its rim are reward enough. And last but far from least, there's the vast Serengeti. From December to April it's the scene of the world's most famous mass migration, when hundreds of thousands of wildebeest pound the path trodden for centuries to the Masai Mara – definitely a sight not to be missed.

Ins and outs

About 80 km west from Arusha on the road towards Dodoma, there is a T-junction at Makuyuni. The entrance to the Tarangire National Park is 40 km to the south of this junction off the Arusha–Dodoma road, whilst the road that heads due west goes towards Lake Manyara, the Ngorongoro Crater and the Serengeti. This road used to be notoriously bad, with deep ruts and potholes, but it was upgraded a few years ago to smooth tar all the way to the gate of the crater, thanks to overseas funding from Japan. The drive to the gate of the Ngorongoro Crater Reserve takes about four hours and is a splendid journey. On clear days, you'll have a view of Mount Kilimanjaro all the way, arching over the right shoulder of Mount Meru. You will go across the bottom of the Rift Valley and at the small settlement of Mto wa Mbu, pass the entrance to the Lake Manyara National Park at the foot of the Great Rift Escarpment. Just beyond the entrance to the park the road climbs very steeply up the escarpment and there are wonderful views back down onto Lake Manyara. From here the country is hilly and fertile and you will climb up to the Mbulu Plateau which is farmed with wheat, maize and coffee. The extinct volcano of Ol Deani has gentle slopes and is a prominent feature of the landscape.

All the safari operators offer at the very least a three day and two night safari of the crater and Serengeti, most offer extended tours to include Tarangire or Manyara, and some include the less visited Ol Doinyo Lengai and Lake Natron. There is the option of self-drive but as non-Tanzanian vehicles attract much higher entrance fees into the parks, this is not normally cost effective. ▶▶ *For more information on national park fees and safaris, see page 9. For safari tour operators in Arusha, see page 109.*

Tarangire National Park → *Altitude: 1110 m.*

Unjustifiably considered the poor relation to its neighbouring parks, Tarangire may have a less spectacular landscape and does make you work harder for your game, but it also retains a real sense of wilderness reminiscent of more remote parks like Ruaha and Katavi. Famous for its enormous herds of elephant that congregate along the river, it is not unusual to see groups of 100 more and there are some impressive old bulls. ▸▸ *For listings, see page 124-126.*

Park fees and information
Tarangire National Park, established in 1970, covers an area of 2600 sq km and is named after the river that flows through it throughout the year. The gate opens at 0630, although an earlier entrance is possible if you have paid the entry fee of US$35 in advance. The best time to visit is in the dry season from July to September when the animals gather in large numbers along the river. Although you may not see as many animals here as in other places, Tarangire is a wonderful park. There are fewer people here than in Ngorongoro and that is very much part of the attraction. One of the most noticeable things on entering the park are the baobab trees that rise up from the grass, instantly recognizable by their massive trunks. As the park includes within its boundaries a number of hills, as well as rivers and swamps, there is a variety of vegetation zones and habitats. The river rises in the Kondoa Highlands to the south, and flows north through the length of the park. It continues to flow during the dry season and so is a vital watering point for the animals of the park as well as those from surrounding areas.

Wildlife
The Tarangire National Park forms a 'dry season retreat' for much of the wildlife of the southern Masailand. The ecosystem in this area involves more than just Tarangire National Park. Also included are the Lake Manyara National Park to the north and a number of 'Game Controlled Areas'. The largest of these are the Lake Natron Game Controlled Area further north and the Simanjiro Plains Game Controlled Area towards Arusha. The Mto wa Mbu Game Controlled Area, the Lolkisale Game Controlled Area and Mkungunero Game Controlled Area are also included. The key to the ecosystem is the river and the main animal movements begin from the river at the beginning of the short rains around October and November. The animals moving north during the wet season include wildebeest, zebra, Thompson's gazelles, buffalo, eland and hartebeest. The elephant population in this park was estimated at around 6000 in 1987 but numbers are believed to have fallen since then because of poaching. At the height of the rainy season the animals are spread out over an area of over 20,000 sq km. When the wet season ends the animals begin their migration back south and spend the dry season (July-October) concentrated around the River Tarangire until the rains begin again.

The number of species of birds recorded in Tarangire National Park has been estimated at approximately 300. These include migrants that fly south to spend October-April away from the winter of the northern hemisphere. Here you may spot various species of herons, storks and ducks, vultures, buzzards, sparrowhawks, eagles, kites and falcons, as well as ostrich.

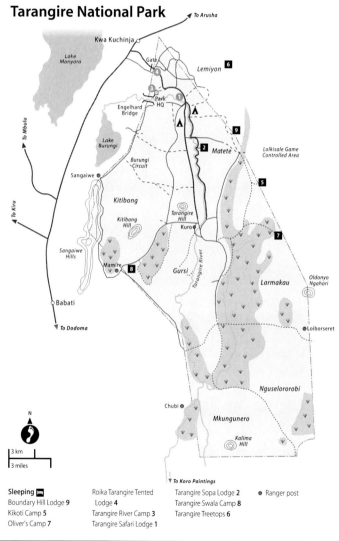

Routes

The park is large enough for it not to feel crowded even when there are quite a few visitors. There are a number of routes or circuits that you can follow that take you to the major attractions.

Lake Burungi circuit

Covering about 80 km, this circuit starts at the Engelhard Bridge and goes clockwise, along the river bank. Continue through the acacia trees until about 3 km before the Kuro Range Post where you will see a turning off to the right. Down this track you will pass through a section of Combretum-Dalergia woodland as you head towards the western boundary of the park. The route continues around and the vegetation turns back to parkland with acacia trees and then back to Combretum as the road turns right and reaches a full circle at the Engelhard Bridge. The lake water levels have fallen and Lake Burungi is almost dry. If you are very lucky you may see leopard and rhino in this area, although the numbers of rhino have reportedly decreased.

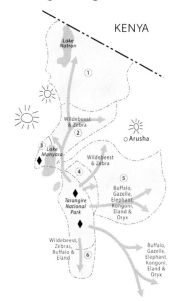

Tarangire migrations

Lake Natron Game Controlled Area **1**
Mto wa Mbu Game Controlled Area **2**
Lake Manyara National Park **3**
Lolkisale Game Controlled Area **4**
Simanjiro Game Controlled Area & Plains **5**
Mkungunero Game Controlled Area **6**

Not to scale

Lemiyon area

This circuit covers the northern area of the park bound on each side by the eastern and western boundaries park and to the south by the river. This is where you will see the fascinating baobab trees with their large silvery trunks and gourd-like fruits. Their huge trunks enable the trees to survive through a number of rain failures and they are characteristic of this type of landscape. Also found here are acacia trees, which provide food for giraffe. Other animals that you expect to see are wildebeest, zebra, gazelles and elephant.

Kitibong Hill circuit

This track covers the west section of the park and is centred on Kitibong Hill. It includes acacia parkland in the east and Combretum-Dalbergia woodland in the west, the Gursi floodplains to the south and the foothills of Sangaiwe Hills, which are along the western boundary of the park. This area homes a variety of plains animals including buffalo and elephant.

The Gursi and Lamarkau circuit

The grasslands found in the south of the park are home to many plain-grazing species. You are also likely to see ostrich here. During the wet season a large swamp forms in what is known as Larmakau – a corruption of the Masai word *'o'llakau'*, meaning hippo, which can be seen here.

Without a 4WD you will not be able to see much of the southernmost section of the park and during the wet season it is often impassable to all vehicles. There are two areas in the south – Nguselororobi to the east and Mkungunero in the southwest corner. The former is mainly swamp, with some plains and woodland, and if you are lucky you might see cheetah here. Mkungunero has a number of freshwater pools that serve to attract many different species.

Tarangire Conservation Area

The Tarangire Conservation Area is a 585 sq km area on the eastern boundaries of the park set aside by the local villages. The region comprises four distinct areas, the Lolkisale Conservation Area, the Naitolia Concession Area, the Makuyuni Elephant Dispersal Area, and the Lolkisale Livestock and Wildlife Zone. The Conservation Area was established to protect the main wet-season migration route from the park and provide the animals with a natural sanctuary from the demands of modern farming methods such as extensive deforestation by illegal charcoal collectors and years of indiscriminate poaching. What makes this whole project unique is that revenue goes directly into the local community and members of these same communities are being employed by tourism-based services within the area (see **Boundary Hill Lodge**, below). The local craftsmen have been involved in building the new lodges in the area using local renewable materials from the surrounding regions; the village councils sit on the board of directors; and women empowerment projects and local schools have received funding from the project. For more information visit www.tarangireconservation.com.

Tarangire National Park listings

For Sleeping and Eating price codes and other relevant information, see pages 7-9.

Sleeping

Tarangire National Park *p121, map p122*

$$$$ Boundary Hill Lodge, located just outside the park within the Lolkisale Conservation Area, T0787-293727 (mob), www.tarangire conservation.com. This lodge – part-owned by the local Masai community and benefiting community projects – has 8 rooms built on the hillside, all affording total privacy with unobstructed views over the savannah and swamps. The rooms are individually designed, some with outdoor baths and toilets with a view. Walking safaris, night drives and fly camping available. Rates from US$240 per person including activities, with special offers on the website.

$$$$ Kikoti Camp, in the conservation area adjoining the park, reservations, Arusha, T027-250 8790, www.safarilegacy.com. A small luxury tented lodge built amongst a landscape of ancient boulders, baobab, mopane and fig trees, with 10 spacious tents with grass roofs and wooden decks. Large eating boma with outside campfire and comfortable deck chairs. Bush breakfast and lunches are served in secluded areas, sundowners on Kikoti Rock. Bush walks as well as game drives on offer and visits to the local Masai village. Rates from US$410 per person.

$$$$ Oliver's Camp, in the eastern part of Tarangire National Park, www.asilialodges. com Intimate small luxury camp with 8 tents, a library and drinks tent, open air dining with the manager and guides who offer walking safaris and game drives during the day. One tent is in a secluded location in the bush for honeymooners, carefully designed to blend into the landscape.

$$$$ Roika Tarangire Tented Lodge, on the banks of the river about 5 km from the park gate, T0787-673338 (mob), www.tarangire roikatentedlodge.com Opened in Jan 2008, this tented camp set in 20 ha has 20 rooms themed to individual animals with stunning wood carvings on everything from lamp stands to bedposts. Rather obscure concrete 'animal' baths extend the theme – check out the elephant bath if you can. It's not as scenically striking as its neighbour the **Tarangire River Camp**, and they seem to have gone overboard on the concrete stones in the bar but it does have a quirky charm. Reduced rates during the low season.

$$$$ Tarangire Sopa Lodge, in the northeast of the park, about 30 km from the main gate, signposted, T027-250 0630/9, www.sopa lodges.com. If you like intimate lodges, then this might disappoint. A large luxury lodge with 75 suites, opulent lounges, bars and restaurant. Excellent food and barbecues, large landscaped swimming pool on the edge of a rocky gorge and a shop. Rooms and the pool area are currently being refurbished. There are less impersonal choices of accommodation in the park. Rates are from US$265 per person full board.

$$$$ Tarangire Swala Camp, on the edge of the Gursi swamp, reservations, Arusha, T027- 250 9816, www.kusini.com. Camp closed during the rainy season Apr-Jun. A first-class site for birdwatching. Comprises 9 extremely comfortable guest tents raised on a wooden deck above the ground under acacia trees, with en suite facilities. Silver service dining. The staff and management team at Swala have initiated a conservation project that has recently led to the building of a school for the children of a village that borders Tarangire. Rates US$490 per person full board (not including drives).

$$$$ Tarangire Treetops, in the conservation area, T027-250 0630, www.elewana.com. The 20 enormous rooms at this lodge take the form of stilt houses, constructed 3-5 m up in huge baobab and marula trees on a wooded hillside overlooking the Tarangire Sand River. It really is a beautiful and luxurious lodge, but its weakness lies in its location, being a considerable distance on rough roads from the main game-viewing areas in Tarangire. Nevertheless, excellent food and service, a swimming pool, walking safaris and night drives on offer. Rates in the region of US$780 per person full board, including game drives and activities.

$$$ Tarangire River Camp, within a concession area set aside for conservation by the local Masai community of Minjingu, which borders Tarangire in the northwest, 3.5 km from the main gate, T027-254 7007, www.mbalimbali.com. In a beautiful setting overlooking the river and the Masai Steppes, and shaded by a giant baobab tree, the 21 well equipped tents have wooden decks and en suite bathrooms. The main building is an elegant elevated thatch and timber structure comprising a main lounge, wildlife reference library, dining room and cocktail bar.

$$$ Tarangire Safari Lodge, 10 km into the park from the gate, lodge T027-253 1447/8, reservations, Arusha, T027-254 4752, www.tarangiresafarilodge.com. This is a lovely lodge with tents set on an escarpment overlooking the Tarangire River with acacia-studded plains and beautiful sunrises. Sleeps 70, good restaurant and bar with a large swimming pool, children's pool with slide, and considerable discounts for children. This area is relatively free of tsetse flies which are a problem in other areas of the park. Excellent value considering its location within the park. Recommended.

Camping

The **National Park's public campsite** is 10 mins into the park from the gate and set amongst a grove of impressive baobab trees. Toilet and shower facilities are simple but above average. US$30.

There are also 12 special campsites, water and firewood are provided but there are no other facilities. Nor have they been sympathetically located in decent positions with nice views. They are, however, generally pleasant and pretty remote. US$50. These are used by the safari operators on camping tours. Further information is available from Tanzania National Parks, head office, see page 89.

Mto wa Mbu to Lake Natron

From the turn off on the Arusha–Dodoma road, the road heads through the small town of Mto wa Mbu, home to many distinctive red-clad Masai. This used to be a popular stop for safari-goers who wanted to rest and have a break from the bumpy road, but these days the smooth tarmac carries vehicles straight through town. It is, however, the closest town to Lake Manyara National Park gate and from here is another road that goes north to Lake Natron. There are fabulous views over Manyara from the road that climbs up this escarpment from Mto wa Mbu towards the crater. In contrast to Kenya, here there is no eastern wall to the Rift Valley which flattens out as the fault continues south.*» For listings, see pages 132-134.*

Ins and outs

Getting there There are community initiatives using the local Masai people as guides who can arrange a visit to this region, for example the **Mkuru Camel Safari Cultural Tourism Programme** (see page 94) or the **Engaruka Cultural Tourism Programme** (see below). Several tour operators also offer cultural tours in this region using the local people as guides. These include **Hoopoe**, **Roy Safaris**, **Takim's Holidays**, and **Klub Africo Safaris** (see Tour operators in Arusha, page 109).

Mto wa Mbu

Mto wa Mbu (meaning Mosquito Creek) is a small, busy market town selling fruit and vegetables grown by the fertile surrounding farms. It is on the route from Arusha to the northern safari circuit of Ngorongoro and Serengeti and only 3 km away from the gate of Lake Manyara National Park. You are likely to be welcomed to the town by people trying to sell the arts and crafts on display in the Masai central market, a cooperative of about 20 curio sellers, behind which is a fresh food market. However, all curios offered here seem to be more expensive than those in Arusha. Mto wa Mbu is a colourful town that's developed over recent years to accommodate its visitors. A new supermarket and bureau de change are due to open, there's a disco (**Safari Park**) near the market, which is popular with backpackers, and bikes are available for hire along the main street. It's worth exploring beyond this main street if you get chance, as you'll find plenty of local bars, a fruit and vegetable market and several local guesthouses for around US$10 a night if you're on a very limited budget.

The area around Mto wa Mbu was dry and sparsely populated until the irrigation programmes began in the 1950s, which transformed the area into an important fruit and vegetable growing region. (Look out for the distinctive red bananas for sale.) The accompanying population growth turned Mto wa Mbu into a melting pot of cultures. There is greater cultural diversity in this area than elsewhere in Tanzania, so in one day you can sample Chagga banana beer, or see a farmer from the Kigoma region make palm oil. The Rangi use papyrus from the lakes to make beautiful baskets and mats, and the Sandawe continue to make bows and arrows, which are used to hunt small game. On the surrounding plains the Masai tend their cattle, and there are occasional Masai cattle markets. Seeing so many red-robed Masai men all together is quite a striking sight.

The **Mto wa Mbu Cultural Tourism programme** ⓘ *further information available from Tanzanian Tourist Information Centre, Arusha, see page 89, or www.infojep.com/culturaltours,* supported by the Tanzanian Tourist Board and SNV, the Dutch Development Organization, offers an opportunity to support the local inhabitants and learn about their lifestyle. Walking safaris with Masai guides through the farms in the verdant oasis at the foot of the Rift Valley can be arranged. There are walks to Miwaleni Lake and waterfall where papyrus plants grow in abundance, or an opportunity to climb **Balaa Hill**, which overlooks the whole town. The Belgian Development Organization ACT has enabled locals to grow flowers commercially for export and there are colourful flower fields, with the wonderful backdrop of the Rift Valley. Alternatively, you can rent a bicycle and cycle through the banana plantations to see the **papyrus lake**. The landscape is awe inspiring with the escarpment rising vertically up into the sky on the one side and the semi-desert stretching away to the horizon on the other. The guides are all former students of Manyara secondary school and they have a reasonable standard of English. Profits from the tours are invested in development projects and for the promotion of energy-saving stoves.

Lake Manyara National Park

Lake Manyara National Park

On the way to Ngorongoro Crater and the Serengeti, Lake Manyara is well worth a stop in its own right. Set in the Great Rift Valley, Lake Manyara National Park is beneath the cliffs of the Manyara Escarpment, and was established in 1960. It covers an area of 325 sq km, of which 229 sq km is the lake. The remaining third is a slice of marshes, grassland and acacia woodland tucked between the lake and the escarpment whose reddish brown wall looms 600 m on the eastern horizon. ▸▸ *For more information on national parks, see page 9.*

Ins and outs
Getting there There is an airstrip near the park gate, and Coastal Air flies daily from Arusha. By car the park, 130 km west of

Sleeping
Kiruruma Tented Lodge 2
Lake Manyara 1
Lake Manyara Serena Lodge 3
Lake Manyara Tree Lodge 6
Panorama Safari Camp 4

Arusha, can be reached via the Arusha–Serengeti road. The drive from Arusha takes about 1½ hours.

Getting around The main road through the park is good enough for most vehicles, although some of the tracks may be closed during the wet season.

Park fees and information The best times to visit the park are December-February and May-July. The entrance fee is US$35.

Background
The lake is believed to have been formed 2- to 3-million years ago when, after the formation of the Rift Valley, streams poured over the valley wall. In the depression below, the water accumulated and so the lake was formed. It has shrunk significantly and was probably at its largest about 250,000 years ago. In recent years it has been noted that lake levels are falling in several of the lakes in the region, among them Lake Manyara. This trend often co-exists with the development of salt brines, the rise of which are anticipated.

Wildlife
The park's ground water forests, bush plains, baobob strewn cliffs, and algae-streaked hot springs offer incredible ecological variety in a small area. Lake Manyara's famous tree-climbing lions make the ancient mahogany and elegant acacias their home during the rainy season, and are a well-known but rather rare feature of the northern park. In addition to the lions, the national park is also home to the largest concentration of baboons anywhere in the world. Other animals include elephants, hippo and plains animals, as well as a huge variety of birdlife, both resident and migratory. At certain times of the year Lake Manyara feeds thousands of flamingos, which form a shimmering pink zone around the lake shore. Other birds found here include ostrich, egrets, herons, pelicans and storks. Also seen are African spoonbills, various species of ibis, ducks and the rare pygmy goose. As with all the other parks, poaching has been a problem in the past and has affected the elephant population in particular. It was a shock when the census of 1987 found that their population had halved to under 200 in just a decade. At the gate of the national park is a small museum displaying some of the park's bird and rodent life.

Routes
A road from the park gate goes through the ground water forest before crossing the Marere River Bridge. This forest, as its name suggests, is fed not by rainfall, but by ground water from the high water table fed by seepage from the volcanic rock of the rift wall. The first animals you will see on entering the park will undoubtedly be baboons. About 500 m after this bridge the road forks. To the left the track leads to a plain known as **Mahali pa Nyati** (Place of the Buffalo), which has a herd of mainly old bulls cast out from their former herds. There are also zebra and impala in this area. This is also a track to the Hippo Pool here, formed by the Simba River on its way to the lake and home to hippos, flamingos and many other water birds.

Back on the main track the forest thins out to bush and the road crosses the Mchanga River (Sand River) and Msasa River. Shortly after this latter bridge there is a turning off to the left that leads down to the lakeshore where there is a peaceful picnic spot. Soon after this bridge, the surroundings change to acacia woodland. This is where the famous tree-climbing lions are found, so drive through very slowly and look for a tail dangling down through the branches.

Continue down the main road crossing the Chemchem River and on to the Ndala River. During the dry season you may see elephants digging in the dry riverbed for water. At the peak of the wet season the river may flood and the road is sometimes impassable as a result. Beyond the Ndala River the track runs closer to the Rift Valley Escarpment wall that rises steeply to the right of the road. On this slope are many different trees to those on the plain and as a result they provide a different habitat for various animals. The most noticeable are the very impressive baobab trees with their huge trunks.

The first of the two sets of hot springs in the park are located where the track runs along the wall of the escarpment. These are the smaller of the two and so are called simply **Maji Moto Ndogo** (Small Hot Water). The temperature is about 40°C, heated to this temperature as it circulates to great depths in fractures that run through the rocks created during the formation of the Rift Valley. The second set of hot springs is further down the track over the Endabash River. These, known as **Maji Moto**, are both larger and hotter, reaching a temperature of 60°C. You are supposed to be able to cook an egg here in about 30 minutes. The main track ends at Maji Moto and you have to turn round and go back the same way. In total the track is between 35 and 40 km long.

North of Mto wa Mbu

Engaruka

Engaruka, one of Tanzania's most important historical sites, is 63 km north of Mto wa Mbu on the road to Ol Doinyo Lengai and Lake Natron. Access along here is really only feasible by 4WD. The village lies at the foot of the Rift Valley escarpment. Masai cattle graze on the surrounding plains and dust cyclones often arise on the horizon. They are feared as the 'devil fingers' that can bring bad luck when they touch people.

In the 15th and 16th centuries the farming community here developed an ingenious irrigation system made of stone-block canals with terraced retaining walls enclosing parcels of land. The site included seven large villages. Water from the rift escarpment was channelled into the canals that led to the terraces. For some unknown reason the farmers left Engaruka around 1700. Several prominent archaeologists, including Louis Leakey, have investigated these ruins but to date there are many questions left unanswered about the people who built these irrigation channels, and why they abandoned the area. The ruins are deteriorating because, with the eradication of the tsetse fly, Masai cattle now come to graze in this area during the dry season, causing extensive damage.

The **Engaruka Cultural Tourism Programme** ⓘ *further details available from Tanzanian Tourist Information Centre, Arusha, see page 89, or www.infojep.com/cultural_tours,* is supported by the Tanzanian Tourist Board and SNV, the Dutch Development Organization. In half a day you can tour the ruins or visit local farms to see current farming and irrigation methods. A Masai warrior can also guide you up the escarpment – from where there are views over the ruins and surrounding plains – pointing out trees and plants the Masai use as food and medicine along the way. In one day you can climb the peak of **Kerimasi** to the north of the village and there is a two-day hike up Kerimasi and then **Ol Doinyo Lengai** volcano (see below). The sodium-rich ashes from the volcano turn the water caustic, sometimes causing burns to the skin of the local Masai's livestock. Moneys generated are used to exclude cattle from the ruins and start conservation work, and also to improve the village primary school. There is no formal accommodation but it is possible to camp.

Ol Doinyo Lengai → *Altitude: 2886 m.*
ⓘ *As the mountain lies outside the conservation area no national park fees are payable.*

Ol Doinyo Lengai, the 'mountain of God', is Tanzania's only active volcano. It is north of and outside the Ngorongoro Conservation area in the heart of Masailand, to the west of the road to Lake Natron. This active volcano is continuously erupting, sometimes explosively but more commonly just subsurface bubbling of lava. It is the only volcano in the world that erupts natrocarbonatite lava, a highly fluid lava that contains almost no silicon, and is also much cooler and less viscous than basaltic lavas.

The white deposits are weathered natrocarbonatite ash and lava and these white-capped rocks near the summit are interpreted by the Masai as symbolizing the white beard of God. The last violent eruption was in 1993 and lava has occasionally flowed out of the crater, indeed there were minor eruptions as recently as 2007 and 2008. Only physically fit people should attempt the climb, note that the summit is frequently wreathed in clouds.

Although it is possible to climb the mountain, the trek up to the crater is an exceptionally demanding one. In parts of the crater that have been inactive for several months the ground is so soft that one sinks into it when walking. In rainy weather the light brown powdery surface turns white again because of chemical reactions that occur when the lava absorbs water. Climbs are frequently done at night as there is no shelter on the mountain and it gets extremely hot. The gradient is very steep towards the crater rim. A guide is required and you are strongly advised to wear sturdy leather hiking boots to protect against burns should you inadvertently step into liquid lava. Boots made of other fibres have been known to melt. Another safety precaution is to wear glasses to avoid lava splatter burns to the eyes.

Lake Natron

This pink, alkaline lake is at the bottom of the Gregory Rift (part of the Great Rift Valley), touching the Kenyan border and about 250 km from Arusha. It is surrounded by escarpments and volcanic mountains, with a small volcano at the north end of the lake in Kenya, and the much larger volcano, Ol Doinyo Lengai, to the southeast of the lake (see above). The lake is infrequently visited by tourists because of its remoteness but numerous Masai herd cattle around here. The route from Arusha is through an area rich with wildlife, depending on the season, particularly ostriches, zebra and giraffe.

The lake has an exceptionally high concentration of salts and gets its pink colour from the billions of cyano-bacteria that form the flamingo's staple diet. There are hundreds of thousands of lesser flamingos here as this lake is their only regular breeding ground in East Africa. Often more of the birds are found here than at either Lake Magadi in Kenya or Lake Manyara. Lake Natron is also an important site for many other waterbird species, including palearctic migrants. A few kilometres upstream to the Ngare Sero River there are two **waterfalls**. Follow the river from the campsite: with the occasional bit of wading, it is a hike of about an hour.

Mto wa Mbu to Lake Natron listings

For Sleeping and Eating price codes and other relevant information, see pages 7-9.

Sleeping

Mto wa Mbu *p127*

$$$$ E Unoto Retreat, 14 km from Mto wa Mbu on the road to Lake Natron, T0787-622 724 (mob), www.maasaivillage.com. A Masai-inspired lodge nestling into the Rift Valley escarpment that resembles an authentic Masai village and blends into the surroundings. The 25 luxurious rooms are in separate bandas with nice views over Lake Miwaleni which is home to many hippo. 4 of the bandas are designed for wheelchair users, and the honey- moon suite has a personal butler and luxurious heavy wood furniture. A small infinity pool overlooks the lake, bikes can be hired and guests are encouraged to interact with the local Masai on guided walks to the top of the Rift escarpment and to local villages, where the hotel owners recently built a school.

$$$$ Lake Manyara View Lodge, signposted on the main road to Ngorongoro about 3 km from Mto wa Mbu, signposted on the left, T027-250 1329, www.lakemanyaraview.com. Recently opened, with spectacular views. Offer a variety of room styles from makouti- roofed bungalows with terraces overlooking the lake, to rather strange rooms built in the shape of baobab trees. Not all have lake views, so choose carefully. There are 33 rooms, although they plan to increase this to 70. The swimming pool overlooking Lake Manyara is still under construction. At US$340 for a double, prices are on the expensive side and it's difficult to judge at this stage whether they'll be justified. Reports welcome.

$$$-$ Jambo Lodge and Campsite, in Mto Wa Mbu, just a few doors away from **Twiga Campsite**, T027-253 9311, www.njake.com. Well maintained gardens and spotless en suite rooms in 2-storey houses with TV, fridge, and terrace or balcony. Swimming pool, restaurant and baobab tree bar. Spacious camping ground with good ablutions facilities, US$7 per person or US$20 if hiring a tent.

$$$-$ Kiboko Bushcamp, 2 km before town on the Arusha Rd, 2 km from the main road, T027-253 9152, www.kibokolodge.com. 10 self-contained permanent tents in a lovely tract of acacia forest, set well apart under thatched roofs, though sparsely furnished with small beds and with unattractive concrete showers and toilets. Also has a large campsite but only 2 toilets and showers. Restaurant and bar in a large thatched building which looks rather tired, can organize Masai dancing.

$$$-$ Migunga, outside the park, just a couple of kilometres before the gate, T0765-043 676 (mob), www.moivaro.com. This lovely tented camp is set in 14 ha of acacia forest in a secluded part of Migungani Village. Bush- buck and other antelope are sometimes seen on the property. 19 spotless, self-contained tents, dining room and bar under thatch. Less luxurious than the normal tented camps, but much more affordable and rates include meals. There's also a shady campsite with 4 'mobile' tents set up with beds inside for US$20 per person or camping with your own tents for US$10 per person. Mountain biking, bird walks and village tours can be arranged. Reduced rates for low season.

$$$-$ Twiga Campsite and Lodge, left of the main road in Mto wa Mbu going towards the gate of Lake Manyara National Park, T027-253 9101, twigacampsite@hotmail.com. There are some decent tent pitches at the back with plenty of shade, hot showers, a curio shop, and a reasonable bar and restaurant area near the swimming pool. Restaurant serves chicken, beef and rice, etc, and plenty of cold beer. The 34 new rooms are an improvement on the old ones and well worth the extra dollars, with TV, fridge, separate dining area. They're at the far end of the camp and so don't get as much noise from the street as the older rooms, which are fairly basic.

Camping
Sunbright Camp, near Mto wa Mbu, signposted on the right off the main road towards Ngorongoro Crater, T0754-815950 (mob), amiriadamu@yahoo.com. This pretty camp site with lovely gardens is a good option with a spacious bar and restaurant and good facilities. US$7 per person.

Lake Manyara National Park *p128, map p128*
$$$$ Kirurumu Tented Lodge, reservations, **Hoopoe Safaris**, Arusha T027-250 7011, T027-250 7541, www.kirurumu.com. Built on the escarpment in a stunning location overlooking the lake, 24 well appointed tents on solid platforms under thatched roofs, with splendid views, excellent service and meals, Relaxing bar with views over Lake Manyara.
$$$$ Lake Manyara Serena Lodge, on the edge of the eastern Rift Valley's Mto wa Mbu escarpment direct lodge number, T027-253 9160, reservations www.serenahotels.com. The main attraction here is the lovely infinity pool with views over to the lake. 67 rooms in round bungalows all with lake views, due to be renovated. 2 rooms available for wheelchair users, close to the hotel and main facilities. Wi-Fi available. Offers 'soft adventures' – mountain biking, forest hikes, nature and village walks, night game drives, canoe safaris when the lake isn't too shallow and children's programmes – available to everyone, not just staying guests. Manyara is perhaps the weaker of the 3 Serena lodges in the area, but remains a good and reliable option with fantastic views. Rates from US$550 full board for a double room.
$$$$ Lake Manyara Tree Lodge, reservations, Johannesburg, South Africa, T+27-11-809 4300, www.andbeyond.com. Set in the heart of a mahogany forest in the remote south-western region, this is the only lodge within the park and is nicely designed to exert minimal impact on the environment. The 10 luxurious treehouse suites are crafted from local timber and makuti palms, with en suite bathroom and outside shower, deck, fans, mosquito nets and butler service. Dining boma where guests can watch what is going on in the kitchen, breakfast and picnics can be organized on the lake shore. Swimming pool. Around of US$950 per person, but for this you get an impeccable safari experience, full board, wine, transfers, game drives and birdwatching safaris included in the price.
$$$$ Lake Manyara Hotel 300 m above the park, reservations, Arusha, T027-254 4595, www.hotelsandlodges-tanzania.com. On the escarpment overlooking the lake and park with wonderful views. Undergoing extensive renovation. There's a beautiful swimming pool in established gardens, a TV room, babysitting service, restaurant and bar (although there have been some negative reports about the food). Village walks and guided mountain bike trails arranged.
$ Panorama Safari Camp, on escarpment overlooking the lake, 500 m from the main road, T027-253 9286. A very good budget option run by Hungarians. 10 large pre-erected tents with thatched roof, veranda and proper beds, US$40. Small tents with mattress are US$10 or camping with your own equipment is US$5. There's a decent ablutions block with hot water, and a bar and restaurant. Peaceful, away from the noise of the town, this is a good option for independent travellers.

National Park accommodation
There are 10 bandas just before the park entrance in a pretty tract of forest, though

mosquitoes are an enormous problem here. Each have an en suite bathroom, sleep 2, and cost US$40 per person. There is also a youth hostel at park headquarters that sleeps 48, with basic facilities. Normally used by large groups only.

Camping There are 2 public campsites at the entrance to the park, with water, toilets and showers that cost US$30. There are 3 special campsites inside the park itself, all of which must be pre-booked as part of a safari and can only be used by one group at a time, US$50. Bookings through Tanzania National Parks head office, Arusha, see page 89.

Lake Natron *p131*
$$ Lake Natron Tented Camp, southwest of the lake, the only local accommodation near Lake Natron, operated by Moivaro, T027-250 6315, www.moivaro.com. 9 self-contained spacious tents with showers and flush toilets, thatched dining room and bar, swimming pool, solar power in all tents and dining room. You can also camp here if you have your own tent. The camp is an excellent base to explore the surrounding area on hikes and from which to climb Ol Doinyo Lengai. The camp can organize the climb and can offer transfers from and to Arusha if you have no transport.

Camping
Independent overlanders report that it is possible to bush camp reasonably close to the lake, or near the waterfalls on the Ngare Sero River, if fully self-sufficient. Remember that lions may visit the area to drink.

◉ Transport

Lake Manyara National Park *p128, map p128*
Air
Coastal Air fly to **Arusha** daily at 1155 from the airstrip near the park gate.

Ngorongoro Conservation Area

The Conservation area encompasses Ngorongoro Crater, Embagai Crater, Olduvai Gorge – famous for its palaeontological relics – and Lake Masek. Lake Eyasi marks part of the southern boundary and the Serengeti National Park lies to the west. The Ngorongoro Crater is often called 'Africa's Eden' and a visit to the crater is a main draw for tourists coming to Tanzania and a definite world-class attraction. A World Heritage Site, it's the largest intact caldera in the world, containing everything necessary for the 30,000 animals that inhabit the crater floor to exist and thrive. Karatu, the busy town known as 'safari junction', 25 km south of the conservation area, is often used by budget travellers who want to visit the Ngorongoro Crater without spending money on a full-on safari from Arusha. You can catch public transport to Karatu, stay overnight and then take a half day safari to the crater the next morning. ▸▸ *For listings, see pages 142-145.*

Ins and outs

Getting there and around Ngorongoro is 190 km west of Arusha, 25 km from Karatu and 145 km from Serengeti and is reached via the Arusha–Serengeti road. At Karatu, is the turning off to Gibb's Farm, 5 km off the main road. From this junction you turn right towards the park entrance and on the approach to **Lodware Gate**; as the altitude increases the temperature starts to fall. Your first view of the crater comes at **Heroes' Point** (2286 m). The road continues to climb through the forest to the crater rim. It is sometimes possible along this road to spot leopard that inhabit the dense forests at the top of the crater. During the long rains season (April-May) the roads in the park can be almost impassable, so access to the crater floor may be restricted. ▸▸ *See also Ins and outs for the crater itself, page 137.*

Park fees and information On top of the daily fee of US$50 for adults and US$10 for children (5-16 years) to enter the Ngorongoro Crater Reserve, there is a hefty US$200 fee per half day excursion to enter the crater itself and a vehicle fee of US$40 per entry. You'll also need to hire a guide at a daily rate of US$20. For more information, www.ngorongoro-crater-africa.org. The best times to visit are December-February and June-July.

Background

The Ngorongoro Conservation Area was established in 1959 and covers an area of 8288 sq km. In 1951 it was included as part of the Serengeti National Park and contained the headquarters of the park. However, in order to accommodate the grazing needs of the Masai people's livestock it was decided to reclassify it as a conservation area. In 1978 it was declared a World Heritage Site in recognition of its beauty and importance. Where the road reaches the rim of the crater you will see memorials to Professor Bernhard Grzimek and his son Michael. They were the makers of the film *Serengeti Shall Not Die* and published a book of the same name (1959, Collins). They conducted surveys and censuses of the animals in the Serengeti and Ngorongoro Parks and were heavily involved in the fight against poachers. Tragically Michael was killed in an aeroplane accident over the Ngorongoro Crater in 1959 and his father returned to Germany where he set up the Frankfurt Zoological Society. He died in 1987 requesting in his will that he should be buried beside his son in Tanzania. Their memorials serve as a reminder of all the work they did to protect this part of Africa.

Karatu → *Phone code 027.*

The small but burgeoning town of Karatu is 25 km from the gate of the Ngorongoro Crater Reserve, 25 km from Lake Manyara, and 140 km from Arusha. The new road from Arusha to the gates of the Ngorongoro Crater which was completed in 2003 was sponsored by the Japanese government. With completion of this road, Karatu has come into its own and now spreads for several kilometres along the highway. It is locally dubbed 'safari junction' and for good reason. All safaris vehicles en route to the parks in the northern circuit pass through here. Because of its proximity to the crater more and more lodges and campsites are springing up. Some offer very good, and in some cases much cheaper, alternatives to staying within the confines of the Ngorongoro Crater Reserve. However, the disadvantage is not having the views that the lodges on the rim of the crater afford. As well as the accommodation options listed below, those on an organized camping safari may find themselves staying at one of the many other campsites around Karatu, as the cheaper companies use these instead of the more expensive campsite at the top of the crater (which, incidentally, is overcrowded, has poor facilities and gets extremely cold). These cater exclusively to the groups who have their own cooks, though there are often also bars to buy beers and soft drinks. There are three banks in town and all have ATMs. For those on self-drive safaris this is the last place to buy provisions and fuel before entering the Ngorongoro Crater Reserve (see Shopping, page 145). Petrol stations spread from one end of town to the other. There are plenty of buses throughout the day between Arusha and Karatu. One option here for budget travellers wanting to visit the Ngorongoro Crater, is to catch public transport as far as Karatu, stay overnight and then take a half day safari to the crater the next morning, and return to Arusha the following afternoon. This is considerably cheaper than booking a safari from Arusha.

Ngorongoro Crater

The crater has an area of 265 sq km and measures between 16 and 19 km across. The rim reaches 2286 m above sea level and the crater floor is 610 m below it. The crater floor is mainly grassy plain interspersed with a few tracts of sturdy woodland. Scrub heath and remnants of montane forests cloak the steep slopes. There are both freshwater and brackish lakes, and the main water source is Lake Migadi in the centre of the crater; a soda lake that attracts flocks of pink-winged flamingos and plenty of contented hippos who remain partially submerged during the day and graze on grass at night. The views from the rim overlooking Ngorongoro Crater are sensational, and you can pick out the wildlife as dots on the crater floor.

Ins and outs
All the lodges and the public campsite are around the rim of the crater. The descent into it is by way of two steep roads, which are both one-way. You enter by the **Windy Gap** road and leave by the **Lerai** road. The Windy Gap branches off the Serengeti road to the right and descends the northeast wall to the floor of the crater 610 m below. The road is narrow, steep and twists and turns as it enters the crater, which is rather like a huge amphitheatre.

Most people go down into the crater on an organized safari from Arusha (see page 109), or join one in Karatu. Access into it and onto its floor is limited to half a day per visitor, and safaris enter either early in the morning or early in the afternoon. Access is restricted to registered tour operators in Tanzanian-registered vehicles, and for most of the year, only 4WDs are allowed. If you have your own vehicle, you are allowed to take it through the Ngorongoro Crater Reserve (and beyond into the Serengeti) but you are not allowed to take it down into the crater. However, there is the option to leave your own vehicle at the top and Land Rovers and drivers can be hired in Crater Village where you pick up the ranger, which is cheaper than hiring through the lodges.

Background
The name 'Ngorongoro' comes from a Masai word *Ilkorongoro*, which was the name given to the group of Masai warriors who defeated the previous occupants of the area, the Datong, around 1800. The sounds of the bells that the Masai wore during the battle that were said to have terrified their enemies into submission, was '*koh-rohng-roh*' and it is from this that Ngorongoro comes. The Masai refer to the Ngorongoro Southern Highlands as '*O'lhoirobi*', which means the cold highlands; while the Germans also referred to the climate, calling these the 'winter highlands'. Ngorongoro is believed to date from about 2,500,000 years ago – relatively recent for this area. It was once a huge active volcano and was probably as large as Kilimanjaro. After its large major eruption, as the lava subsided its cone collapsed inwards leaving the caldera. Minor volcanic activity continued and the small cones that resulted can be seen in the crater floor. To the northeast of Ngorongoro crater are two smaller craters, Olmot and Embagai. From the crater on a clear day you should be able to see six mountains over 3000 m.

Wildlife
The crater is home to an estimated 30,000 animals and visitors are almost guaranteed to get a good look at some or all of the Big Five. About half of this number are zebra and wildebeest. Unlike those in the neighbouring Serengeti, these populations do not need to migrate thanks to the permanent supply of water and grass through both the wet and the dry seasons. Thanks to the army of pop-up minibuses that go down each day the animals are not afraid of the vehicles and it's not unusual for a pride of lions to amble over and flop down in the shade of a minibus. However, recently introduced regulations limit the number of vehicles around an animal or kill to five, in an effort to reduce the distress and impact of hordes of over-eager safari vehicles when surrounding the wildlife. The crater's elephants are mostly old bulls with giant tusks. The females and calves prefer the ●

forested highlands on the crater rim and only rarely venture down into the grasslands. There are no giraffe. Because of the crater's steep sides they can't climb down, and there is a lack of food at tree level.

In early 2001 huge swarms of *Stomoxys* flies were harmful to many animals and particularly lions, of which six died and 62 were seriously damaged and they apparently left the crater in an attempt to escape. In a previous outbreak of the flies, in 1962, the lion population was decimated, with only eight lions surviving. Numbers have slowly increased since that time, but the Ngorongoro lions, generally bigger and stronger than lions elsewhere, are in danger of extinction, not least because the lack of genetic diversity within the population leaves it vulnerable to events such as *Stomoxys* attacks and disease. There have been reports that since the middle of 2000 many other animals have died of unknown causes, including over 300 buffalo, 200 wildebeest, over 60 zebra and a few hippo and rhino.

Ngorongoro Conservation Area

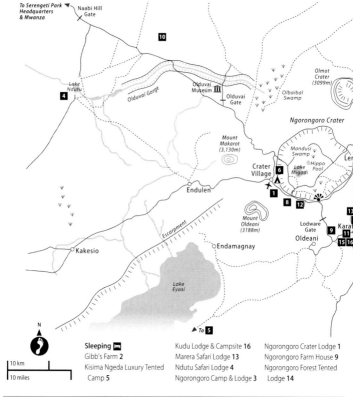

Sleeping
Gibb's Farm 2
Kisima Ngeda Luxury Tented Camp 5
Kudu Lodge & Campsite 16
Marera Safari Lodge 13
Ndutu Safari Lodge 4
Ngorongoro Camp & Lodge 3
Ngorongoro Crater Lodge 1
Ngorongoro Farm House 9
Ngorongoro Forest Tented Lodge 14

Embagai Crater

Embagai Crater (also spelt Empakaai) can be visited in a day from any lodge at the Ngorongoro rim. The caldera is approximately 35 sq km. You can walk down to the 80-m deep, alkaline Lake Emakat, which partly occupies the caldera floor. The vegetation is predominantly highland shrubs and grassland but there are small patches of verdant, evergreen forest in the southern part of the caldera. Buffalo, hyenas, leopards and various species of bats may be seen. Birdlife is prolific and includes the lammergeyer, Egyptian vulture, Verreaux's eagle, pelicans, storks, flamingos, duck, sandpiper, doves, kingfishers and ostrich. This is an isolated, beautiful place, accessible by 4WD only. You need to be accompanied by a ranger because of the buffaloes.

Lake Ndutu is a soda lake in the Ndutu woodlands in the western part of the Ngorongoro Conservation Area. Rarely visited, it is home to many flamingo, plains game mammals and their attendant predators.

Ngorongoro Serena Lodge 6
Ngorongoro Sopa Lodge 7
Ngorongoro Wildlife Lodge 8
Octagon Safari Lodge 15
Olduvai Camp 10
Plantation Lodge 11
Rhino Lodge 12

Olduvai Gorge

Olduvai Gorge, a water-cut canyon up to 90 m deep, has become famous for being the site of a number of archaeological finds and has been called the 'cradle of mankind'. Lying within the Ngorongoro Conservation Area to the northwest of the crater, the site is about 10-15 minutes off the main road between Serengeti and Ngorongoro. Olduvai comes from the Masai word *oldupai*, which is the name for the type of wild sisal that grows in the gorge.

Archaeological finds

Olduvai Gorge first aroused interest in the archaeological world as early as 1911 when a German, Professor Katurinkle, while looking for butterflies in the gorge, found some fossil bones. These caused great interest in Europe and in 1913 an expedition led by Professor Hans Reck was arranged. They stayed at Olduvai for three months and made a number of fossil finds. At a later expedition in 1933 Professor Reck was accompanied by two archaeologists, Dr Louis Leakey and his future wife Mary.

The Leakeys continued their work and in July 1959, 26 years later, discovered 400 fragments of the skull *Australopithecus-Zinjanthropus boisei* – the 'nutcracker man'

– who lived in the lower Pleistocene Age around 1,750,000 BC. A year later the skull and bones of a young *Homo habilis* were found. The Leakeys assert that around 1.8-2 million years ago there existed in Tanzania two types of man, *Australopithecus-Zinjanthropus boisei* and *Homo habilis*. The other two, *Australopithecus africanus* and *arobustus*, had died out. *Homo habilis*, with the larger brain, gave rise to modern man. *Habilis* was a small ape-like creature and, although thought to be the first of modern man's ancestors, is quite distinct from modern man. Tools, such as those used by *Homo erectus* (dating from 1-1½ million years ago), have also been found at Olduvai as well as at Isimila near Iringa. Other exciting finds in the area are the footprints found in 1979 of man, woman and child at Laetoli (a site near Olduvai) made by 'creatures' that walked upright, possibly dating from the same period as *Australopithecus afarensis*, popularly known as 'Lucy', whose remains were discovered near Hadar in Ethiopia in 1974. Dating back 3.6-3.8 million years they pushed back the timing of the beginnings of the human race even further. In 1986 a discovery at Olduvai by a team of American and Tanzanian archaeologists unearthed the remains of an adult female dating back 1,800,000 years. In total the fossil remains of about 35 humans have been found in the area at different levels.

Prehistoric animal remains were also found in the area and about 150 species of mammals have been identified. These include the enormous Polorovis with a horn span of 2 m, the Dinotherium, a huge, elephant-like creature with tusks that curved downwards and the Hipparion, a three-toed, horse-like creature.

At the site there is a small **museum** ⓘ *open until 1500, may be closed during the wet season (Apr-end Jun), entrance US$3*. The building was built in the 1970s by the Leakeys to house their findings. It holds displays of copies of some of the finds, a cast of the footprints and pictures of what life was like for Olduvai's earliest inhabitants. You can go down into the gorge to see the sites and there will usually be an archaeologist to show you around.

Nearby places of interest include **Nasera Rock**, a 100-m monolith on the edge of the Gol Mountain range – it offers stunning views of the southern Serengeti and is a great vantage point from which to watch the annual **wildebeest migration**. This is sometimes called the Striped Mountain, so named for the streaks of blue-green algae that have formed on the granite. **Olkarien Gorge**, a deep fissure in the Gol Mountains, is a major breeding ground of the enormous Ruppell's griffon vulture.

A geological feature of this area are shifting sand-dunes, or *barchan*, crescent-shaped dunes lying at right angles to the prevailing wind. They usually develop from the accumulation of sand around a minor obstruction, for example a piece of vegetation. The windward face has a gentle slope but the leeward side is steep and slightly concave. The *Barchans* move slowly as more sand is deposited; they range in size from a few metres to a great size, as seen in the Sahara or Saudi Arabia.

Lake Eyasi

ⓘ *Access to Lake Eyasi is from the Kidatu–Ngorongoro road. The journey takes about 1½-2 hrs, driving southwest of Karatu and the Ngorongoro Crater. There are few tourist facilities here but in recent years it has been included in walking safaris by several companies. There are no set itineraries for the 5 day and 4 night hiking and camping tours but they generally start at Chem Chem Village from where the guides start their search for a Hadzabe camp. Once there, hikers can freely participate in the Hadzabe daily activities, including* mending bows, collecting herbal poisons for the arrows, actual hunts, gathering of firewood, plants, water, etc.

This soda lake, one of several lakes on the floor of the Rift Valley, is sometimes referred to as the 'forgotten lake'. It is larger than Lakes Manyara or Natron and is situated on the remote southern border of the Ngorongoro Conservation Area, at the foot of Mount Oldeani and the base of the western wall of the Rift Valley's Eyasi Escarpment. The Mbula highlands tower to the east. Seasonal water level fluctuations vary greatly and, following the trend in the region, the lake levels are falling and salt brines have developed. It is relatively shallow even during the rainy season. Lake Eyasi mostly fills a *graben*, or elongated depression of the earth's crust, areas that are commonly the sites of volcanic and/or earthquake activity. The Mbari River runs through the swampy area to the northeast of the lake known locally as **Mangola Chini**, which attracts much game.

Two ancient tribes inhabit this area. The **Hadzabe** people (also called the Watindiga) who live near the shore are hunter-gatherers, still live in nomadic groups, hunt with bows and arrows and gather tubers, roots and fruits. These people are believed to have their origins in Botswana, their lifestyle is similar to the San (of the Kalahari) and the Dorobo (of Kenya). It is estimated that they have lived in this region for 10,000 years. Their language resembles the click language associated with the San. Their hunting skills provide all their requirements – mostly eating small antelopes and primates. Their hunting bows are made with giraffe tendon 'strings', and they coat their spears and arrows with the poisonous sap of the desert rose. They live in communal camps that are temporary structures constructed in different locations depending on the season.

Nearby there is a village of **Datoga** pastoral herdsmen, also known as the Barabaig or Il-Man'ati (meaning the 'strong enemy' in the Masai language). The Datoga are a tall, handsome people who tend their cattle in the region between Lake Eyasi and Mount Hanang. The Masai drove them south from Ngorongoro to Lake Eyasi about 150 years ago, and remain their foes. They live in homes constructed of sticks and mud, and their compounds are surrounded by thornbush to deter nocturnal predators. Like the Hadzabe, the Datoga speak a click language and they scarify themselves to form figure of eight patterns around their eyes in a series of raised nodules.

The northeastern region of the lake is a swampy area fringed by acacia and doum palm forests. Nearby are some freshwater springs, and a small reservoir with tilapia fish. These springs are believed to run underground from Oldeani to emerge by the lakeshore. There are several *kopjes* (see page 151) close by the lake. Wildlife includes a profusion of birdlife including flamingos, pelicans and storks as well as leopards, various antelope, hippos and many small primates.

Archaeological excavations of the nearby **Mumba cave shelter** were undertaken in 1934 by Ludwig and Margit Kohl-Larsen, and their discoveries included many fossilized hominoid remains: a complete prehistoric skull, molars and prehistoric tools such as knives and thumbnail scrapers. Animal remains included rhino, antelope, zebra, hippo and catfish. The Mumba cave also contained ochre paintings. It is believed that the Mumba cave shelter was occupied over the years by various people.

Ngorongoro Conservation Area listings

For Sleeping and Eating price codes and other relevant information, see pages 7-9.

Sleeping

Karatu *p136, map p138*

$$$$ Gibb's Farm, 4 km from Karatu, T027-253 4040, www.gibbsfarm.net. At the edge of a forest facing the Mbulu Hills to the southeast. This charming 80-year old farmhouse set in lush gardens is still a working farm and coffee plantation, originally built by German settlers in 1929. Accommodation is in 22 luxurious farm cottages, recently upgraded and all with private verandas, garden bathrooms and open fireplaces. The restaurant produces excellent meals using organic vegetables grown on the farm. And there's a spa with a difference – a traditional Masai healer provides treatments made from local plants and materials, either in your cottage or in his thatched house, the Engishon Supat. Recommended.

$$$$ Ngorongoro Forest Tented Lodge, along the same road as Marera until you reach a junction signposted to the right to **Ngorongoro Forest Tented Lodge** and to the left for **Marera Safari Lodge**. T027-250 8089, www.ngorongoroforestlodge.com. Also overlooking the Ngorongoro Forest Reserve, this stylish new lodge has 7 spacious and attractive tented rooms elegantly furnished and with both indoor and outdoor showers. The lounge bar overlooks the forest reserve and the wildlife corridor to Lake Manyara, with vast windows and a telescope for stargazing. US$245 per person full board.

$$$$ Plantation Lodge, 4 km towards the crater, 2 km from the main road, badly signposted so look hard, T027-253 4405 www.plantation-lodge.com. Accommodation in exquisitely stylish rooms on a coffee estate. A huge amount of detail has gone into the safari-style decor. The 16 individual and spacious rooms are in renovated farm buildings throughout the grounds. There are several places to sit and drink coffee or enjoy a sundowner and you can choose to eat at grand dining tables on your veranda, in huge stone halls, in the garden, or in the main house with the other guests. The honeymoon suite has a vast bed, fireplace, jacuzzi and sunken bath, some units are whole houses which are ideal for families. Swimming pool.

$$$$-$$$ Ngorongoro Farm House, on a 200-ha coffee farm 4 km from the Lolduare Gate of the crater, T0784-207727 (mob), www.tan ganyikawildernesscamps.com. There are 50 rooms spread between 3 separate camps, attractively built in the style of an old colonial farm. In the main thatched building is the barand a newly renovated restaurant with a wooden terrace overlooking the farmland and flower beds. Swimming pool. Excellent food using fresh vegetables from the farm.

$$$ Marera Safari Lodge, 4 km off the main Arusha–Ngorongoro Rd, signposted, with **Ngorongoro Forest Tented Lodge** on the right. T027-250 4177, info@mareratours.com. Lovely location on the top of the hill over-looking Ngorongoro Forest Reserve. Each of the 7 en suite tents is on a wooden platform with thatch shelter and a terrace that looks over the forest. There's a restaurant and a bar, and guides are available for walks into the forest and local villages. At US$160 for a double room, a more affordable option than staying on the Crater Rim.

$$$ Octagon Safari Lodge and Irish Bar, 1 km outside Karatu signposted on the left off the main road towards Ngorongoro Gate, T0754-650324 (mob), www.octagonlodge. com. Owned by Rory and Pamela, an Irish-man and his Tanzanian wife, this lodge is set in beautiful African gardens. The 12 wood and bamboo chalets all have a Masai theme, are en suite and have balconies looking out onto the gardens. The Irish bar has plenty of whiskies to choose from, along with Guinness, and the food has received good reports. Rates US$125 per person full board.

$$$-$ Kudu Lodge and Campsite, signposted to the left if going out of town towards the crater, 600 m off the main road, T027-253 4055, www.kudulodge.com. Established and popular lodge in mature gardens with experienced staff. Accommodation in comfortable rondavaals. There's a variety of options: doubles from US$140, triples US$220, brand new family cottages with kitchen from US$165. A 50% discount is available in low season. The large shady campsite, often used by safari groups, has separate cooking shelters and good ablution blocks with hot water. Camping US$10. Enormous bar with satellite TV, pool table, fireplace and lots of couches, internet café, gift shop and restaurant. Safaris can be organized. Accepts payment in US$, £, € and credit cards.

$$$-$ Ngorongoro Camp and Lodge, on the main road in the middle of Karatu next to a petrol station and bank, T027-253 4287, www.ngorongorocampandlodge.net. This is a good mid-range option, with 32 neat and tidy double rooms with space for extra beds and good showers with plenty of hot water. Full breakfast included, cosy (though expensive) bar with fireplace and satellite TV, restaurant, supermarket. Room rates are overpriced at US$140 for a double but nevertheless, a friendly and comfortable place to stay. Camping is available for US$7 per person. The campsite is 100 m from the main lodge on one of the back roads and there is a bar and kitchen area for the safari cooks. Safaris organized, especially good value are half-day crater tours for US$150 and full day for US$160.

Ngorongoro Crater p136, map p138
For other accommodation options within 20 km of the Ngorongoro Crater, outside the conservation area's boundary, see Karatu, page 142.

$$$$ Ngorongoro Crater Lodge, central reservations, Johannesburg, South Africa, T+27-11-809 4300, www.andbeyond.com. A lodge has been on this spot since 1934, but it was completely rebuilt in 1995, and the architecture and style is simply magnificent. It's the most luxurious lodge on the rim of the crater, very romantic and opulent. The individual cottages offer butler service, sumptuous decor, a fireplace and even an ipod station. With unobstructed views down into the crater even from the bathrooms, this is a special place to stay. Very expensive at US$655-1450 per person per night depending on season, but fully inclusive of meals, drinks and game drives The lodge supports local schools, clinics and health initiatives.

$$$$ Ngorongoro Serena Lodge, T027-250 4058, www.serenahotels.com. Luxury development built to the highest inter- national standards out of wood and pebbles. Stunningly perched on the rim of the crater and each of the rooms has its own rock enclosed balcony. Telescope provided on main balcony to view the crater. The centre of the public area is warmed by a roaring fire and lit by lanterns. Friendly staff, good food and has its own nursery in the gardens to plant indigenous plant species. Offers hiking and shorter nature walks. Local Masai make up 25% of staff. Rates from US$350 per person.

$$$$ Ngorongoro Sopa Lodge, central reservations, T027-250 0630, www.sopa lodges.com. Luxury lodge with 92 suites on the exclusive eastern rim, all enjoying uninterrupted views into the crater. Spectacular African rondavaal design with magnificent lounges, restaurant and entertainment areas, swimming pool and satellite TV. Most of the lodges are on the southern or western crater rim but the Sopa is on the unspoilt eastern rim, way off the beaten track. Unfortunately, this involves an extra 45-50 km journey (one way) over poor quality roads.

$$$$ Ngorongoro Wildlife Lodge, T027-254 4595, www.hotelsandlodges-tanzania.com. An ugly 1970s concrete block on the rim of the crater with wonderful views, the facilites are fine. 75 rooms with balconies overlooking the crater. Geared to fast throughput of tours. Bar with log fire, TV room with satellite TV, restaurant serving either buffets or à la carte, although there have been poor reports about the quality. Zebra can be seen on the lawns.

$$$ Rhino Lodge, T0762-359055 (mob), www.ngorongoro.cc. Jointly owned by Coastal Aviation and the Pastoralists Council of Ngorongoro, which represents local Masai communities. This former home of the first conservationist to the area was reopened in 2008 after extensive rebuilding and helps to support 6 local Masai villages. It's the only mid-budget option on the crater rim and offers good value with 24 simply furnished, Masai-inspired rooms, all en suite with balconies overlooking the forests. Restaurant and bar area are simple with huge fireplaces. Rates are US$110 per person half board.

National Park campsites

Simba Campsite, about 2 km from Crater Village. A public campsite with showers, toilets and firewood, but facilities have deteriorated and water supplies are irregular – make sure that you have sufficient drinking water to keep you going for the night and the game drive the next day. Given that you are camping at some elevation at the top of the crater, this place gets bitterly cold at night so ensure you have a warm sleeping bag. It gets very busy with tour groups, with up to 200 tents at any one time. The hot water runs out quickly – so don't expect to have a shower here. Many budget safari companies use this site, though **Karatu** is quite frankly a better option. If in your own vehicle, there is no need to book. Just pay for camping (US$30 per person) along with park entry when you enter at the gate.

Elsewhere in the reserve there are 5 special campsites (US$50 per person), usually used by the safari companies going off the beaten track.

Olduvai Gorge p139, map p138

$$$$ Ndutu Safari Lodge, reservations Arusha, T027-250 2829, www.ndutu.com. Established in 1967 by professional hunter George Dove, Ndutu is one of the earliest permanent lodges in the Crater/Serengeti area and has become something of an institution over the years. On the southern shore of Ndutu soda lake, amongst acacia woodland, in a good position for the migration in the calving season, midway between the Ngorongoro Crater and Seronera Lodge in the Serengeti, 90 km to both and near to the Olduvai Gorge. Sleeps 70 in 34 stone cottages. Bar and restaurant, fresh ingredients from Gibb's Farm, restricted use of water as it is trucked in. Rates in the region of US$385 full board for a double room, discounts available in low season. Ndutu was home for over 20 years to the famous wildlife photographer Baron Hugo van Lawick, one of the first filmmakers to bring the Serengeti to the attention of the world. He died in 2002 and was granted the honour of a full state funeral before being buried at Ndutu.

$$$$ Olduvai Camp, just south of the Serengeti border, closest lodge to the Olduvai Gorge, reservations through UK T+44-(0)1306 880 770, www.africatravelresource.com. The 3 head guides are all Masai warriors from the villages immediately around the camp and there is the opportunity to go walking with them in the Ngorongoro highlands. Facilities are simple, the 17 tents are of a modest size with thatched roofs and wooden floors, furnished with the basic essentials, en suite bathrooms with flush toilets and bladder showers. The public spaces are limited to 2 small thatched rondavaals and an open fire pit. Has a generator, and lanterns are provided at night. Rates US$455 per person, including all meals, walking guide, park fees and game drive. Compared to the other giant impersonal concrete lodges in the Ngorongoro Conservation Area, this is an intimate, rustic camp that offers the opportunity to sleep on the plains amongst the local Masai.

Lake Eyasi *p140, map p138*
$$$$ Kisima Ngeda Luxury Tented Camp, on the shores of Lake Eyasi, a remote southern corner of Ngorongoro Conservation Area, at the foot of Mount Ol Deani, www.kisimangeda.com. Tents with thatched roofs next to lake, en suite stone baths, wooden furniture, electric lights and plenty of space. Swimming in the lake, all activities on offer including meeting the Hadzabe people.

Eating

Karatu *p136, map p138*
Bytes, in the middle of town behind a petrol station. Very stylish café-bar with cane furniture, home-made cakes, good coffee, imported alcoholic drinks, delicious daily specials such as Mexican wraps and curries, and internet access. Next door is a shop selling local farm produce and coffee beans.

Shopping

Karatu *p136, map p138*
For those on self-drive safaris this is the last place to buy food and before entering the Ngorongoro Crater Reserve. There's a market on the left hand side of the road if coming from Arusha which has a good variety of fresh food; meat can be bought from the small butcher at the back and bread from the kiosks.

Directory

Karatu *p136, map p138*
Banks There are 3 banks in town, the **National Bank of Commerce**, on the main road next to the Ngorongoro Safari Lodge and Bytes restaurant; **Exim Bank** on the left as you're driving towards the crater; and the **National Microfinance Bank**, on the right, further up from Exim. All have ATMs.

Serengeti National Park

The Serengeti supports the greatest concentration of plains game in Africa. Frequently dubbed the eighth wonder of the world, it was granted the status of a World Heritage Site in 1978, and became an International Biosphere Reserve in 1981. Its far-reaching plains of endless grass, tinged with the twisted shadows of acacia trees, have made it the quintessential image of a wild and untarnished Africa. Large prides of lions laze easily in the long grasses, numerous families of elephants feed on acacia bark, and giraffes, antelope, monkeys, eland and a whole range of other African wildlife is here in awe-inspiring numbers. The park is the centre of the Serengeti Ecosystem – the combination of the Serengeti, the Ngorongoro Conservation Area, Kenya's Masai Mara and four smaller game reserves. Within this region live an estimated three million large animals. The system protects the largest single movement of wildlife on earth – the annual wildebeest migration. This is a phenomenal sight: thousands upon thousands of animals, particularly wildebeest and zebra, as far as the eye can see. ›› *For more information on national parks and safaris, see page 9. For listings, see pages 152-155.*

Ins and outs

Getting there There are several airstrips inside the park used by charter planes arranged by the park lodges and by Coastal Air.

By road, the Serengeti is usually approached from the Ngorongoro Crater Reserve. From the top of the crater the spectacularly scenic road with a splendid view of the Serengeti plains winds down the crater walls on to the grasslands below. Along here the Masai tribesmen can be seen herding their cattle in the fresher pastures towards the top of the crater. Shortly before the Serengeti's boundary there is the turning off to Olduvai Gorge where most safari companies stop. Then entry is through the **Naabi Hill Gate** to the southeast of the park where there is a small shop and information centre. From here it is 75 km to **Seronera**, the village in the heart of the Serengeti, which is 335 km from Arusha. Approaching from Mwanza or Musoma on the shore of Lake Victoria, take the road east and you will enter the Serengeti through the **Ndabaka Gate** in the west through what is termed as the Western Corridor to the Grumeti region. This road requires 4WD and may be impassable in the rainy season. There is a third, less frequently used gate in the north, **Ikoma Gate** that lies a few kilometres from Seronera. This also goes to Musoma but again is not a very good road.

Getting around Most tourists use a safari package from either Arusha or Mwanza but it is possible to explore in your own vehicle. However, the roads are quite rough and you can expect hard corrugations, (especially the road from Naabi Hill to Seronera) where there are deep ruts, and in many regions of the park there is a fine top soil known locally as 'black cotton', which can get impossibly sticky and slippery in the wet. This is especially true of the Western Corridor. The dry season should not present too many problems. The

Serengeti National Park

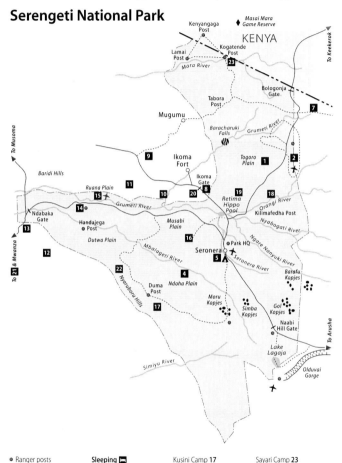

● Ranger posts

Sleeping
Bilila Lodge Kempinski **19**
Faru Faru Lodge **10**
Grumeti Serengeti Tented Camp **15**
Ikoma Bush Camp **8**
Kijereshi Lodge **12**
Klein's Camp **7**

Kusini Camp **17**
Lobo Wildlife Lodge **2**
Mapito Tented Camp **20**
Mbalageti **22**
Mbuzi Mawe **18**
Migration Camp **1**
Sabora Lodge **11**
Sasakwa Lodge **9**

Sayari Camp **23**
Serena Kirawira Camp **14**
Serengeti Serena Lodge **16**
Serengeti Sopa Lodge **4**
Serengeti Stopover **13**
Seronera Wildlife Lodge **5**
Speke Bay Lodge **21**

Park Headquarters are at Seronera and there are airstrips at Seronera, Lobo and Grumeti, and at many of the small exclusive camps.

Park information and entry fees The entry fee is US$50 for adults and US$10 for children aged between 5 and 16 years.

Climate The dry season runs from June to October, the wet between March and May and in between is a period of short rains, during which time things turn green. At this time of year there are localized rain showers but it's more or less dry. With altitudes ranging from 920 to 1850 m, average temperatures vary from 15 to 25 °C. It is coldest from June to October, particularly in the evenings.

Background

The name is derived from the Masai word '*siringet*' meaning 'extended area' or 'endless plains'. A thick layer of ash blown from volcanoes in the Ngorongoro highlands covered the landscape between 3-4 million years ago, preserved traces of early man, and enriched the soil that supports the southern grass plains. Avoided by the pastoralist Masai because the woodlands had tsetse flies carrying trypanosomiasis (sleeping sickness), the early European explorers found this area uninhabited and teeming with game. Serengeti National Park was established in 1951 and at 14,763 sq km is Tanzania's second largest national park (after Selous). It rises from 920-1850 m above sea level and its landscape

Serengeti migrations

varies from the long and short grass plains in the south, the central savannah, the more hilly wooded areas in the north and the extensive woodland in the western corridor. The **Maswa Game Reserve** adjoins its western border.

Wildlife

During the rainy season the wildebeest, whose population has been estimated at around 1,500,000, are found in the eastern section of the Serengeti and also the Masai Mara in Kenya to the north. When the dry season begins at the end of June the annual migration starts as the animals move in search of pasture. Just before this, they concentrate on the remaining green patches, forming huge herds, the rutting season begins and territories are established by the males, who then attempt to attract females into their areas. Once mating has occurred, the herds merge together again and the migration to the northwest begins. The migrating animals do not all follow the same route. About half go west, often going outside the park boundaries, and then swing northeast. The other half go directly north. The two groups meet up in the Masai Mara in Kenya. To get to the west section of the Serengeti and the Masai Mara, where they will find pasture in the dry season, the wildebeest must cross a number of large rivers and this proves too much for many of them. Many of the weaker and older animals die during the migration. Needless to say predators follow the wildebeest on their great trek and easy pickings are to be had. The animals have to cross the Mara River where massive Nile crocodiles with thickset jaws lick their lips in anticipation of a substantial feed. For any visitor to Tanzania, the herds are a spectacular sight. They return to the southeast at the end of the dry season (October-November) and calving begins at the start of the wet season (March).

☾ *This migration to the Masai Mara and back again usually lasts seven to eight months and the biggest concentration of wildebeest can be seen in the Serengeti between November and June before they begin to head north again.*

The Serengeti is also famous for cheetah, leopards and lions, some of which migrate with the wildebeest while others remain in the central plain. Prides of lions are commonly seen, leopards are most frequently detected resting in trees during the daytime along the Seronera River, whereas cheetahs are usually spotted near the Simba Kopjes. The elephant population in Serengeti was estimated to have fallen fivefold during the mid 1970-1980s thanks to poaching, though since then the numbers have slowly increased. Birdlife is prolific and includes various species of kingfishers, sunbirds and rollers, ostrich, egrets, herons, storks, ibis, spoonbills and ducks. Birds of prey include Ruppell's vulture and the hooded vulture, several varieties of kestrels, eagles, goshawks and harriers.

Routes

If you are approaching the Serengeti from the southeast (from the Ngorongoro Crater Conservation Area), **Lake Ndutu**, fringed by acacia woodland, lies southeast of the main road. Lake Ndutu is a soda lake, with a substantial quantity of mineral deposits around the shoreline. It is home to many birds, including flamingos. During the rainy season it offers excellent opportunities to see a large variety of animals including predators. Next you will reach the **Short Grass Plains**. The flat landscape is broken by the **Gol Mountains**, to the right, and by kopjes. The grass here remains short during both the wet and dry seasons. There is no permanent water supply in this region as a result of the nature of the soil. However, during the rains water collects in hollows and depressions until it dries up at the end of the wet season. It is then that the animals begin to move on.

Take a walk on the wild side

Imagine walking along the iconic plains of the Serenegti, wandering silently past wildlife, taking in all the smells and sights and sounds of the bush on foot, worlds away from the noise and confines of a Land Rover crammed with tourists ...

Until very recently, although an option in game controlled areas and in private concessions on the park borders, walking safaris in the Serengeti National Park itself were prohibited. However, following demand from tour operators and the increasing dual pressure of raising ever more revenue from tourism while minimizing its impact on the environment, TANAPA, the Tanzanian Parks Authority, have finally relented.

Available all year apart from in the rainy season during April and May, the walks themselves are on pre-assigned routes and can last anything from 45 minutes to three days or more. Short walks can be booked through the visitor centre at Seronera (see page 151) and can take you around the Serengeti side of Lake Ndutu in the south of the park or along the Grumeti River near Migration Camp. At the time of writing, other short walks were planned around the Mbalageti River area in the Western Corridor and by the Mara River near Kogatende in the north. The longer, multi-day walks need to be booked well in advance, and allow you to explore the Togoro Plains area between Mbuzi Mawe and Lobo on the northeastern side of the park.

Not surprisingly, the authorities have introduced strict controls and regulations. Walking groups are limited to a maximum of eight people and must be accompanied by a TANAPA armed ranger, who stays at the front of the single-file group, and by a TANAPA guide. The routes are limited to just one group at any one time, so you will effectively have your area of the Serengeti all to yourselves, maintaining its amazing wilderness environment.

Although the walking itself won't be tough – the terrain is mostly gentle and flat – don't underestimate the heat and the potential lack of shade. Take sensible precautions such as plenty of water, a sun hat, a high factor sunscreen and strong shoes, and then relax and enjoy the experience.

Fees and information Park fees range from US$20 for trails up to an hour long, US$50 for trails up to three hours and US$100 per day for multi-day walks and camping. For further information, contact TANAPA, T027-250 3471.

Tour operators On the longer walks, you'll need a tour operator to deal with all the logistics, and it must be one that's been approved by TANAPA to take walking safaris. At present, there are very few of these and a recommended approved operator is **Wild Frontiers**, based in Johannesburg, South Africa, T+27-117 022 035. They will organize food and fly camping (sleeping out in the bush) for overnight stops, have a support vehicle, first aid and communications equipment, and a specially trained guide to accompany you, along with the armed ranger.

The **Southern Plains** provide nutritious grasses for the wildebeest, and when the short rains come in November these mammals move south to feed. In February-March, 90% of female wildebeest give birth and the plains are filled with young calves.

Naabi Hill Gate marks the end of the Short Grass and beginning of the **Long Grass Plains**. Dotted across the plains are **kopjes**. These interesting geological formations are made up of ancient granite that has been left behind as the surrounding soil structures have been broken down by centuries of erosion and weathering. They play an important role in the ecology of the plains, providing habitats for many different animals from rock hyraxes (a small rabbit-like creature whose closest relation is actually the elephant) to cheetahs.

The kopjes that you might visit include the **Moru Kopjes** in the south of the park to the left of the main road heading north. You may be lucky enough to see the Verreaux eagle, which sometimes nests here. The Moru Kopjes have a cave with Masai paintings on the wall and a rock called **Gong Rock** after the sound it makes when struck with a stone. There are also the **Simba Kopjes** on the left of the road before reaching Seronera, which, as their name suggests, are often a hideout for lions.

Passing through the Long Grass Plains in the wet season from around December to May is an incredible experience. All around, stretching into the distance, are huge numbers of wildebeest, Thompson's gazelle, zebra, etc.

The village of **Seronera** is in the middle of the park set in the **Seronera Valley**. It forms an important transition zone between the southern grasslands and the northern woodlands. The area is criss-crossed by rivers, and as a result this is where you are most likely to spot game. It is reached by a gravel road, which is in fairly good condition. Seronara is the best area to visit if you can only manage a short safari. It has a visitor centre and the research institute is based here. It also contains a small museum noted for its giant stick insects (near the lodge). In the approach to Seronera the number of trees increases, particularly the thorny acacia trees. You can expect to see buffalo, impala, lion, hippo and elephant. If you are lucky you might see leopard.

About 5 km north of Seronera the track splits. To the right it goes to Banagi and Lobo beyond, and to the left to the Western Corridor, about 20 km north of Banagi Hill, which is home to both browsers and grazers. At its base is the **Retima Hippo Pool** about 6 km off the main track at Banagi. Banagi was the site of the original Game Department Headquarters before it became a national park. North of here the land is mainly rolling plains of both grassland and woodland with a few hilly areas and rocky outcrops.

In the northeast section of the park is the **Lobo Northern Woodland**. Wildlife remains in this area throughout the year including during the dry season. The area is characterized by rocky hills and outcrops, where pythons sunbathe, and woodlands frequented by elephants fringe the rivers. Lobo is the site of the **Lobo Lodge**, 75 km from Seronera. Further north is the Mara River with riverine forest bordering its banks. This is one of the rivers that claims many wildebeest lives every year during the migration. You will see both hippo and crocodile along the river banks.

If you take the left-hand track where the road splits north of Seronera you will follow the **Grumeti Western Corridor**. The best time to follow this track is in the dry season (June-October) when the road is at its best and the migrating animals have reached the area. Part of the road follows, on your right, the Grumeti River, fringed by lush riverine forest, home to the black and white colobus monkey. On the banks of the river you will also see huge crocodiles basking in the sun. The Musabi and Ndoha Plains to the northwest and west of Seronera respectively can be viewed if you have a 4WD. The latter plain is the breeding area of topi and large herds of up to 2000 will often be found here. All but the main routes are poorly marked.

Serengeti National Park listings

For Sleeping and Eating price codes and other relevant information, see pages 7-9.

Sleeping

Serengeti National Park *p146, map p147*
Inside the park

$$$$ Bilila Lodge Kempinski, about 20 km north of the Retima Hippo Pool, www.kempinski-bililalodge.com. This lodge is due to open in Jun 2009. It promises to set the benchmark for luxury hotels in the region, with 80 rooms having all the mod cons you'd expect plus a telescope in each room. Suites have their own plunge pools and there's an infinity pool with views over the plains. There will also be a gym, a spa, a library, a business centre, a wine cellar, a boma, a pub and 2 restaurants. Rooms start at US$675.

$$$$ Grumeti Serengeti Tented Camp, Western Corridor, 93 km west of Seronera and 50 km east of Lake Victoria, central reservations Johannesburg, South Africa, T+27-11-8094300, www.andbeyond.com. Overlooks a tributary of the Grumeti River teeming with hippo and crocodiles. The wildebeest migration also passes through. Real African bush country with an abundance of birdlife including Fisher's lovebird. Central bar/dining area near the river, swimming pool, 10 charming, custom-made tents with stylishly colourful decor, private shower and WC. Solar electricity minimizes noise and pollution. Expensive at US$950 per person in the high season, including all meals and drinks and game drives, but fantastic service and a great location, especially during the migration. Balloon safaris are also available from the lodge.

$$$$ Kusini Camp, at the Hambi ya Mwaki-Nyeb Kopjes in the southwest, near the border with the Maswa Game Reserve, reservations Arusha, T027-250 9816/7, www.kusini.com. Closes during the rainy season Apr-May. Well off the usual tourist track, the camp is situated in a conchoidal outcrop of kopjes, offering superb views. 12 stylish tents, 1 of which is a honeymoon suite. Hospitable camp managers arrange sundowners on cushions up on the kopjes and candlelit dinners each evening. There's also a library and lounge. Rates US$650 per person or US$715 for a full game package.

$$$$ Lobo Wildlife Lodge, northeast of Seronera in the Lobo area, 45 km from the border with Kenya, reservations, Arusha, T027-254 4595, www.hotelsandlodges-tanzania.com. The 75 rooms built entirely of wood and glass around clusters of large boulders remain almost invisible from distance. The swimming pool and bar, both dug into the rock, afford good views over the savannah.

$$$$ Mbuzi Mawe, in the northeast of the park, about 45 km from Seronera, T028-262 2040, www.serenahotels.com. Built around rocky kopjes, Mbuzi Mawe means Klipsringer in Swahili and you'll see several of them skipping up the rocks here, no longer shy of people. It's a charming, understated camp with 16 tents stylishly decorated with private verandas, a relaxing bar and restaurant and friendly staff. US$570 for a double room full board.

$$$$ Mbalageti, in the Western Corridor of the park, T0787-969150 (mob), www.mbalageti.com. In an attractive location on Mwamyeni Hill, with 360° views over the plains and Mbalageti River. The 24 luxury tented chalets are set out in 2 groups – those facing sunrise and those facing sunset, all beautifully furnished and the suites have outdoor baths on private terraces. The lounge is full of African tribal carvings and antiques and the swimming pool, restaurant, bar and outdoor spa with tranquillity pool have fantastic views over the plains. Rates from US$585 for a double room. There are also 14 lodge rooms costing US$395.

$$$$ Migration Camp, built within the rocks of a kopje in the Ndassiata Hills near Lobo, over- looking the Grumeti River, T027-250 0630, www.elewana.com. Provides excellent views of the migration. Jacuzzi, swimming pool and restaurant. The 20 richly decorated tents include a secluded honeymoon tent and a family tent sleeping 6, each one is surrounded by a 360º veranda, and there are many secluded vantage points linked by timber walkways, bridges and viewing platforms. Resident game includes lion, leopard, elephant and buffalo. Rates in the region of US$680, or US$780 for a full game package per person.

$$$$ Sayari Camp, in the far north of the Serengeti, near the Kenyan border, reservations through Asilia Lodges, Arusha, T027-250 2799, www.asilialodges.com. Formerly a mobile camp that followed the migration, this permanent camp was established in Jun 2006 and is still the only camp in this remote region. 8 luxurious and comfortable tents with en suite bathrooms. The mess tent has a bar, lounge and restaurant centred around a camp fire. Attentive service, rates are all-inclusive. Income from the camp supports education and employment in the nearby villages.

$$$$ Serena Kirawira Camp, western Serengeti, T027-250 4058, central reservations www. serenahotels.com. A luxuriously appointed all-inclusive tented camp 90 km from Seronera in the secluded Western Corridor area. A member of Small Luxury Hotels of the World group. All the 25 tents have Edwardian decor and great views across the plains. The central public tent is adorned with exquisite antiques, including an old gramophone, and the swmming pool overlooks the plains. Rates US$890 per person inclusive.

$$$$ Serengeti Serena Lodge, 20 km north of Seronera Village, central reservations T027- 250 4058, www.serenahotels.com. Another super-luxurious establishment in an idyllic central location with superb views towards the Western Corridor. Set high overlooking the plains, the lodge is constructed to reflect the design of an African village. Each of the 66 rooms are stone-walled and thatched rondavaals, with wooden balcony, natural stone bathrooms, a/c, central heating, carved furniture and are decorated with Makonde carvings. Also has beauty centre and infinity pool with views over the Serengeti. Rates US$320 per person.

$$$$ Seronera Wildlife Lodge, in the centre of the Serengeti, near the village of Seronera, T027-254 4595, www.hotelsandlodges- tanzania.com. This large lodge really is at the heart of the Serengeti. Good game viewing year round, but also significant visitor traffic. The public areas are very cleverly built into a rocky kopje, as is the new swimming pool (making it look like an attractive natural pool). The bar is especially nice, but the 75 rooms are in unattractive and old-fashioned accommodation blocks built in the 1970s. Restaurant, shop, bar and viewing platform at the top of the kopje (beware of the monkeys). Campers at the nearby public campsites are allowed into the bar in the evenings (suitably dressed), as driving around the immediate vicinity of Seronera is permitted until 2200.

$$$$ Serengeti Sopa Lodge, in the previously protected area of Nyarboro Hills north of Moru Kopjes, central reservations T027-250 0630, www.sopalodges.com. Luxury all-suite lodge with 75 suites . Excellent views of the Serengeti plains through double-storey window walls in all public areas, multi-level restaurant and lounges, and conference facilities, double swimming pool and satellite TV, way off the beaten track involving an extra 50 km drive over poor roads (one way).

$$$$ Serengeti Wilderness Camp, 40 km east of Seronera, overlooking the Tagora Plains, reservations through Wild Frontiers, Johannesberg, South Africa, T+27-117 022

035, www.wildfrontiers.com. You really feel you're in the heart of the bush at this camp, which is semi-permanent and moved every 3 months or so depending on the season to follow the game movement, producing minimal impact on the environment. Unpretentious and friendly, guests here rave about the quality of the food. There's a large dining tent and bar, with a separate lounge area. The 10 comfortable tents are en suite with bucket showers and solar powered lighting. A great option if you want more of a bush experience but one that comes with home comforts. Recommended.

National Park campsites There are several public campsites around Seronera. Be prepared to be totally self-sufficient and if you are self-driving bring food with you as there is little available in Seronera Village. It is not necessary to pre-book the public campsites; you simply pay for camping when you enter the park. Facilities vary but most have nothing more than a long drop and are completely unfenced. The animals do wander through at night so ensure that you stay in your tent. Camps are regularly visited by hyenas each night scavenging for scraps, and lions have also been known to wander through in the middle of the night.

Outside the park

$$$$ Klein's Camp, on a private ranch on the north eastern boundary of the park just south of the Kenyan border, central reservations, Johannesburg, South Africa, T+27-118 094 300, www.andbeyond.com. Named after the American big game hunter Al Klein, who in 1926 built his base camp in this valley. The ranch is located on the Kuka Hills between the Serengeti and farmland, which forms a natural buffer zone for the animals and overlooks the wildlife corridor linking the Serengeti and the Masai Mara. 10 stone and thatch cottages each with en suite facilities. The dining room and bar are in separate rondavaals with commanding views of the Grumeti River Valley, and there's a swimming pool and solar power electricity. Night drives and game walks. US$950 per person per night all inclusive, reductions for low season.

$$$$ Sasakwa Lodge, Sabora Lodge and **Faru Faru Lodge**, these 3 lodges are located in a 140,000 ha private concession area owned by Singita near the Grumeti River and Ikoma Gate, www.grumetireserves.com. **Sasakwa** has 7 luxury cottages with private pools set on a hill with stunning views over the main migration route. Facilities include a gym and yoga room, an equestrian centre and a helicopter for transfer to the local airstrip. This flagship property costs a hefty US$1600 per person. **Sabora** and **Faru Faru** are both classic tented camps reminiscent of the 1920s safari style, both costing US$995 per person.

$$$$-$$$ Ikoma Bush Camp, 2 km from Ikoma Gate, central reservations T027-255 3242, www.moivaro.com Has the concession for the area to operate game viewing drives and walks, and works in close collaboration with the local villages. This is slightly cheaper than some of the more luxurious tented camps above, and rates are US$180 per person full board in the peak season. The camp is comfortable and secluded, with 39 spacious en suite tents There is hot and cold running water and flush toilets. Electricity is provided by solar power as is the hot water. There is a dining room and bar under thatch.

$$$$-$$$ Mapito Tented Camp, 5 km outside the park, signposted left off the main road, 1 km from Ikoma Gate then about 4 km drive on a dirt-track, T0732-975210 (mob), www.map ito-camp-serengeti.com. More affordable than lodges within the park at around US$200 per person full board, this relaxing camp has 10 large en suite tents with hot water bucket showers and solar powered electricity. They can arrange walking safaris and night game drives as well as cultural visits to villages.

$$$ Speke Bay Lodge, on the shores of Lake Victoria off the main road 15 km from Ndabaka Gate towards Mwanza, T028-262 1236, www.spekebay.com. A lovely, cheaper alternative to staying in the Serengeti if you fancy a break from the bush. Run by a Dutch couple, this lodge has 8 round bungalows (although more are planned) on the shores of Lake Victoria. Rooms are spacious and spotless with a mezzanine floor for triple beds. The bar and restaurant are on a terrace overlooking the beach. With well-established gardens, over 250 bird species and a pod of 10 hippos within its 85 ha, it's a mini nature reserve in its own right. The lodge offers bird walks, canoe trips with local fishermen and boat hire.

$$-$ Kijereshi Lodge, just outside the far end of the Western Corridor near the Ndabaka Gate, T028-262 1231, www.kijereshiserengeti.com. 23 tents and bungalows, with en suite bathrooms, though not in the same class as some of the other tented camps. Excellent restaurant in an old homestead that some-times has game meat on the menu, cosy lounge and bar with fire in winter, swimming pool, gift shop, TV room with wildlife videos. This is usually fairly quiet, although it is used by overlander groups at times, but is convenient if you want to enter or exit the park at the Ndabaka Gate from Mwanza or Musoma. The campsite is US$15 and campers can use the other facilities at the lodge. Be warned though – the campsite is 1 km or so from the lodge; exercise extreme caution if walking back in the dark, animals are present. Camping fees are paid directly to the lodge reception here and not on entry to the park.

$$-$ Serengeti Stopover, along the Mwanza–Musoma Rd on the western edge of Serengeti, 141 km east of Mwanza and 1 km west of Ndabaka Gate, T028-262 2273, www.serengetistopover.com. A good basic restaurant that does the best fish and chips in the area, caught fresh that day from Lake Victoria, which is within walking distance. 10 simple self-contained chalets with TVs, fans and nets, some with verandas and lounge areas, and a campsite. On the border of Kijereshi Game Reserve and the Serengeti, its proximity to the park means that game can be present and you could avoid park entrance fees. Unlike safaris from Arusha, the lodge can arrange day trips to the park that can be very good value. It is run as a community initiative with the local Sukuma people, and tours can be arranged to the local villages. Recommended for budget travellers, you can jump off any of the buses that go between Mwanza and Musoma.

▲ Activities and tours

Serengeti National Park p146, map p147
Balloon Safaris
Seronera Lodge and **Grumeti Serengeti Tented Camp**, see Sleeping, above, UK office T+44 (0) 122 587 3756, www.balloon safaris.com. Balloon safaris are available for US$499 per person; 1-hr balloon flight at sunrise, with a champagne breakfast and transport from your lodge. Especially during the months of the migration, this is often the highlight of visitors' trips to Tanzania. Although expensive, the experience is well worth the treat. Given that there are only 3 balloons, it is essential to pre-book.

◯ Transport

Serengeti National Park p146, map p147
Air
Coastal Air, www.coastal.cc, flies from the Grumeti Serengeti Tented Camp airstrip to **Arusha** daily at 0940 (3 hrs); from the Seronera Wildlife Lodge airstrip to **Arusha** daily at 1105 (3 hrs). From Grumeti Serengeti Tented Camp to **Mwanza** daily at 1355 (3 hrs); from Seronera Wildlife Lodge to **Mwanza** daily at 1540 (3 hrs). These flights stop at the other lodge airstrips on demand.

Index

A

accident and emergency 13
accommodation 7, 8
Ahmadiyya mosque 28
altitude sickness 75
Arusha 85
　activities and tours 109
　bars and clubs 108
　cultural tourism programmes 94
　directory 115
　eating 106
　excursions 93
　getting around 88
　getting there 88
　Ins and outs 88
　safety 88
　shopping 108
　sights 89
　sleeping 100
　tour operators 109
　tourist information 89
　transport 114
Arusha Declaration Monument 92
Arusha International Conference Centre (AICC) 92
Arusha National Park 96
　background 98
　Ins and outs 97
　listings 105
　Mount Meru 100
　wildlife 98
Askari Monument 24
Atiman House 27

B

Banda Beach 30
biosphere reserves 10
Bongoyo Island 34

C

camel riding 109
casuarina trees 29
Cenotaph 25
climbing Kilimanjaro 76
climbing Mount Meru 99
consulates
　foreign in Tanzania 50
　Tanzanian abroad 13
cost of travelling 15
credit cards 15
currency 14

D

dala-dalas 48
Dar es Salaam
　activities and tours 45
　air 47
　bars and clubs 42
　directory 50
　diving 34
　eating 40
　embassies and consulates 50
　entertainment 43
　excursions from Dar 31
　Ins and outs 22
　internet 51
　Northern Beaches 33
　shopping 43
　sights 24
　sleeping 35
　tour operators 46
　transport 47
Darkhana Jama'at-Khana 28
diving 34

E

Embagai Crater 139
embassies
　foreign in Tanzania 50
　Tanzanian abroad 13
Engaruka 130
Engaruka Cultural Tourism Programme 130
exchange 14

G

game reserves 10
Gezaulole 33
Greek Orthodox Church 28
Gymkhana Club 30

H

halau 8
health 13
Hemingway, Ernest 74
hotels 7
How to organize a safari 111

I

Ibaddhi Mosque 28
Ilkiding'a village 94
immigration 18
　office in Dar es Salaam 51

K

Karatu 136
　listings 142
Kariakoo 30
Karimjee Hall 27
Kifuni 80
Kigamboni 31
Kilimanjaro marathon 71
Kilimanjaro National Park 74
　approach 74
　climbing 78
　formation 77
　ins and outs 74
　Loitkitok Trail 84
　Marangu trail 79
　Mweka trail 84
Kisarawe 34
Kivesi 94
Korogwe 56
　listings 60
Kunduchi beach 33

L

Lake Duluti 93
Lake Eyasi 140
   listings 145
Lake Manyara National Park 128
   listings 133
Lake Manyara NP
   formation 129
   routes 129
Lake Masek 139
Lake Natron 127, 130, 131
   listings 134
Leakey finds at Olduvai Gorge 139
Loitokitok trail, Kilimanjaro 84
Lukozi 59
Lushoto 57
   listings 61
Lutheran Cathedral 24

M

Machame 66
Machame trail, Kilimanjaro 83
Maji Moto 130
Maji Moto Ndogo 130
Makumbusho Village Museum 31
Mamba 67
Manolo 59
Marangu 64, 66
   listings 69
Marangu trail, Kilimanjaro 79
Marangu/Mamba Cultural Tourism Programme 66
Masumbae Forest Reserve 59
Mbudya Island 34
Meaning of Kilimanjaro, The 81
medicines 13
Memon Mosque 28
Meru, Mount 99
Meserani Snake Park 93
Mkomazi Game Reserve 59
   listings 63
Mkomazi Rhinos resettlement project 60
Mkuru camel safari 94
Mlalo 59
Mombo 56
money 14
Moshi 64, 65
   excursions 66
   listings 67
Mosques
   Ahmadiyya 28
   Ibaddhi 28
   Memon 28
   Sunni 28
Mount Hanang 95
Mount Kilimnajaro
   climbing 78
Mount Longido 95
Mount Meru 100
Mount Seguruma 59
Msasani Peninsula
   eating 41
   sleeping 37
Mtae 59
Mto wa Mbu 127
   listings 132
Mulala village 94
Mumba cave shelter 141
Museums
   National 28
Mweka trail, Kilimanjaro 84

N

Nasera Rock 140
National Museum 28
national parks 9, 10
National Parks
   Arusha 96
   Kilimanjaro 74
   Mkomazi GR 59
   Olduvai Gorge 139
   Tarangire 121
Ndekia 59
Ng'iresi village 94
Ngorongoro Conservation Area 135
   background 135, 137
   ins and outs 135
   listings 142
Ngorongoro Crater 136
   ins and outs 137
   listings 143
Ngurdoto Crater 98
Njeche 94
North to Kilimanjaro and Moshi 53
Northern Circuit Game Parks 117
nyama choma 8
Nyumba ya Sanaa Complex 30

O

Ol Doinyo Lengai 131
Old Yacht Club 25
Olduvai Gorge 139
   archaeological finds 139
   listings 144
Olkarien Gorge 140
opening hours 15
Oyster Bay 31

P

parks 9
police 15
post 16
price codes 8
Pugu Hills Forest Reserve 34
Pugu Kaolin Mine 35

R

reserves 9
restaurant price codes 8

S

safari 9
   how to organize one 111
   tipping 12
   transport 12
   what to take 12
safety 16
Same 59
   listings 63
security 16
Serengeti National Park 146
   background 148
   ins and outs 146
   listings 152
   routes 149
   sleeping 152
   wildlife 149
Seronera 151
Seyyid Barghash 27
Shira Plateau trail, Kilimanjaro 83
Simga 59
sleeping 7
Solomon, King 78
Soni 57
   listings 61
St Albans Church 28
St Joseph's Roman Catholic

Cathedral 28
St Peter's Catholic Church 28
Sunni mosque 28

T

Tanzania Tourist Board 17
Tanzanian embassies and
 consulates abroad 13
Tarangire National Park 121
 Lake Burungi circuit 123
 listings 124
 routes 123

telephone 16
The Flying Doctors 13
time 17
tipping 17, 76
tourist information 17
 websites 17
travellers' cheques 15

U

ugali 8
Uhuru Monument 29
Umbwe trail, Kilimanjaro 80

Usambara Mountains 57

V

visas 18
voltage 13

W

Western Usambara Mountains
 Cultural Tourism Programme
 58
wildlife 9

Titles available in the Footprint *Focus* range

Latin America	UK RRP	US RRP
Bahia & Salvador	£7.99	$11.95
Buenos Aires & Pampas	£7.99	$11.95
Costa Rica	£8.99	$12.95
Cuzco, La Paz & Lake Titicaca	£8.99	$12.95
El Salvador	£5.99	$8.95
Guadalajara & Pacific Coast	£6.99	$9.95
Guatemala	£8.99	$12.95
Guyana, Guyane & Suriname	£5.99	$8.95
Havana	£6.99	$9.95
Honduras	£7.99	$11.95
Nicaragua	£7.99	$11.95
Paraguay	£5.99	$8.95
Quito & Galápagos Islands	£7.99	$11.95
Recife & Northeast Brazil	£7.99	$11.95
Rio de Janeiro	£8.99	$12.95
São Paulo	£5.99	$8.95
Uruguay	£6.99	$9.95
Venezuela	£8.99	$12.95
Yucatán Peninsula	£6.99	$9.95

Asia	UK RRP	US RRP
Angkor Wat	£5.99	$8.95
Bali & Lombok	£8.99	$12.95
Chennai & Tamil Nadu	£8.99	$12.95
Chiang Mai & Northern Thailand	£7.99	$11.95
Goa	£6.99	$9.95
Hanoi & Northern Vietnam	£8.99	$12.95
Ho Chi Minh City & Mekong Delta	£7.99	$11.95
Java	£7.99	$11.95
Kerala	£7.99	$11.95
Kolkata & West Bengal	£5.99	$8.95
Mumbai & Gujarat	£8.99	$12.95

Africa	UK RRP	US RRP
Beirut	£6.99	$9.95
Damascus	£5.99	$8.95
Durban & KwaZulu Natal	£8.99	$12.95
Fès & Northern Morocco	£8.99	$12.95
Jerusalem	£8.99	$12.95
Johannesburg & Kruger National Park	£7.99	$11.95
Kenya's beaches	£8.99	$12.95
Kilimanjaro & Northern Tanzania	£8.99	$12.95
Zanzibar & Pemba	£7.99	$11.95

Europe	UK RRP	US RRP
Bilbao & Basque Region	£6.99	$9.95
Granada & Sierra Nevada	£6.99	$9.95
Málaga	£5.99	$8.95
Orkney & Shetland Islands	£5.99	$8.95
Skye & Outer Hebrides	£6.99	$9.95

North America	UK RRP	US RRP
Vancouver & Rockies	£8.99	$12.95

Australasia	UK RRP	US RRP
Brisbane & Queensland	£8.99	$12.95
Perth	£7.99	$11.95

For the latest books, e-books and smart phone app releases, and a wealth of travel information, visit us at:
www.footprinttravelguides.com.

footprinttravelguides.com

Join us on facebook for the latest travel news, product releases, offers and amazing competitions: www.facebook.com/footprintbooks.com.